TRANSATLANTIC VOICES

TRANSATLANTIC VOICES

Interpretations of Native North American Literatures

EDITED BY ELVIRA PULITANO

UNIVERSITY OF NEBRASKA PRESS | LINCOLN AND LONDON

© 2007 by the Board of Regents of
the University of Nebraska
All rights reserved. Manufactured
in the United States of America
⊚

Library of Congress
Cataloging-in-Publication Data

Transatlantic voices :
interpretations of Native North
American literatures / edited by
Elvira Pulitano.
    p. cm.
Includes bibliographical references
and index.
ISBN 978-0-8032-3758-2
    (cloth : alkaline paper) —
ISBN 978-0-8032-6034-4
    (paperback : alkaline paper)
1. American fiction — Indian
authors — History and criticism.
2. Criticism — Europe.
3. Characters and characteristics
in literature. 4. Indians of
North America — Intellectual life.
5. Indians in literature.
    I. Pulitano, Elvira, 1970–
PS153.I52T73 2007
810.9'897 — dc22   2007016818

Set in Quadraat by Bob Reitz.
Designed by A. Shahan.

FOR LOUIS OWENS
IN MEMORIAM

Contents

Acknowledgments

This work would not have been possible without the help, encouragement, and insight of many people, to whom I owe a debt of thanks.

Gerald Vizenor offered generous comments and suggestions from the very early stages, and I wish to acknowledge his constant support, willingness to listen to new ideas, and trickster spirit during the numerous conversations we engaged in. John Purdy was a continuous source of encouragement, support, and humor, and I would like to thank him for his precious editorial suggestions and commentary and for putting up with my deadlines-related anxiety. A. Robert Lee provided generous help, useful comments and critique, and wild humor from his Pacific University base and encouraged the project from its very first inception. I also wish to acknowledge Lee Schweninger, who, from within the experience of his own transatlantic academic travels, offered generous suggestions for potential contributors, provided excellent feedback when needed, and helped me track down transatlantic sources. Chris LaLonde has also been a source of inspiration and warm encouragement since I first met him at the American Indian Workshop (AIW) in Torino, Italy, in 2003, and I would like to thank him for his generous comments on my work. The growing transdisciplinary scholarship on Native North American Studies in Europe has significantly inspired this volume, and I would like to acknowledge the founders of the Society for Multi-Ethnic Studies: Europe and the Americas (MESEA) for giving me the opportunity to present papers at their international conferences and for such stimulating conversations around and across the Atlantic.

For allowing this project to take full shape, I also owe special thanks to a few other individuals who trusted my judgment and endorsed my enthusiasm along the way: Susan Castillo, at Glasgow University, who, unable to contribute an essay herself, generously suggested potential names; LaVonne Ruoff, for being such an inspiring model, with her own transatlantic approaches to Native American literatures and overall critical insight (her pioneering essay "The Influence of Elio Vittorini's *In Sicily* on James Welch's *Winter in the Blood*" would often resonate in my mind as I considered various aspects of the Native-European literary encounter); Laura Coltelli, at the University of Pisa, who, having had to decline my invitation to join the project, also offered warm support and encouragement; last but not least and always, Mario Corona, at the University of Bergamo, for being such an inspiring scholar, for his continuous interest in my "transatlantic moves," and for helping me grow along the way and across these routes.

Following my own transatlantic crossings, this project has also received endorsement and enthusiasm from esteemed colleagues, on both sides of the Atlantic, whose wisdom, generosity, and intellectual insight I have been fortunate enough to benefit from these past few years. Agnese Fidecaro, Deborah Madsen, Myriam Perregaux, Denis Renevey, Paul Taylor, Sheila Collingwood-Whittick, Erika Scheidegger, and Lukas Erne in the English Department at the University of Geneva have supported my ideas for this collection of essays all the way through, and I wish to acknowledge their valuable comments during endless conversations. Special thanks to Agnese for tolerating my presence in the office we shared for almost three years and for her challenging questions. I also wish to acknowledge all my colleagues in the English Department at Lausanne University for a most warm welcome and enthusiastic response to my scholarship on Native American Studies during the year that I taught there. All the more enthusiastic has been the response from my colleagues in the Ethnic Studies Department at California Polytechnic State University — Victor Valle, Kate Martin, Karen Muñoz-Christian, and Aaron Rodrigues — to whom I owe many words of thanks for making my transition across the Atlantic so much easier.

Not least do I offer many thanks to my students, in Lausanne, Geneva, and Albuquerque, New Mexico, and currently San Luis Obispo, California, for teaching me so much about cross-cultural communication. Finally, my greatest debt, as usual, goes to my family in Sicily for their unconditional love and support and for encouraging my transatlantic academic experiences, which ultimately and inevitably continue to keep us apart yet always so close. To my dearest friends on both sides of the Atlantic (a geography that encompasses southern and northern Italy, Switzerland, as well as New Mexico and California), I also owe a special debt of thanks. Grazie a tutti. Grazie di cuore.

ELVIRA PULITANO

Introduction

Transatlantic Voices: Interpretations of Native North American Literatures brings together fourteen scholars from Europe. These scholars have contributed original, critical studies of contemporary literature by Native North Americans in the past few years. The essays in this collection present their most recent critical interventions on Native North American literary studies.

European critical practices and theoretical discourses transcend the boundaries of nations, disciplines, and academic traditions. A collection of essays on Native North American literatures by scholars in Europe takes the Atlantic as a site of cross-cultural exchange and circulation of ideas, a bridge linking the Old and New Worlds, in the attempt to overcome historical and ideological differences. Reflecting the most recent critical debates surrounding the discipline of American Studies in the United States and Europe, *Transatlantic Voices* significantly points toward transnational and transcultural practices and methodologies.[1]

Recent scholarship on the Atlantic has focused on the cross-cultural exchanges originating with the transatlantic slave trade, a rhizomorphic system that in the years between 1500 and 1800 would alter considerably the boundaries of the Old World. Greatly aided by Paul Gilroy's influential study of transatlantic modernity, *The Black Atlantic* (1993), scholars interested in transnational and intercultural perspectives have found in the Atlantic a fruitful, creative space around which to articulate ideas on ethnicity, race, gender, class, sovereignty, nationalism, migration, and language in an increasingly globalized world. As the editors of the journal *Atlantic Studies* point out: "Scholars genuinely interested in exchanges between the east and west coast of the Atlantic—Africa, South America, the Caribbean and Canada, as well as Europe and the United States—are coming to think that the project can best be managed in a multipolar world. In fact the Atlantic perspective is best perceived within older and currently evolving forms of globalization" ("Editorial").

What, nevertheless, necessitates more critical attention within emerging Atlantic perspectives is the importance of the Atlantic for contemporary Native North American Studies. In "Crossroads of Cultures" Shelley Fisher Fishkin mentions the research of Annette Kolodny on Viking contact with Native North American tribes in Canada and Maine, pointing out how "transnational questions and approaches can complicate Native American issues in American studies in fascinating ways" (29). Transatlantic journeys linking Europe to the Americas have significantly characterized the history of the two continents since Columbus's first voyages. We know, for instance, that one of the admiral's first gestures, upon arriving on the North American continent, was to ship a group of Tainos back to Spain so that they could "learn to speak" (quoted in Owens 3). And "famous" Indian historical figures such as Pocahontas, Black Elk, Luther Standing Bear, and others would travel to major European cities—whether to prove Europeans' successful attempts at "civilizing" the Indian or simply to become a source of entertainment in Buffalo Bill's Wild West Show. Undoubtedly, key moments in the history of the relationship between Indians and Europe, such transoceanic journeys are not, however, the primary concern of the present volume.

The essays collected in *Transatlantic Voices* take Gilroy's idea of the Atlantic as a complex system of cultural and political exchanges in order to present the most recent, original interpretations on Native North American literatures by scholars on the other side of the Atlantic (Gilroy 4).[2]

Since the publication in the late 1960s and 1970s of four major Native American novels—*House Made of Dawn* (1968) by N. Scott Momaday, *Winter in the Blood* (1974) by James Welch, *Ceremony* (1977) by Leslie Marmon Silko, and *Darkness in Saint Louis Bearheart* (1978) by Gerald Vizenor—to be followed, in the 1980s aftermath, by Louise Erdrich's

Love Medicine, Native North American literary voices have stimulated a great amount of critical attention in Europe. Translations of some of the most critically acclaimed works of the so-called Native American Renaissance into European languages have been in circulation for the past twenty years or so; at the same time, essays and critical articles in English, often published by small European university presses and frequently included in American (and European) journals and essay collections, have initiated a serious critical tradition of European scholarship on Native North American Studies. Moreover, the regular annual gathering of these same scholars to discuss themes and issues concerning Native North American literatures and its place within contemporary American and world literature provide evidence of the growing interest in the Native American literary production by critics on the other side of the Atlantic.

In 1980, during the annual meeting of the European Association of American Studies in Amsterdam, a group of European scholars first discovered their common interests in "Indian issues" and decided to stay in touch. Such gathering of many of these scholars originated an informal American Indian Workshop (AIW), which would be held annually in a different European city and which would be organized around a single theme. It was out of the 1984 AIW in Rome that Christian Feest edited *Indians and Europe: A Collection of Interdisciplinary Essays*, published in 1987. The *European Review of Native American Studies* was established later that year. Despite the interdisciplinary approach (with essays ranging from anthropology to art history and sociology and from history to music and zoology) and despite the large breadth of the historical period covered (from the sixteenth to the twentieth centuries), *Indians and Europe* remains essentially what its editor describes:

> [It is a work that deals] specifically with European views of this relationship, with images that are part of the Old World's cultural heritage. In those instances in which Native American visitors seem to offer their opinions on Europe and the Europeans (especially some of Catlin's and Buffalo Bill's Indians as described in

this volume), there is reason to believe that, either they themselves or those who wrote or spoke for them, stood firmly in a European tradition. (2)

Feest's historical and anthropological orientations undoubtedly account for the lack of critical attention to Native North American literary works in *Indians and Europe*. Today it isn't surprising why Feest's edited volume, published at a time when Native American literature was blossoming with creative and imaginative works and when critical analyses of this same literature had already been attempted in Europe, ultimately ignores Native American literary voices.[3] It might be that, as we read in the editor's postscript, "a simple explanation for the reasons of the special relationship between Europeans and the native populations of North America is that no such relationship exists. Under closer scrutiny it becomes apparent that all that interested and interests Europeans is 'Indians,' a wholly fictional population inhabiting the Old World mind rather than the New World land" (609).

While these words might ring true for the essays gathered in Feest's 1987 interdisciplinary volume, they are not at all representative of critical approaches to Native North American literatures as we have seen them developing in Europe in the past two decades or so.[4] Scholars in France, Germany, Italy, Switzerland, the Netherlands, the United Kingdom, Turkey, Austria, Bulgaria, and Scandinavia have come a long way from a simply romantic fascination with "American Indians." Their critical and literary interpretations, often focusing on discourses of hybridity, intertextuality, and transculturation, have increasingly underscored the cross-cultural nature of Native North American literatures, a discourse that, in its essential "conjunction of cultural practices" (Krupat 18), has been powerfully challenging essentialist claims to identity and authenticity as well as romantic, stereotypical images of Indians.

Clearly, scholars in Europe have learned to see Natives (not *indians*, in Gerald Vizenor's terms) inhabiting the "New World land" rather than the "Old World mind." A quick overview of the "Native American Voices" panel at the 2004 European Association of American Studies conference in Prague (which included, among the others, papers focusing on the reappropriation of language in Linda Hogan's *Power* and Thomas King's *Green Grass Running Water* as well as a discussion of the Native American novel within the context of cosmopolitanism) clearly suggests European scholars' change of direction in their critical interpretations of Native North American literatures.[5] From the earliest anthropological and historical approaches, the legacy of Europe's fascination with the myth of the noble savage, and from close textual readings often characterized by rigid (Western) aesthetic standards, scholars in Europe have turned increasingly to different theoretical approaches.

Discussions of Native North American literatures in the context of postcolonialism and globalization have characterized the nature and content of recent essays included in collections on world literature in English and multiethnic American literatures published by various European university presses. At the same time, considering the consistent erasure of Native American literary voices on the part of orthodox postcolonial theory, scholars in Europe have begun to critique the applicability of postcolonial methodologies to indigenous texts. Along with Native and North American critics, scholars in Europe have begun to question to what extent postcolonial theory, in its heavily Western, Eurocentric discursive modes, can indeed explicate the complex layering of Native American literary texts and the Native aesthetics within which such texts are deeply enmeshed. Moreover, considering the discursive parallels of Native North American literatures and the theoretical discourse of postcolonialism, some scholars have argued the necessity of "expanding the canon" of orthodox postcolonial literatures (Madsen, *Postcolonial Literatures*). A significant change of direction seems to be signaled by the most recent indigenist theoretical approaches. European scholars have become more sensitive to theoretical positions originating out of Native indigenous cultural contexts and epistemologies such as, for instance, the storytelling quality of Greg Sarris's *Keeping Slug Woman Alive* (1993) or the more radical and subversive trickster hermeneutics of Gerald Vizenor's critical narratives.[6] By embracing Native writers' and critics' forceful call for a Native/indigenous theory as a legitimate and commensurate tool of analysis and literary interpretation for indigenous texts, scholars in Europe have contributed and continue to contribute to the radical shift in theoretical approaches toward Native North American literatures. Such a change of direction inevitably concurs with the critical orientation we have seen developing in the United States and Canada over the past few years.

The purpose of Transatlantic Voices is to bring together, perhaps for the first time since Feest's edited collection, a wide number of European scholars with common interests concerning the study of Native North American literatures and to present the most recent, innovative critical approaches and directions.[7] As my remarks hopefully suggest, I think it is time for a more "literary" collection from European critics, one initiating what I hope will become an original and stimulating conversation open to future scholarly collaboration. Due to the fact that very little, if any, attention is often given in the United States to the scholarship on Native American literatures produced in European countries, it is my hope that the essays collected in the present volume will direct American readers (Native and non-Native alike) to the growing, exciting body of scholarship generated across the Atlantic.

My objective is not to construct some kind of rigid binary system by means of which I argue that European scholars are generating critical approaches that depart substantially from interpretations of Native North American literatures as produced in the United States and Canada. My purpose in Transatlantic Voices has been to point out that recent critical interpretations offered on the other side of the Atlantic reveal indeed a level of sophistication comparable to the recent production in North America, a shift from ethnographic and anthropological studies to literary theory in a global context. Having said that, however, I cannot deny the fact that our "strategic locations"—to use Edward Said's famous epithet in describing the author's position with regard to his or her subject of investigation—does indeed matter in our approach to Native North American literatures. The fact that we do not have a Native/indigenous background, and therefore approach this material as outsiders, is certainly an important factor to take into account in our critical interpretations. All the more important is the fact that we are not even Americans (no matter our complex heritage and/or personal history—as Americanists—of transatlantic travels), being therefore twice removed from the subject of our scholarly interest. Within this context I would concur with Alfred Hornung that there is indeed "a different political agenda in Europe," with regard to the field of ethnic and cultural studies, from the ideological conception frequently emerging in the United States. The fact that Europeans' interest in U.S. "minority" writers is often and inevitably linked to "the subaltern status of minority groups in the countries where we teach and work" inevitably calls for comparative, interdisciplinary approaches (Hornung, "Message"). And the fact that some of us do ultimately belong to such subaltern minority groups in various European countries is definitely another important factor to consider. In the light of Europe's recent remapping of its own territorial borders—a remapping that has brought a significant reconceptualization in our ideas of nation and national identity—our approach to the study of Native North American literatures inevitably calls for transnational and transcultural discursive methodologies.

Diverse and wide-ranging in scope and motifs, the essays gathered in *Transatlantic Voices* explore, for the most part, various aspects of the Native-European encounter as it can be traced in contemporary Native North American writing. While the emphasis upon fiction in the volume might raise some questions, I would like to point out that the term *fiction* in Native North American writing needs to be interpreted with a certain elasticity. Addressing this same issue in his comparative study of multicultural American literature, A. Robert Lee argues that the term *fiction* "is meant to embrace novellas, stories and story-cycles, autobiography as implicated in its own kind of fictionality, even a number of verse chronicles . . . all, and however different the one from the other, *ficciones* in the spirit of Jorge Luis Borges" (*Multicultural* 2). Considering the contributors' "fictional" subjects of investigation in this volume—whose range include, among others, N. Scott Momaday's "Man Made of Words," Gordon Henry's autobiographical "entries,"

Louis Owens's mixed-genre collection, *I Hear the Train*, Wendy Rose's and Jim Barnes's poetic oeuvres, Gerald Vizenor's *Bearheart*, and Leslie Marmon Silko's *Almanac of the Dead*—Lee's observation fits neatly the kind of genre crossing and boundary breaking that is a distinctive feature of Native North American literatures.

The first part of the collection introduces the idea of "Theoretical Crossings" as a locus for exploring notions of "story," "history," and "transculturality." All crucial landmarks in contemporary debates on Native North American identity and authenticity, they become all the more controversial when viewed by critics operating on this side of the Atlantic. As critics not directly implicated in the politics involved in such debates, European scholars are often able to maintain a critical distance that, from within the perspective of tribally specific contexts, might at first appear inappropriate or misinformed.

Contextualizing the notion of story, or narrative, within the wider panorama of contemporary Anglophone literary theory and criticism, Hartwig Isernhagen's essay considers the implications of the frequently used (and abused) theorem "they have stories" for Native American literatures and identity. While tracing the essentially holistic nature of *story*, a conflation of what later on was referred to as *myth* and *history*, Isernhagen points out the paradox in the way critical orthodoxy has turned such holism into a dualism, "in a gesture of devaluating history and the written." The term *story*, he argues, has been used to construct Native American literature (and identity) as essentially "other," when that same theorem "is at the same time a key to central reflections on all cultures in our time." Stretching his reflections to include contemporary debates on trauma—itself a dangerous measure of authenticity (as we have seen in the case of Holocaust narratives)—and (auto-)biography, Isernhagen fuels a debate that, as I indicate later on, has recently drawn a significant amount of critical attention on both sides of the Atlantic.

Crisscrossing some of Isernhagen's reflections, Bernadette Rigal-Cellard explores the function of history in Native North American literatures, a process that becomes particularly challenging for Europeans because, as she puts it, ours is the continent that supposedly "brought

History to America and imposed it upon the Natives through the violence of the Conquest." Whether Native writers reject History as being another Eurocentric weapon of colonization (such as, for instance, in the case of Vizenor) or rely on it in order to rehabilitate their past, the two strategies, she contends, ultimately and inevitably intersect. The fact that Vizenor, in *The People Named the Chippewa: Narrative Histories* (1984), draws from official books of history, which he imaginatively recreates as "Narrative Histories," is for Rigal-Cellard a clear example of some of the ambiguities of History that Native North American writers inevitably face. If, in novels of the so-called Native American Renaissance, the fusion of the historical and the mythical ends up anesthetizing the potential "to operate active and open political rebellion against the domineering society," more recent novels such as, for instance, LeAnne Howe's *Shell Shaker* (2001) "reorient" the meaning of History as to point out the inextricable link with Myth. For Rigal-Cellard, Howe's novel might signal a new phase in contemporary Native North American fiction, one in which History, along "with the benevolent assistance of mythic protectors" (including trickster, rabbit, and Mother Porcupine) help the protagonists shape and "self-define their future." Such reorientation, for Rigal-Cellard, ultimately occurs in Vizenor's work as well. Both his analysis of socialist China, in *Griever* (1987), and of imperial Japan, in the most recent *Hiroshima Bugi* (2003), skillfully blend fiction with nonfiction, Myth and History, and provocatively weave a complex "mythic thought fit for our times and our global community."

Helmbrecht Breinig focuses on two concepts of cultural and individual identity formation, *transculturality* and *transdifference*, as they were originally formulated in European discussions of cultural contact and applies them to Native America. Unlike models of *mestizaje, creolization*, and *transculturation*, and essentially different from Homi Bhabha's (in)famous notion of *hybridity*, transdifference, Breinig argues, "does not refer to an ongoing and basically Derridean deconstruction of difference," but quite the contrary. Rephrasing Wolfgang Welsch's notion of transculturality, according to which "there is no longer anything absolutely foreign" in his globalized version of transculturation, Breinig ultimately contends that in the history of Native and European Americans as it has been developed for more than five hundred years there has been and will always be "something absolutely foreign." In other words, phenomena of transculturality and transdifference are not mutually exclusive but, rather, are complementary. Using the witty self-positioning of Anishinabe novelist and critic Gordon Henry as well as narratives from the boarding schools experience, Breinig points out how the overwriting of Native cultures on the part of Eurocentric America "has not resulted in a total and permanent erasure" but, rather, in "a kind of palimpsest" (Klaus Lösch's concept).

The essays in part 2, "From Early Fiction to Recent Directions," trace the development of the Native American novel from the 1930s to the present while exploring some interesting facets of the Native-European encounter. Gaetano Prampolini's essay provides a contrastive reading of John Joseph Mathews's *Sundown* (1934) and D'Arcy McNickle's *Surrounded* (1936), novels that, for the first time, "activate the paradigm of realism" centering on the protagonists' more or less successful journey back into Indianness (a paradigm that was widely adopted by native North American novelists of later generations well into the 1980s). As novels of great—although not yet fully recognized—literary merit, *Sundown* and *The Surrounded*, Prampolini argues, master the rhetoric of a distinctively Western narrative genre while giving it some significant "subversive twists."

In the attempt to answer the question of how "American" or "cosmopolitan" Native American novels ultimately are, Brigitte Georgi-Findlay traces interesting "new directions" in recent novels by Leslie Marmon Silko, James Welch, and Louise Erdrich, directions that inevitably add to recent debates on multiculturalism.[8] Both *Gardens in the Dunes* (1999) and *The Heartsong of Charging Elk* (2000) ironically portray the Native "discovery" of Europe, as Silko and Welch, respectively, send their protagonists on a transatlantic journey that, to a certain extent, reverses Europeans' arrival in the New World. In *The Master Butchers Singing Club* (2003), Georgi-Findlay argues, the transatlantic encounter occurs in an immigrant context, as Erdrich explores the German part of her mixed-blood heritage. And in Erdrich's novel *The Last Report on the Miracles at Little No Horse* (2001) Georgi-Findlay detects a "more intense questioning of culturally constructed gender roles" through the "heavily manufactured" pose of the character Agnes / Father Damien. Georgi-Findlay concludes her overview by arguing that "all four novels explore the boundaries of cultures by pointing to transcultural connections and the instability of ethnic and national identities." More important, these four novels significantly rewrite the concept of "American" by pointing toward a cosmopolitan, transnational dimension in the narratives produced today by Native mixed-blood authors in North America.[9]

A transnational perspective, as it appears more prominently in the prose and poetry of Native North American women writers, becomes the focus of part 3, on "Trauma, Memory, and Narratives of Healing." The fact that trauma studies (with its most focal object of discussion, the Holocaust) have not found, at least until recently, easy applicability in interpretations of Native North American literatures is indeed intriguing, all the more so—as Isernhagen accurately remarks in his theoretical investigation—if we consider that Native American writers frequently and consistently "have preserved the strong connection between story and healing" ("They Have Stories"). A certain resistance (especially among Jewish scholars) to explore the meaning of the Holocaust in relation to other genocides might obviously account for such a "critical silence."[10] And yet, as new clinical approaches to trauma blend Western tools with indigenous knowledge and methods, comparative critical approaches to trauma might become all the more necessary and productive. Within this context recent critical debates on both sides of the Atlantic clearly suggest that theoretical accounts of trauma can indeed offer an interesting lens to approach Native North American texts.[11]

Entering such an embattled critical field, Debora L. Madsen reads Paula Gunn Allen's *The Woman Who Owned the Shadows* (1983) as a novel that "actively engages and disputes dominant Western fictions of 'trauma' in a Native American context." Focusing on the narrative's treatment of time, Madsen questions the position of influential trauma theorists who have conceptualized a "belated temporality" to explain the narrative nature of trauma and its representation. Through a close reading of Allen's fragmented narrative, which takes into account a tribally informed perspective, Madsen ultimately argues for a revisionist approach in current debates on trauma. Such an approach, for Madsen, "can uncover for us a larger truth about identity de/formation under conditions of trauma."

If the connection between the Holocaust and Native American genocide can provide interesting venues for critical debates at the beginning of the twenty-first century, the same is true for the relation between the plight of Native North American peoples and other indigenous communities around the world. In her essay on Wendy Rose's poetry Kathryn Napier Gray explores the analogy of "looking" and "seeing" as a means by which Rose engages her Indian invisibility, her European heritage, and the invisibility of indigenous peoples across continents. While previously concerned mostly with her American Indian heritage, only recently, Napier Gray argues, has Rose come to terms with her European lineage—as her most recent collection of poems, *Itch Like Crazy* (2002) clearly suggests. At the same time, by considering Rose's anthropological background, Napier Gray explores the transnational perspective of Rose's traveling "eye/I," as it engages with the practice of placing indigenous peoples "in museum display cases" across the hemispheres. By telling the story of Truganinny (the last of the Tasmanian people) and Julia Pastrana (a mid-nineteenth-century Mexican Indian and circus performer), Rose, according to Napier Gray, "travels across continental, political, and 'genetic' borders . . . and imaginatively re-creates the experience of different indigenous and mixed-blood women." Upholding the strength of her "wide awake eyes," Rose ultimately constructs a "contact zone" that allows her to face the most painful elements of her complex mixed-blood existence.

The final essay in this section explores the transnational dimension of Leslie Marmon Silko's monumental novel *Almanac of the Dead* (1991). Responding to those critics who have attacked Silko for losing sight of "tribal sovereignty" in her multicultural, visionary approach, Rebecca Tillett focuses on the transcultural, hybrid space that Silko's narrative creates in order to discuss the novel's recovery of tribal "histories/ memories" as a powerful counterforce against America's historical amnesia. By erasing all borders—"between time and space; between history and geography; between living and dead; between forms of oppression; between nation-states; between continents"—*Almanac of the Dead*, Tillett suggests, grounded as it is on a Native indigenous epistemology that promotes a holistic approach, ironically becomes the most "indigenous," or "tribally conscious," novel written by a mixed-blood author with an eye toward the transnational/global scenario.

Focusing mostly on Europe but moving beyond Europe's bounded territory, the essays in part 4 of *Transatlantic Voices* follow two distinct but interrelated themes: comparative mythologies and transatlantic journeys. So far, comparative readings of Native and European mythologies have received considerably scarce critical attention in scholarship of Native North American literatures on both sides of the Atlantic. Myth and mythic language go back to the origins of Native and Western cultures and in both convey the generic, creative force that shapes the communal identity of the cultures (*múthos* in Greek meaning both "word" and "story"). Within this context critical interpretations of the mythological interlacing of Native and Indo-European worldviews, rather than functioning as a further act of (Western) epistemic imperialism—with European scholars always trying to impose Eurocentric discursive modes on indigenous material—might illustrate, instead, the essentially heteroglot and dialogic nature of Native American literatures as well as its subversive character. Crucial in such an interpretative process is the concept of "conjoining," a term—as Paul Taylor suggests—used by French medieval criticism "to identify the artistic process of changing a traditional form by appropriating it for a new use." By *conjoining* Native and Western mythological discourses, Native American authors forcefully articulate the political and subversive nature of their writing in terms of "abrogation" and "(re)appropriation" of Eurocentric discourse while forcing Eurocentric readers to consider indigenous Native epistemologies.[12]

Authors such as James Welch, N. Scott Momaday, Leslie Marmon

Silko, Louise Erdrich, Gerald Vizenor, Aaron Carr, Louis Owens, to
mention a few, consciously or not have superbly and subversively appropriated Greek and Roman mythology as well as European Middle Age
and Renaissance cultural myths and fused them with Native American
mythic lore. If, as the Jorge Luis Borges's epigraph to Momaday's novel
The Ancient Child (1989) reads, "myth is at the beginning of literature,
and also at its ends," it might be useful to investigate in detail the nature
of such a statement and its relevance for contemporary Native North
American writers (and European critics) operating at the crossroads of
cultures. Such is the scope of the first three essays in part 4.

Paul Beekman Taylor's essay explores the "mythic connections" in
Vizenor's *Darkness in Saint Louis Bearheart* (1978). As a novel that "emanates and constitutes three overlapping mythic and post-mythic genre
paradigms: exodus, pilgrimage, and quest," *Bearheart* bears overt echoes
of the biblical tale of Moses, medieval morality plays, as well as of Chaucer's fourteenth-century human comedy, *The Canterbury Tales*. Taylor's
journey into Vizenor's "prototexts" and "paratexts" is indeed far-reach-
ing, as he also considers "European mythic searches for tokens of eternal life," exemplified by, among others, the Greek myth of Theseus's
and Demeter's descent to the Underworld and by the Celtic quest for the
Holy Grail. "Conjoining" not only Greek myths and medieval quest narratives but the overall corpus of European literature, "taking off where
Cervantes ended," *Bearheart*, Taylor argues, has its literary correspondences in classical American literature as well: *Leaves of Grass* (1855),
Moby-Dick (1851), and, most prominently, *The Adventures of Huckleberry
Finn* (1884). These are all texts with which Vizenor's "mythopoeia" effectively and all the more ironically converses. As he plunges more and
more into his close reading, *à la recherche* of Vizenor's "pretexts and paratexts," Taylor ultimately characterizes *Bearheart*'s chronicle as "a manual
of escape," one that tells us "how to emigrate" from "terminal beliefs
and blinded visions to a non-mixed-blood universality of being."

Christian and Native water imagery in Erdrich's early novels are the
focus of Mark Shackleton's essay. Along with those critics who read
Erdrich's fusion of Western and Native mythologies "as an instance of

cross-fertilization," Shackleton cross-reads Christian and Anishinabe water symbols in *Love Medicine* (1984, rev. 1993) and *Tracks* (1988) and illustrates how "the two cultures contrast, interpenetrate, and at times ironize each other." Drawing on Greg Sarris's comments on reading *Love Medicine*, Shackleton also addresses the critic/reader's position in making these kinds of cross-cultural transactions. While acknowledging his Eurocentrism, his "greater knowledge of the Bible than Anishinabe myths and legends," Shackleton is, nevertheless, willing to take up the challenge of cross-cultural reading, ultimately arguing that Erdrich's "Christian and Native mythologies mak[e] large but rewarding demands on her readers" while challenging epistemological assumptions for both Native and Western audiences.

Following a discussion with N. Scott Momaday, in which the Pulitzer Prize–winning novelist recounted his visits to Bulgaria while the country was still under Communist rule, Yonka Krasteva "began to perceive a mode of reciprocity between Bulgarian traditional literature and that of Native peoples." By taking such a comparative approach, Krasteva reads Linda Hogan's *Power* (1998) as a borderland text, a novel conveying a cosmic message of healing. While critiquing Hogan's overt binary thinking in her validation of Native American spirituality versus Judeo-Christian religion, Krasteva maintains that "the dynamic symbiosis between cultural epistemologies and symbolism in the construction of the sacred" that the novel promotes ultimately defies such a separatist ethos. Addressing the "rewriting of ancient myths" in Bulgarian culture, defined by Krasteva as "another marginalized, non-Western culture," and in the ceremonial literature that draws from it, Krasteva's cross-cultural reading, which takes into account recent perspectives in Native Christian discourse, ultimately complies with Hogan's primary intent in her art: "I think of my work as part of the history of our tribe and as part of the history of colonization everywhere" (qtd. in Wilson, *Nature* 233).

The last three essays in the collection turn to the motif of the transatlantic journey while pointing out Native American writers' reinvention of Europe. Ulla Haselstein reads James Welch's final novel, *The Heartsong of Charging Elk*, as a form of "double translation," with the protagonist taking up residence in Europe while maintaining "an unbroken commitment to Lakota cultural tradition and spirituality." Unlike Native American Renaissance novels, which focused around the "homing in" trope (Bevis), Welch's novel, Haselstein maintains, clearly suggests a significant change of direction. While focusing on the protagonist's adventures in France, Haselstein also addresses the "cultural politics of Welch's novel in the context of American minority histories" and briefly compares it with another, previous novel also set in Marseille—namely, Claude McKay's *Banjo* (1929). While arguing that "there is no equivalent to the black Atlantic of multiple transatlantic journeys" in the experience of Native Americans, Haselstein nevertheless maintains that Welch's protagonist does experience the conditions of other immigrants in nineteenth-century France, his life ultimately providing "the narrative framework for an interpretation of Native America identity as diasporic."[13]

Simone Pellerin's essay explores issues of racialism, class, stereotype, and spectacle in narratives by Louis Owens. Focusing on the "French pieces" included in *I Hear the Train: Reflections, Inventions, Refractions* (2001), Pellerin "travels" along the reversed "racial gazes" Owens in turn adopts in the attempt to make sense of the extravagantly maddening experience of his French publishing tour. Reading between the lines and making very clear that her reaction to Owens's narratives is dictated not so much by her being "more or less French" but, rather, by the memory of a brief personal encounter she had with Owens himself in Paris, Pellerin, in her retroactive reading (following Owens's tragic death in 2002), is deeply disturbed by Owens's painful honesty in these pieces. The story "The Dancing Poodle of Arles," for Pellerin, clearly "illuminates" the autobiographical essay about Owens's French travels. With echoes from Van Gogh's paintings and Van Gogh's life, this story, Pellerin maintains, seems to explain why she cannot see "any irony" in Owens's "discoveries in France" but only a powerful, disturbing inability "to cope with that incoherent power over the self that seems to overcome even the bravest of strong words on the page and colors on the canvas."

A. Robert Lee explores the "different geographies of Jim Barnes's life" in an essay that presents one of the first, if not the first, critical analyses devoted to Barnes's distinctive poetry. From the Great Southwest to the Pacific Northwest and to Missouri, all the way to a European traveling experience that has included brief residences in Como, Lausanne, Munich, and Paris, among various other places, Barnes's poetry is significantly characterized by all these locales, "sites" that become, Lee argues, "at once exterior but intricately, and always, inward landscape." As he travels through the rich repertoire of Barnes's poetry, briefly referring to the poet's work-in-progress—the story collection "A Good Place in the World" and new poetry to be titled Visiting Picasso (2007)—Lee maintains that Barnes's Europe is appropriately linked with his America, "the mutuality of both sites" providing a "wholly distinctive signature."

This is not a comprehensive collection of critical ideas or theoretical interpretations. Rather, the essays here serve as a forum, a discursive venue by means of which scholars in Europe contribute to a debate on Native North American literatures while calling attention to the most recent, original interpretations offered on the other side of the Atlantic. From Finland to Germany and Italy, from the United Kingdom and France to Switzerland and Bulgaria, contributors to Transatlantic Voices favor "the inescapable hybridity and intermixture of ideas" proposed by Gilroy that, far from affirming nationalistic, ethnically absolute approaches—European approaches—ultimately point toward the transnational and transcultural (xi). Such a critical orientation, I argue, is compatible with the ideological message that Native North American writers themselves have been sending for the past few decades and which now, at the beginning of the new millennium, seems to have become their most distinctive feature. In my view a collection such as this should invite attention in North America if only to suggest to both Native and non-Native readers that European scholars invested in issues concerning Native North American literatures and theory have, surely no less than their American colleagues, come a long way from earlier anthropological approaches and stereotypical views on Indianness.

More important, a collection such as this might indeed, in the era of increasing transnationalism, bridge the distance between two continents and worldviews kept apart by centuries of colonial history and cultural dominance.

This collection is dedicated to the memory of Louis Owens, a valued friend to some of the contributors, a generous mentor and friend to the editor. It was July 2002 when Louis and I first began discussing the potential for this volume. In a series of e-mail exchanges Louis encouraged me to pursue the project, adding that my upcoming appointment in the English Department at the University of Geneva (to start that fall) would have put me in an ideal position to initiate, develop, and complete a collection of essays on European criticism of Native North American literatures. A few days after his last message, in which—as I recall now—he had offered additional advice on editorial matters, I found out about his tragic, sudden death, as all of us did. Today I regret that I have lost those messages, magically and mysteriously disappeared in the meanders of cyberspace. More important, of course, I regret Louis's decision to end his life in such a tragic manner. I regret the fact that he could not ultimately find an alternative way to get rid of that "outside shadow" (a Choctaw expression Owens frequently used to explain his life) that determined his life. As A. Robert Lee points out, "His self-loss was our loss, untimely to a fault" ("Outside Shadow" 21).

Louis Owens first gave me the idea for this edited collection. Today, four years after his death, I can only be pleased that his idea has come to full completion. Louis Owens was and remains an important, original voice in Native North American Studies. As I hope these fourteen essays show, his legacy has not remained in vain. Thanks to all the contributors for making this project come true. Along with them I present, from both sides of the Atlantic, my belated, heartfelt tribute to Louis.

Genève, June 2006;
San Luis Obispo, December 2006

Notes

1. The Atlantic Ocean and its adjacent land formations, a geography that inscribes the historical triangle of the transatlantic slave trade, have become the focus of attention in recent European scholarship of multiethnic literatures. As the president of MESEA, the Society for Multi-Ethnic Studies: Europe and the Americas, points out, both the society and its affiliated Routledge journal, *Atlantic Studies*, were born out of the desire on the part of the committee members "to expand beyond the horizon of ethnic studies in the United States to include other geocultural areas having an equally strong multi-ethnic presence" (Hornung, "Message"). See the society's Web site, www.mesea.org. For additional interdisciplinary scholarship on transatlantic themes in Europe, see the ongoing research program at the University of Padova, Italy, "Sea Changes: Bodies, Practices and Discourses across the Atlantic" (www.maldura.unipd.it/seachanges/overview.html), a program that, starting in 2004, has so far produced two stimulating international conferences and collections of essays, *Approaching Seachanges: Metamorphoses and Migrations across the Atlantic* (2005) and *Rethinking the Black Atlantic* (forthcoming). For recent critical assessments on the transnational turn in American Studies in the United States, see Shelley Fisher Fishkin's 2004 Presidential Address to the American Studies Association, "Crossroads of Cultures."

2. Although I am aware that a distinct boundary between Canada and the United States should not be drawn when discussing the literatures of the indigenous populations in North America, my use of the term *Native North American literatures* in the present volume is meant as a response to the ambiguity and complexity that current debates on nomenclature ultimately raise. With the exception of Beatrice Culleton Mosionier, whose 1983 novel is discussed, among others, by Bernadette Rigal-Cellard, all the other Native authors considered in *Transatlantic Voices* are based in the United States. Despite such a heavily "American" Native presence, I have, nevertheless, opted for the term *Native North American literatures* (which I use in the plural), arguing that the study of indigenous literatures in the United States ultimately calls for a comparative approach.

3. The notable exception in Feest's volume is Fedora Giordano's bibliographical essay, "North American Indians in Italian (1950–1981): A Bibliography of Books," which lists the Italian translations of *House Made of Dawn*, *Winter in the Blood*, *Ceremony*, and *Storyteller*.

4. Such is also the contention of Laura Coltelli's brief overview on European responses to Native American literatures. While lamenting the heavily historical and anthropological orientation among "European Indianists," Coltelli nonetheless points out the increasing research devoted to contemporary Native American literature (341).

5. The papers from this workshop have appeared in a recent volume of *Litteraria Pragensia*, a periodical published by Prague University, edited by Klára Kolinská and Brigitte Georgi-Findlay.

6. My own study, *Toward a Native American Critical Theory* (2003), intends to be a modest contribution to such a critical change of direction.

7. A 1996 issue of *Studies in American Indian Literatures*, edited by Birgit Hans, was devoted to European writings on Native American literature. Interdisciplinary in nature, the issue brought together linguists, literary critics, and historians working on Native American issues.

8. One of such new directions—most notably, the "turn to Europe"—in recent Native American novels has also been investigated by scholars in the United States. See Ruoff; and Schweninger, the latter providing useful bibliographical information on the topic.

9. Within the context of the most recent "Native American" novels I should at least mention one of the most significant absences in the present volume, Gerald Vizenor's *Hiroshima Bugi: Atomu 57* (2003). A "dynamic mediation on nuclear devastation," to use the publisher's description, Vizenor's novel is also a penetrating examination and critique of Japanese culture, and, as such, it can be placed along the same line as *Griever: An American Monkey King in China* (1987), Vizenor's previous novel on cultural parallelism. For an example of earlier novels exploring the interaction of Native and European cultural traditions, see A. A. Carr's *Eye Killers* (1995). Published in the American Indian Literatures and Critical Studies Series by the University of Oklahoma Press, Carr's novel skillfully combines Eastern European legends of vampires with Navajo mythology.

10. For an interesting view on this rather controversial topic, see Friedberg; and Churchill.

11. For recent U.S. scholarship on the subject, see Jennifer Lemberg, "'Concealed Memory': Considering Multigenerational Trauma and James Welch's *The Death of Jim Loney*," a paper presented at the 2004 MLA convention in Philadelphia, at a panel in honor of James Welch. Lemberg's overall study, a

dissertation tentatively titled "Missing Women: Trauma, Absence, and Identity," spans the clinical, the literary, and the theoretical in order to map the connections between ethnic American literature, gender theory, and trauma studies. Texts analyzed include, among others, Theresa Cha's *Dictee*, Art Spiegelman's *Maus*, Welch's *Death of Jim Loney*, Silko's *Ceremony*, Chang-rae Lee's *Gesture Life*, and Tim O'Brien's *In the Lake of the Woods*. For previous studies, see "Storytelling and Trauma: Gender, Identity, and Testimony in a Contemporary Context," a dissertation submitted by Theresa Laurel Brown at the University of Chicago in 1994. Laurel Brown's study compares works by Leslie Marmon Silko, Audre Lorde, and Eleanor Wilner.

12. For representative pieces, see Taylor; Rigal-Cellard; and Wilke.

13. Much like the contested debates on trauma, discussion on diaspora and diasporic consciousness as it applies to the experience of Native indigenous populations in North America have only recently begun to take shape. Both Louis Owens and Jace Weaver have used the term *diaspora* to characterize the situation of many contemporary Native American writers operating within mainstream American academic institutions, individuals often far from their traditional homelands and communities and for whom writing ultimately becomes the only vehicle to re-create a Native identity and culture. As I have argued elsewhere, the literary production of contemporary Native American writers can provide significant revisions to the theoretical panorama of diaspora discourse today ("Racial Memory," MS).

Works Cited

Bevis, William. "Native American Novels: Homing In." In *Recovering the Word: Essays on Native American Literature*. Ed. Brian Swann and Arnold Krupat. Berkeley: University of California Press, 1987. 580–620.

Breinig, Helmbrecht, ed. *Imaginary (Re-)Locations: Tradition, Modernity, and the Market in Contemporary Native American Literature and Culture*. Tübingen: Stauffenburg Verlag, 2003.

Churchill, Ward. *A Little Matter of Genocide: Holocaust and Denial in the Americas, 1492 to the Present*. San Francisco: City Lights Books, 1997.

Coltelli, Laura. "European Responses to Native American Literatures." In *Handbook of Native American Literature*. Ed. Andrew Wiget. New York: Garland Publishing, 1996. 339-45.

Feest, Chris, ed. *Indians and Europe: An Interdisciplinary Collection of Essays.* Aachen: Rader Verlag, 1987.

Fisher, Shelley Fishkin. "Crossroads of Cultures: The Transnational Turn in American Studies—Presidential Address to the American Studies Association," November 12, 2004. *American Quarterly* 57.1 (2005): 17–57.

Friedberg, Lilian. "Dare to Compare: Americanizing the Holocaust." *American Indian Quarterly* 24.3 (2000): 353–80.

Gilroy, Paul. *The Black Atlantic: Modernity and Double Consciousness.* Cambridge: Harvard University Press, 1993.

Hans, Birgit, guest ed. "European Writings on Native American Literature." *SAIL* 8.4 (1996): 1–86.

Hornung, Alfred. "Editorial." *Atlantic Studies* 1.1 (2004).

———. "Message from the President." *Atlantic Studies* 1.1 (2004).

Kolinská, Klára, and Brigitte Georgi-Findlay, eds. "Contemporary Aboriginal Literature in North America." *Litteraria Pragensia* 30.15 (2005): 3–64.

Krupat, Arnold. *The Turn to the Native: Studies in Criticism and Culture.* Lincoln: University of Nebraska Press, 1996.

Lee, A. Robert. *Multicultural American Literature: Comparative Black, Native, Latino/a, and Asian American Fictions.* Edinburgh: Edinburgh University Press, 2003.

———. "Outside Shadow: A Conversation with Louis Owens." In *Louis Owens: Literary Reflections on His Life and Work.* Ed. Jacquelyn Kilpatrick. Norman: University of Oklahoma Press, 2004. 20–52.

Madsen, Deborah L., ed. *Postcolonial Literatures: Expanding the Canon.* London: Pluto Press, 1999.

———, ed. *Beyond the Borders: American Literature and Post-Colonial Theory.* London: Pluto Press, 2003.

Oboe, Annalisa, ed. *Approaching Seachanges: Metamorphoses and Migrations across the Atlantic.* Padova: Unipress, 2005.

Oboe, Annalisa, and Anna Scacchi, eds. *Rethinking the Black Atlantic.* London: Routledge, forthcoming.

Owens, Louis. *Mixedblood Messages: Literature, Film, Family, Place.* Norman: University of Oklahoma Press, 1998.

Pulitano, Elvira. "Racial Memory, Oral Tradition, and Narratives of Survivance: Re-writing Diaspora in Contemporary Native American Literature." MS, first presented at the 2003 international MESEA conference, "Ethnic Communities in Democratic Societies," in Thessaloniki, Greece.

———. *Toward a Native American Critical Theory.* Lincoln: University of Nebraska Press, 2003.

Rigal-Cellard, Bernadette. "Doubling in Gerald Vizenor's *Bearheart*: The Pilgrimage Strategy or Bunyan Revisited." SAIL 9.1 (1997): 93–114.

———. "Western Literary Models and Their Native American Revisiting: The Hybrid Aesthetics of Owens's *The Sharpest Sight.*" In *Native American Representations: First Encounters, Distorted Images, and Literary Appropriations.* Ed. Gretchen M. Bataille. Lincoln: University of Nebraska Press, 2001. 152–65.

Ruoff, A. LaVonne. "Images of Europe in Leslie Marmon Silko's *Gardens in the Dunes* and James Welch's *The Heartsong of Charging Elk.*" In *Sites of Ethnicity: Europe and the Americas.* Ed. William Boelhower, Rocío Davis, and Carmen Birkle. Heidelberg: Universitätsverlag, 2004. 179–98.

Sarris, Greg. *Keeping Slug Woman Alive: A Holistic Approach to American Indian Texts.* Berkeley: University of California Press, 1993.

Schweninger, Lee. "Claiming Europe: Native American Literary Responses to the Old World." *American Indian Culture and Research Journal* 27.2 (2003): 61–76.

Taylor, Paul B. "Native Americans Translating Culture: Momaday and Anaya." SPELL (*Swiss Papers in English Language and Literature*) 6. Ed. Balz Engler. Tübingen: Narr, 1992. 133–50.

Wilke, Gundula. "Re-Writing the Bible: Thomas King's *Green Grass, Running Water.*" In *Across the Lines: Intertextuality and Transcultural Communication in the New Literatures in English.* Ed. Wolfgang Klooss. Amsterdam: Rodopi, 1998. 83–90.

Wilson, Norma C. *The Nature of Native American Poetry.* Albuquerque: University of New Mexico Press, 2000.

TRANSATLANTIC VOICES

1. THEORETICAL CROSSINGS

1 "They Have Stories, Don't They?"

Some Doubts Regarding
an Overused Theorem

The notion of *story*, or *narrative* (the two terms will be taken to be synonymous for purposes of this argument), is so central in the practice, criticism, and theory of Native American literature that around it gather—or it actively attracts to itself—many of the major issues in that literature. At the same time, the notion is necessarily modified by interaction with those issues, as they provide the larger contexts for its use. This essay will attempt to trace some such interactions and contexts as well as to place the entire complex within the wider context of contemporary anglophone literary theory and criticism.

The single most influential text in establishing the centrality of a notion of story to any definition of *Indianness* must be N. Scott Momaday's "The Man Made of Words," though the impact that ethnographic practices and interests had on American Indian literature should not be underestimated. More than other "new" literatures, it has in various ways attempted to ground itself in traditional (and more broadly cultural) material,[1] which is certainly one reason why there is greater closeness between the literary and the ethnographic in Native American literature than, for example, in Maori or Samoan literature—a difference that affects the genre systems of these literatures by, for example, making of the life history a literary genre in the American Indian context, which elsewhere it is not, or not to the same degree.[2]

Momaday's speech can in fact be read as an attempt to marry the ethnographic with a programmatically modernist, myth/symbol-based conception of literature in a gesture of defining the Indian. *The word,* represented in the argument by Momaday's often-repeated story of the arrowmaker, is linked to the land in a definition of selfhood that is both universal and separatist. One need not deny the foundational nature of the land as a source of value in this worldview to argue that it relies more fundamentally on the notion of story insofar as it is through narrative that the value of the land and of close interaction with it becomes actual, that the land becomes part of lived culture, that it is historicized—even if only as that which transcends history.

"Story": Integrity, Value, and a Loss of Distinctions

Story oscillates between a very wide and a fairly narrow meaning. Like "The Man Made of Words," Momaday's essay "The Native Voice" uses story in combinations such as "story and myth and primal song" and in enumerations such as "songs, prayers, spells, charms, omens, riddles, and stories" (5, 6), which indicate a division of labor among language products of which story is only one, but Momaday also talks in the singular of "the language of story and myth and primal song," and "all the stories of the world" are said to "proceed from" the primal scene of the drawing of a prehistoric image, in a gesture that almost makes story and culture synonymous. In the same vein "stories, as such, constitute but one of many constructions within the oral tradition" (10), but the story of the arrowmaker comes to stand for the oral tradition, for the human imagination in its encounter with Reality, and in this manner for a, or perhaps the, most fully realized form of humanity: "there is a sense in which the arrowmaker has a quality of being that is more viable than that of other men in general" (13).

In both meanings, the very specific and the very general, story/stories are associated with the realization of values in language.

It is particularly in "minority" literatures that individual stories will talk about and dramatize certain specific group values. Thus, among traditional narratives those about transformation have had their obvious uses for the self-constitution of Native senses of identity: they narrativize the preservation of an essential selfhood through a series of destructions or the preservation of sameness in difference or survival in and through conflict. The extreme example in the American Indian context would be Coyote; other trickster figures embody the principle in less extreme forms.[3]

These values, if ascribed to Native stories, typically support critical arguments such as Dunsmore's:[4] "These stories also express another kind of human self, another, older way of being. They are stories of a greater kinship that Euro-America has chosen to forgot [sic]. They are the stories that are necessary now for us to re-member our selves among the earlier nations of the earth" (163).

Different knowledge, selfhood, interconnectedness with the animate and inanimate world, community—these motifs validate a corpus that other critics, such as Dennis Tedlock, for example, would validate via the ascription of aesthetic value and that more politically inclined ones (such as Forbes and Cook-Lynn) would validate via that of cultural activity: stories, then, are salient articulations of individual and group identity and as such cannot not have value.

There is thus a generalizing tendency already in such arguments regarding individual stories: it is less and less the specific message that gives value to a story; it is ultimately as story (any story) that stories acquire their fundamental and foundational value. As Clayton, for example, argues for a particular prominence of narrative in minority fiction, which he places within the framework of a general resurgence of narrative in American literature, it is from the first sentence (which introduces "an old Chippewa . . . using stories to hold off his own death") linked to survival. This linkage is in the material itself but not primarily in its contents—if stories again and again provide strength, this includes the strength to commit suicide, even if, "more often, stories provide the strength to live rather than to die."

Narrative as such, then, is valuable. The motifs we have just encountered in Dunsmore, however, recur on this level. Above all, story is conceived as holistic and thus as embodying the value of wholeness. It is a conflation of what critics such as Cassirer discussed as *myth* and *history*. If Western criticism has since the Enlightenment worked with strong oppositions between the two terms, *story* serves as a holistic notion that subverts the distinction and with it the differential truth values that have traditionally been ascribed to myth and history. It is designed to ascribe a lived truth to all stories that are advanced in a spirit of sense making. And such holism itself becomes value because the division of cultural labor has supposedly become the fragmentation of culture. At the same time, there is a tendency to convey to story the differential levels of prestige of both—but above all the reality-making power of myth. For there is a paradox here. While the holism becomes an attribute of story, because it transcends the distinction, it is ascribed to one side: to myth, to the oral tradition, in a gesture of devaluating history and the written. (This gesture is certainly most strongly developed in ethnocriticism.)

The value of holism, in other words, is employed iteratively, on different levels of the discussion. Where it is used to separate myth from history, it will endorse a process of emancipation, legitimation, and healing: myth, and especially etiological myth with its concern with origins, will offer a guarantee of cultural difference, of the survival of that different knowledge just mentioned. History will above all be that story of Indian-white conflict that almost inexorably leads one toward some sense of victimization of the "minority." The two stories will thus tend to embody different evaluations of past, present, and future—evaluations that underwrite the patent transition from history to myth that informs the plots and thematic structures of salient early works of the Native American Renaissance, such as Momaday's *House Made of Dawn* and Leslie Marmon Silko's *Ceremony*.[5] Arguably, on the other hand, some of the difficulty and interest of *Almanac of the Dead* results from its refusal to accept the distinction as worthy of engagement—from the fact that it draws on myth and history, on orality and literacy, but places neither above the other, perhaps because it ultimately cannot accept their essential difference. This novel may, in other words, be among the first that operate fully in terms of a holistic notion of story that truly transcends the myth/history distinction.

The notion of story may then also enable one to understand that crossover between orality and literacy that, according to Axtell, characterized the situation of first contact between Indians and whites. Orality was recognized as lacking the stability and security of transmission that characterizes literacy, literacy as maybe having affinities with shamanistic power that "normal" oral discourse lacks.[6] Story, again closing a gap, thus mirrors the situation of first contact itself, in which the parallel oppositions oral/written and Indian/white were both operative and inoperative: "Writing [originally 'white'], therefore, did not banish magic from the native world, but enhanced and extended it. The native headmen who agreed to send their children to schools in Europe or colonial towns were induced partly by a desire to acquire the new magic through the younger generation" (Axtell 306).

Story here transcends cultural barriers. Similarly, it serves critics as a neutral term that stands outside of specific critical traditions and thus enables them to avoid the trap of ethnocentric categorization. If the critics' "attempts to develop theories of and about post-colonialism [have been] vitiated by a critical vocabulary which relies heavily on Eurocentric concepts of literary classification and textual analysis," as Huggin recognized already in 1989 (27), story has contributed considerably to overcoming this problem.

At the same time, the pluralization of stories that has come with this move has taken place in a thoroughly postmodernist gesture, under the mediate or immediate influence of Lyotard's master narrative of the death of master narratives: Huggin recognizes, in the same breath, "the impetus for a different kind of assimilation, this time involving the reincorporation of the various post-colonial heterodoxies within the admittedly pluralist and decentred, but now increasingly institutionalized, domain of European/American 'post-modernism'" (27; cf. Clayton 383–84). This observation and my earlier reference to Cassirer are intended to indicate that the criticism and practice of Native American literature have been influenced by the critical orthodoxy and that the term story has at one and the same time served to define the difference between that literature and others and to obscure it. We have here the normative impact of a white academy that cannot but create perspectives of sameness. This becomes clearest perhaps in the pervasive concern with culture, literature, and texts as conflicts, or contests, of stories. If Zamir argues that "both the juxtaposition of antithetical Native American narratives and the dialectical articulation of western and oral traditions in *Ceremony* constitute a contest of stories, in which narratives are competing to describe and explain a Pueblo world radically dislocated by the penetrations of a capitalist political economy" (397), *story* equals *interpretation*, and as such it is always partial, in the several senses of the word. It has become intimately associated with power, and it cannot be conceived as not being in some sense against another story or other stories. Culture and society are seen as fields for the playing out of conflicts of stories—an approach to contemporary realities, and above all to intercultural phenomena, that has its obvious uses. *Story/narrative* has here as elsewhere become the name for what one might call the very "heart" of cultural reproduction: "Culture circulates through science no less than science circulates through culture. The heart that keeps the circulatory system flowing is narrative—narratives about culture, narratives within culture, narratives about science, narratives within science."[7] With all its skewed metaphoricity—first narrative is the heart that pumps (what precisely?), in the end it is narrative that is pumped and circulates—this quotation nicely represents a tendency to use the term for several interconnected but distinct purposes: it links different objects by ascribing the same underlying element to them, as science and culture are united by narrative; it abolishes conventional borders between them and attempts to arrive at an innovative perspective; it is used to search for a shared principle of vitality or power that might account for the continuity of cultural production; it stresses process, rather than product.

What is, then, supposed to be a defining aspect of the Native American and what has obviously become part of Native American self-representation—the story/narrative theorem—is at the same time a key to central reflections on all culture in our time. To point this out is neither to contest nor to confirm the "truth" of the notion that "they have stories," precisely because by so obviously becoming part of Native self-definitions it has acquired the self-evident truth of lived experience.

"They have stories" precisely because they say and are said to have them. But their being said to have them can, and needs to, be contextualized in the current critical and theoretical scene. And we can even define the "bridge" between the specific and the general in this instance: it is the self-reflexive aspect of minority self-representations *as* minoritarian, which comes with their identity function: it entails a degree of self-theoretization on the part of the "other." Quite early, for example, Robert F. Gish saw that "storytelling becomes not just the means and process of Fools Crow; rather, it becomes the very subject itself" (350), and there are few Native American texts about which basically the same statement has not been made. This perspective dovetails, of course, with the general interest in self-reflexiveness and metafiction in the late 1900s—a confluence of motifs that may have aspects of "influence" because the same market impinges on both sides, minority and majority, but that is certainly not an influence from one side only on the other.

Story in this manner ambivalently and ambiguously contributes to the construction of otherness (or even becomes its foundation), at the same time that it becomes universal. It may be local, and it may come with strong relativist implications, but, as the human animal is defined, again and again, as a narrating one, storytelling becomes a universal capability. This is why the term is also perilously stretched not only between relativism and universalism but between a postulate of untranslatablity and one of universal translatability. Cheyfitz has, of course, dealt at length with the resulting problem that both perspectives may lend themselves to exploitation and to a commodification that necessarily entails trivialization, but American Indian material has perhaps been more ruthlessly exploited through the perspective of otherness. As representing other forms of knowledge—preferably "untranslatable" ones—it has again and again become a convenience: appropriated by "white" (hegemonic) criticism because it "transcends" and thereby more or less automatically heals the perceived deficits of the hegemonic culture, though without materially affecting it.[8] The other stories that Indians have, then, become *contributions* to the hegemonic culture—this word proliferates in some discussions, and the tributary relationship is frequently patent enough.[9]

If story thus plays a role in games of exploitation, it also contributes to the culturalization of social conflict in and through the humanities. It supports the view that indigenous cultures (rather than societies) interact with the hegemonic culture (rather than society): a thoroughly dematerializing rhetorical move. The material (political or economic, for example) interaction among living humans in a physical environment becomes abstract, and it does so in a paradoxical way: the pragmatic question *how to do things with words* is slanted in the direction of "mere words," rather than "words that result in actions with material consequences." The area where the axiom that "they have stories" becomes most materially effective is therefore neither the humanities classroom (despite its claim to form consciousness and conscience) nor the review of books but the courtroom, where stories can support material claims so that the culturalization can be reversed in favor of the material.

Several of the aspects of the story/narrative theorem that I have tried to isolate may, finally, come together to produce an unintended loss of criteria for the evaluation of stories. If, as has here been argued, the notion of narrative "is designed to ascribe a lived truth to all stories that are advanced in a spirit of sense making," this is a circular process: true is that to which truth is ascribed. It becomes difficult to determine the merit of specific stories through appeal to either fact or shared rationality. In the American(ist) context the myth/symbol school, for example, had preserved the distinction between ideology and fact and with it the potential for a concretely critical perspective—how fully realized is a different question.[10] In the current climate, on the other hand, narrative is supposed to be therapeutic, emancipatory, and empowering per se: "an oppositional technique because of its association with unauthorized forms of knowledge, what Foucault has called 'subjugated' and Morrison 'discredited' knowledge" (Clayton 378; cf. his summary of de Certeau on 381–82). Similarly, the link between story and community is undoubtedly good, and it produces good, as "storytelling educates Milkman [in Toni Morrison's novel *Song of Solomon*] in the virtues of community, in the importance of an organic link to the past and to the lives of those who surround him" (Clayton 383; cf. 386–89). Story has again become a value term—but that this is patently problematic is indicated by Clayton's uncomfortably edifying rhetoric toward the end.

The problem is that, if Clayton, in an entirely canonical gesture that is being repeated day in, day out, summarizes Lyotard to the effect that narratives "must be judged not by the standards of truth or falsehood but by those of usefulness" (384), he insists on our competence to judge them. There are, then, more and less useful narratives and perhaps even useless or dangerous or pernicious ones—a position intuitively acceptable probably to just about everyone. But, if this position does not become outright untenable in the current climate, at the very least it becomes impossible to act/speak from it because there is within the paradigm of multiplication of stories/knowledges no criterion of choice. Basically, stories can only be judged from within themselves, not from within competing stories. (The entire discussion of the question of voice, of who has the right to speak not only for but about whom, has to do with this quandary.) Clayton's correct insistence that "postmodern legitimation is oriented toward the local" in the last analysis means that the very conflict of stories that he attempts to view as emancipatory can only be resolved by power (384), by a survival of the fittest stories—that it cannot be adjudicated or mediated by rational discussion.[11]

"Story": Memory, Trauma, Time, Identity

In *The Man Made of Words* the word *story* becomes more or less synonymous with language and thought, and in its coupling with the notion of identity it becomes strongly normative. It conveys strong demands regarding authenticity and consistency: an Indian would not be an Indian unless he or she continuously realized his or her identity with the greatest possible imaginative force in story. In this sense, even where story becomes manifold, it remains always one story: the story of identity.

This story has for the last two or three decades come under the influence of the trauma discussion and through it associated with the theme of the Holocaust. As a fundamental threat to identity that requires a working through in narrative, trauma has been at the center of the most salient story of identity; it has become a foundational item of identitarianism. And the Holocaust discussion has shaped critical views of identity and memory: the dying off of the generation of witnesses as well as (with it) the threatened loss of any possibility of reparation, however pitifully inadequate, has foregrounded the theme of memory to the point where it has usurped the scene of identity. The trauma of the Holocaust has shaped our view of time and history, and the undoubted and indubitable problematics of an insupportable crime has displaced other possible views of history.[12]

Trauma has become the central term in a twentieth-century master narrative about history, suffering, and selfhood. In comparison with earlier such narratives that centered, for example, on tragedy or revenge, it is a comparatively or even fundamentally pacific one. Therapy is not achieved in heroic transcendence that devalues those that inflict suffering, if only as the instruments of the gods, as it is in many classical and classicist tragedies. (Who will not despise Creon when he imposes the death sentence on Antigone?) Therapy is not achieved either in inflicting reciprocal violence—an eye for an eye. But the pacifism of the trauma narrative is only comparative or fundamental, which is at least in part due to the contamination of these narratives with one another. We have seen trauma become a weapon in the struggle for recognition, in a spirit of tragic heroism or revenge. Here begins the exploitation of the narrative for purposes that may be ideological, political, or economic and that will, because they are exercises of power or even violence, generate resistance: it will perpetuate the conflict that in the classical trauma scheme is intended to reach closure.

Even where this degeneration has not overtaken the trauma discourse, trauma has in dangerous ways become a measure of authenticity, which has led to its commodification in the battle for status in the sociocultural marketplace. Both as a critical concept and as the theme and subject matter of literary texts, it has been caught in an inflationary cycle: as trauma guarantees relevance and authenticity, authenticity has come to require trauma, which has created a culture of victimization that has its built-in tendencies to self-perpetuation. (To address these dangers is not to deny the reality and gravity of trauma. The opposite is the intention of the argument: to save trauma from commodification and professionalization.) Compared to other literatures, Native American literature—or at least the Native American Renaissance—has arguably avoided this development to a considerable extent. In comparison, for example, with African-American literature, in which the towering figure of Toni Morrison cannot be discussed without acknowledging the dominance of trauma, authors such as Momaday, Silko, Welch, and Vizenor have in their very different ways (and differently in different works) avoided making trauma the central term in their reading of history, though it may (if only for reasons of historical truth) be there in their texts in a subordinate position. At the same time, however, they have preserved the strong connection between story and healing. The traditional and (at least until recently) ongoing embedding of storytelling processes in American Indian cultures, as well as the intact working of ritual, may have made it unnecessary to underpin the notion of healing with the notion of trauma.

But with this linkage of story and therapy Native American writing faces a danger that trauma literature, too, has to face: that behind the notion of story hides not only a definition of identity but an answer to the question of the good life that too often embodies the automatic acceptance of wholly conventionalized, and therefore necessarily culture-specific, values. On one level this introduces an unquestioned and frequently sentimental moralism into literature and criticism; on another it produces censorship and authorial self-censorship—story types that do not tend toward the therapeutic are marginalized or excised from the canon. A glance at South Pacific literature, for example, shows that a whole range of alternatives, between satire and tragedy, is available, and it seems that it is American criticism in particular that has accepted the therapeutic or affirmative axiom/postulate as a guideline for cultural production in general—perhaps under the impact of a traditional belief in progress but certainly also yielding to the more immediate pressures of political correctness.[13]

But the greatest problem in current identitarian writing, whether under the aegis of trauma or not, to my mind lies in the unquestioned close link among the three terms *narrative*, *memory*, and *identity*, which mutually underwrite one another in ways that strongly rely on a foundational notion of time. In a sense this is the almost inevitable outcome of a struggle over the nature of time that dominated the twentieth century. Under the auspices of the theory of relativity, the question whether time is "real" (or "absolute") or relative has spilled over from science to literature and to culture at large. It has produced literary change in at least two ways: as the radical subjectivization and interiorization of time that we have in stream of consciousness, the frozen moment, and other discursive formations that have characterized the modernist canon; and as a more direct attempt to shape narrative structures as, for example, in the work of Wilson Harris and Lawrence Durrell. Time, in this manner, has been subjected to a theorization that unites C. P. Snow's two cultures, attesting to their cohabitation along the same cultural continuum. But the theorization has been confined to high cultural productions and popular productions derived from them, such as the vast array of science fiction and fantasy material that daily flickers over our screens. It has not directly affected our lives: theory has remained separate from practice, as may very well be proper. We continue to experience time as continuous and absolute—partly, no doubt, in recognition of the simple road from birth to death that we all have to travel. Yet, at the same time that our experience has remained unaffected by the theorization, the conflict of views has immeasurably enhanced the status of time as a key to the discussion of the meaning of life: time has not become an interpretive tool so much as a frame category for that discussion, whose subjects are value, coherence, and integrity. These three terms have, of course, been amalgamated into *identity*, strongly conceived.

At the same time, then, that there is considerable conflict over the relative merits of different conceptions of time (notably, cyclical versus linear), which in themselves become the bases of different types of knowledge, representation, and self-construction, there is very little or no conflict over the centrality of time in the discussion of identity. And *memory* has played a privileged role in the foregrounding of narrative as a category of writing and criticism because it has been taken to guarantee time: "Memory is a crucial concept in the attempt to understand time, since the past is one of time's extensions. Time can be described as a triple system, consisting of the past, the present, and the future; mankind operates constantly on the interface between these levels of time, so that the past and memory condition our perception of the present and our expectations of the future."[14] This is representative of an origin-oriented and (as the verb *to condition* indicates) almost inevitably deterministic "framing" of memory that has shaped the entire discussion of identity: "All narrative accounts of life stories, whether they be the ongoing stories which we tell ourselves and each other as part of the construction of identity, or the more shaped and literary narratives of autobiography or first-person fictions, are made possible by memory. . . . It is commonly accepted that identity, or a sense of self, is constructed by and through narrative: the stories we all tell ourselves and each other about our lives" (King 2). The repetition of the argument, down to the ritualized phrase "stories/narratives we tell ourselves and others," indicates that it has become an enabling axiom—or a cliché. It is used by King to introduce a book about autobiography, and in this function it obviously has its good uses. But the phrasing indicates that story as a narrative of memory is given a saliency that derives from its postulated paradigmatic character: it stands for self-awareness, or "a sense of self," as such.

The notion of identity that is here so "naturally" linked with time and memory is neither natural nor of great antiquity. There is a disturbing tendency in contemporary criticism to regard its talk about identity as the continuation of a long-standing discussion, when in reality it is comparatively recent in origin. In his book on autobiography, for example, King leaves a quotation from Locke dangling in unresolved contradiction with his own argument and misuses another to introduce a notion of two voices present in one autobiographical narrative (2, 3). The fact that neither problem can affect his central line of argument is immaterial to my concern, which is that, in using Locke at all, King (like many others) overlooks a radical break between classical and contemporary discussions of "identity." The former deals with an experience of individual difference: the title of Locke's relevant section in the *Essay* is "Of Identity and Diversity," and it asks above all how I can know that I am not another and what it is that makes me different from all others. Memory is central, in this context, as the faculty that guarantees coherence among the ideas (derived from impressions) of a person, rather than any type of temporal continuity. If anything, it is "spatial": indispensable to the empiricist project precisely not as linear story but as a repertoire of ideas and of associations among them. We need not remember the origins of ideas that we use in the present—in the empiricist project we must, in fact, not remember them because such remembrance would only burden our use of them with unnecessary associations. Time, in this discussion, is a corrosive medium that threatens the richness and coherence of the body of associated ideas that makes the individual. And the governing value would seem to be the uniqueness of that body.

The contemporary discussion, on the other hand, is conducted in and as an answer to a general fragmentation and destruction of values. It raises the question of the meaning and meaningfulness of the existence of individuals and groups (potentially in radically non- or even anti-individualistic ways) and attempts to answer it with the concept of identity itself, which then itself becomes a value. To be oneself is an aim in itself. Authenticity is consistency of the self with and within itself and through time: continuity that realizes consistency. It is with this implication and aim that, under the impact of the trauma discussion as well as the concern with the workings of memory, all representation, and especially all self-representation, has become "narrative." Selfhood has thereby been pressed into the mold of a narrative-based identitarianism, which is a debilitatingly restricted view of that spatiotemporal complex that Bakhtin called the "chronotope."

Such time-oriented identitarian conceptions of selfhood are product and achievement oriented. The construction of a consistent self that constitutes, integrates, and in the moment of (quasi-[auto]biographical) narration interprets its own anterior story (and to some degree that of

the group) becomes the major work of living, self-reflexively and potentially narcissistically. The achieved self may, of course, enable a future. It
may be strongly conceived in this manner. But that future is usually not
concretized except, once again, self-reflexively: as the continuation of
the achieved self in time.[15]

The achievement orientation has become normative. The achieved
self is measured by what it has overcome or worked through: it derives
whatever authenticity will be accorded it from its struggle to achieve itself. This produces a scale for the evaluation of lives: the greater the
threat, the greater the danger to the self that is overcome in its realization, the greater the achievement and with it the merit that lies in it. This
is where trauma confers value and where the competition for traumatic-
ity that has already been alluded to will hence all to easily (and in all too
vulgar a manner) arise.

The search for authenticity via the time/memory/identity nexus has,
in other words, led to profound inauthenticity. This is not a necessary
development but is contingent on larger cultural and political trends.
This insight does not force us to give the nexus up but suggests caution
and skepticism in using it. It also suggests a search for alternatives.

Coda: "Identity" and the (Auto-)Biographic Deformation of the Chronotope

The strongly identitarian narrative is the "inside narrative" par excel-
lence. Whether patterned on the *Entwicklungsroman* or on the autobiography—"biographic" patterns both—it draws the sum of a life. But it does
so only insofar as that sum is accessible to the (auto-)biographer or the
developing subject. Being an inside narrative, it ignores what comes after the moment of drawing the sum; it holds onto the achieved moment
of self-interpretation and pretends that there will be no falling off from
it, no degeneration, no loss, of that selfhood that has been articulated.
Making of the moment of narrative mastery the supreme moment, or
"peak," of a life story, it creates a position of mastery and achievement;
it demonstrates achievement supremely achieved. The story of identity
thus ignores (and helps the culture ignore) the descent toward death; it

is a form of artificial curtailment of the full trajectory of life from birth to death. This is the benevolent mendacity built into the story: its immense potential for solace. This is its idealism and its refusal of tragedy, both of which may account for its prominence in the American market.

Momaday's successful attempt to postulate for the dying Francisco a series of loosely floating remembrances that are "naturally" (that is, authorially) linked to one another thematically and as a body transferred to Abel's life—and, one is led to believe, his consciousness—is a case in point. Here, as elsewhere, "survival" literature—even if handled so cautiously, so tentatively, as in *House Made of Dawn*—is a literature of solace, or of self-deception. It postulates a "good" where there is very little evidence of it. It is motivated by an inordinate desire for meaning that jumps to conclusions because there is no other way to them.

These problematic aspects of the story of identity may be avoided by other, currently subdominant types of narrative. Our discussion, in other words, remains within the field of story but attempts to modify it. The human chronotope can take radically different shapes, some of which are far less memory-and-time-bound than those that take precedence in current discussions. The representation of selfhood, or the question of identity that is foundational to and in Native American writing in our time, can make use of other types of rhetoric—ones that will not be identitarian in the narrow sense generated by the memory/time nexus and that may in the course of time be recognized as emergent ones.

There are, to begin with, other stories that handle their own linearity and teleology differently. What I have been addressing is a quest pattern. One of its age-old competitors is the picaresque, with its repetitiveness (rather than linearity), its static interpretation of cyclical patterns (rather than the spiral that constitutes the quest's adaptation of the cycle), and its conventional ending that signals its own artificiality. Whereas the quest either fails or ends in achievement, the picaresque ends because every story has to end. When the picaresque (anti-)hero withdraws into the garden (as, for example, in *Candide*) or into the hermit's cell (as in Grimmelshausen's *Simplicissimus*) or even into the English country house, nothing has been achieved, very little has been learned, except that the world is best avoided. And such avoidance does not constitute the achieved identity we have been talking about: it is precisely the negation of all those affirmations that the identitarian pattern fosters and demands. The integrity of the picaresque, in other words, lies precisely in the artificiality of its endings, which do not provide closure but evasion and thereby signal that there is no closure to the problems that the text has raised or attempted to raise.

Let us also remember the saliency of the *image* in Bakhtin's discussion of the chronotope: "All the novel's abstract elements . . . gravitate towards the chronotope and through it take on flesh and blood, permitting the imaging power of art to do its work. . . . any and every literary image is chronotopic" (250–51). Where image organizes narrative, there is, most significantly, the mystical, or epiphanic, moment that catapults the self out of the time-bound reality that it has been inhabiting so far and that in the same act catapults the self out of itself, into a transcendent other that is paradoxically conceived as its highest self-realization.

And there is what one might very well regard as the polar opposite of mystical transcendence: work, simple work, as the attempt to shape a thoroughly mundane reality. This is, then, the accidental or incidental, the non-self-reflexive, shaping of a life through dedication to a task that is utterly outside the self and that has been chosen for its own sake, not because it offers an opportunity for self-realization. This is, in other words, the rejection of narcissism. We may find something close to it in Welch's *Heartsong of Charging Elk*.

All of these writing strategies, and others undoubtedly, would in the present situation get one on the way to truer, more "realistic" narratives that would again and again also have to proceed from the outside, in order to render what the story's subject cannot (or can no longer) communicate: the loss of the very ability to communicate fully or an experience that is defined as incommunicable. Such a narrative is "truer" not because the loss is all there is to selfhood but because it is part of it and in many respects constitutes its innermost problem. It is also truer because it does what the story of identity only pretends to do: place the

self fully in its own time, in its whole time, and in the destructive full-
ness of its time.

Notes

1. Differences among the new literatures in English are greater than some
postcolonial theories allow for, to the point where some such literatures, their
practitioners, and their critics may very well implicitly or explicitly reject the
very designation *new*. Native American literature is one of them.

2. See Isernhagen, "Anthropological Narrative"; and "Native American Autobiography."

3. That Sedna fulfills a similar function in the Inuit context seems to me
doubtful. There is the same ambivalence of destruction and creation in that
figure as in the Indian tricksters, but everything in her story seems to be so
clearly readable in didactic terms and so much geared toward the dramatization of the everyday job of surviving in a threatening environment that the
more general expression of a worldview may be less important. For a useful
introduction to the Sedna complex, especially in relation to twentieth-century
Inuit art, see Seidelman and Turner.

4. I cannot and need not provide a survey, let alone a history, of such arguments; the examples are purely illustrative.

5. There is a third type of story that may acquire greater importance as the
myth-history approach of the Native American Renaissance becomes a convention of the past: a story that one may call anecdotal in a wide sense of the
term because it is less concerned with the grand sweep of the other two types
than with recognitions of moments of significance.

6. Axtell 306–8. The vulnerability of the oral tradition is, of course, a minor persistent motif in Momaday's reflections on the word but is almost completely ignored elsewhere.

7. Hayles 21–22. I am indebted to Manuela Rossini for bringing this quotation to my attention.

8. See Isernhagen, "(Un)Translatable?"

9. Dunsmore, for example, struggles valiantly against the danger by focusing on the historical guilt of Anglo-American society with regard to the indigenous populations of North America. But the discussion and acknowledgment of guilt are easily commodified as well; cf. Ricoeur.

10. Cf. Henry Nash Smith's comments, in his "Preface to the Twentieth Anniversary of Printing [of *Virgin Land*]," on the insufficiently theorized relation between the "planes" of myth and fact and his difficulty in recognizing "that there is a continuous dialectic interplay between the mind and its environment"—phrases that preserve a difference that his following remarks on the contents on the book explore (viii–ix).

11. This is a very rough statement of a position that should only be advanced with much greater caution than is possible here for reasons of space. But I do believe I am identifying a basic tendency that distinguishes, for example, a climate of discussion shaped by pragmatists such as Rorty from one that would rely on pragmatists such as Mead or Dewey.

12. This is one of the problems that I take to be at the center of Paul Ricoeur's recent monumental *Memory, History, Forgetting*, a book whose complexity I cannot even begin to engage here.

13. Cf., for example, Goodwin—especially in his very apt sketches of Kasaipwalova (22–23), Soaba (24, 29–31), and Wendt (2529). I believe East and West African literatures, too, would furnish examples.

14. Olilla 16. I am indebted to Minori Takei for bringing this title to my attention.

15. It is in this sense that the conception is product, rather than process, oriented, however much *process* may go into the definition of a particular self. This would, in fact, be the case with many ethnic selves who are opposed, conceptually and ideologically, to a supposedly more rigidly product-oriented "Western" (that is, European or Euro-American) self.

Works Cited

Axtell, James. "The Power of Print in the Eastern Woodlands." *William and Mary Quarterly* 44.2 (1987): 300–309.

Bakhtin, Mikhail. "Forms of Time and of the Chronotope in the Novel: Notes towards a Historical Poetics." In *The Dialogic Imagination: Four Essays by M. M. Bakhtin*. Ed. Michael Holquist, trans. Caryl Emerson and Michael Holquist. Austin: University of Texas Press, 1981.

Cassirer, Ernst. *Philosophie der symbolischen Formen*. Berlin: B. Cassirer, 1923–31. Esp. vol. 2, *Das mythische Denken* (*The Philosophy of Symbolic Forms*. New Haven: Yale University Press, 1996.)

Cheyfitz, Eric. *The Poetics of Imperialism: Translation and Colonization from "The Tempest" to "Tarzan"*. Expanded ed. Philadelphia: University of Pennsylvania Press, 1997.

Clayton, Jay. "The Narrative Turn in Recent Minority Fiction." *American Literary History* 2.3 (Fall 1990): 375–93.

Dunsmore, Roger. "The Power of Kinship." In *Native American Literature: Boundaries and Sovereignties*. Ed. Kathryn W. Shanley. Special Issue of *Paradoxa* 15 (2001): 158–69.

Gish, Robert F. "Word Medicine: Storytelling and Magic Realism in James Welch's *Fools Crow*." *American Indian Quarterly* 14 (1990): 349–54.

Goodwin, Ken. "'A History of Ignorance.'" *New Literatures Review* 20 (1990): 19–31.

Hayles, N. Katherine. *How We Became Posthuman: Virtual Bodies in Cybernetics, Literature, and Informatics*. Chicago: University of Chicago Press, 1999.

Huggin, Graham. "Opting Out of the (Critical) Common Market: Creolization and the Post-Colonial Text." *Kunapipi* 11.1 (1989): 27–40.

Isernhagen, Hartwig. "Anthropological Narrative and the Structure of North American Indian (Auto-)Biography." In *The Structure of Texts*. SPELL: Swiss Papers in English Language and Literature, 3. Ed. Udo Fries. Tübingen: Narr, 1987. 221–33.

———. "(Un)Translatable? Constructions of the Indian and the Discourse(s) of Criticism." *European Review of Native American Studies* 11.1 (1997): 11–17.

———. "Native American Autobiography as 'Art.'" In *Writing Lives: American Biography and Autobiography*. Ed. Hans Bak and Hans Krabbendam. Amsterdam: VU University Press, 2000. 136–45.

King, Nicola. "Introduction: 'But we didn't know that then.'" *Memory, Narrative, Identity: Remembering the Self*. Edinburgh: Edinburgh University Press, 2000. 1–10.

Momaday, N. Scott. "The Man Made of Words." *Indian Voices: The First Convocation of American Indian Scholars*. San Francisco: Indian Historian Press, 1970. 49–62.

———. "The Native Voice." In *Columbia Literary History of the United States*. Ed. Emory Elliott. New York: Columbia University Press, 1987. 5–15.

Olilla, Anne. "Introduction: History as Memory and Memory as History." In *Critical Perspectives on Memory*. Ed. Anne Olilla. Helsinki: SHS, 1999. 7–18.

Ricoeur, Paul. *Memory, History, Forgetting.* Chicago: University of Chicago Press, 2004.

Seidelman, Harold, and James Turner. *The Inuit Imagination: Arctic Myth and Sculpture.* Vancouver: Douglas and McIntyre; Seattle: University of Washington Press, 1993.

Smith, Henry Nash. "Preface to the Twentieth Anniversary Printing." *Virgin Land: The American West as Symbol and Myth.* Cambridge: Harvard University Press, 1970. vii–x.

Zamir, Shamoon. "Literature in a 'National Sacrifice Area': Leslie Silko's *Ceremony.*" In *New Voices in Native American Literary Criticism.* Ed. Arnold Krupat. Washington DC: Smithsonian, 1993. 398–415.

BERNADETTE RIGAL-CELLARD

2 Plotting History

The Function of History in Native North American Literature

Trying to understand the function of History in Native American and Canadian literature is a rather challenging process for Europeans. We live indeed on the continent supposed to have invented "History" as opposed to "Myth," the continent that furthermore brought History to America and imposed it upon the Natives through the violence of the Conquest. History and Myth have always collided in myriad directions that have found their way into contemporary literature, and in a particularly forceful way in the writings of many Native North American authors. History can be briefly defined as a narration about the past based on the records of specific events, records that have to be verifiable, available for consultation in order to be constantly tested against other narrations. As a science, History relies on writing, for written documents guarantee permanency. If these records are originally oral, they must at some point be frozen forever (on tapes or written on paper) for future use. On the contrary, in oral societies events are reinterpreted constantly in the telling; they vary considerably from generation to generation, for details are deleted and others added, without allowing for the possibility to go back to initial events and check their authenticity.

To comfort its seriousness, History is associated with chronology, the precise counting of passing time irremediably viewed as a vector oriented from one point, the past, to another point, the future. Yet this view is deceptively simple: meditating on the birth of History, François Châtelet explains that as historical beings we in the West believe that our actions and words are elements of a dynamic reality, both irreversible and significant, and that our individual fate cannot be detached from the future of mankind. Historic time governs man, who ceases to consider himself as depending on God or gods or on mythology (for the mythology he keeps fabricating belongs to the profane realm) and feels engaged in the long evolution of humanity. To the question "what is man?" the answer rests in the closed and dark universe of the collective past (that only the science of history can read) and in the yet undecipherable gap of the present that we call "future" (*La Naissance de l'histoire* 7–13).

We know that History appeared in Greece first as a means to perpetuate properly the oral stories, the myths, and then as a means to record actual events. In the process myths became synonymous with fantasy, imagination, and possibly lies. The term is often understood in everyday language as fabricated fiction, not worthy of attention, but it is not so for many societies for whom myths produce meaning. This form of high Myth, like History, rests on the transmission of stories to give meaning to the present, but it does not depend on records or archives; it is constant reinvention. Mythic time is understood as permanent present and ignores evolution from an imperfect past to a better future. Yet, in spite of their opposite bases, History and Myth are not necessarily at variance. Indeed, if we accept History as a subjective (individual or collective) interpretation of events, we can contend that the historical discourse can veer itself into the mythic, in the sense of an interpretation of the past that cannot be rationally proved. Archives are deposited once and forever, but historians interpreting them forever reinvent the past. It is thus extremely difficult to separate History from Myth radically.

The rift between the two stems in fact from the power exerted at any given time by their specific proponents. This is particularly explicit in a colonial situation in which the conqueror "makes History" and forcibly imposes his version of it, dismissing as myth what the conquered believe in. Now, in a postcolonial situation, History can be used as an effective weapon against its inventors, for one of the specificities of Western colonization was to open schools that taught reading and writing in order to give the same interpretative keys to everyone. These schools fostered both obedience through the acceptance of the "historical proofs" of Conquest and eventually its exact opposite, Rebellion, because they offered the very tools that would permit the individual's intimate understanding of these historical facts. The colonized subject in turn could (and has) become an active historian with access to the records. As Bill Ashcroft, Gareth Griffiths, and Helen Tiffin put it (quoting Abdul JanMohamed) in *The Empire Writes Back*:

> Literacy leads to the development of historic consciousness. It allows scrutiny of a fixed past. It enables distinctions to be made between truth and error and so permits the development of "a more conscious, critical, and comparative attitude to the accepted world picture" . . . . Literacy, then, eventually produces a "sense of change, of the human past as an objective reality available to causal analysis, and of history as a broad attempt to determine reality in every (diachronic) area of human concern. This in turn permits a distinction between 'history' and 'myth.'" (81–82)

Many Native American novels center their plots on conflicts, past or present, deriving from Conquest, events that have been dutifully recorded in archival vaults and whose interpretation rests in the hands of historians. They thus offer captivating variations on the process Jan-Mohamed describes, for, while their authors accept the advantages of causal analysis, they also mock its pretensions. Although the modes with which they play with History are varied, I see them as following three major tracks (that can be combined within a given novel). I will first look at the way History serves as the defining root of personal and collective identity, and Beatrice Culleton's *In Search of April Raintree* (1983) will be my guide; then the way History structures the plot lines in order to be reappropriated and reoriented, as, for example, in LeAnne Howe's *Shell Shaker* (2001); finally, the way History attacks Myth, as Gerald Vizenor explains in *The People Named the Chippewa: Narrative Histories* (1984). Interestingly, however, in all these stories Myth resists and seems to swallow History in its timeless convolutions.

Even if *In Search of April Raintree* is obviously grounded in historical events
(the deterritorialization of the Métis, their lack of rights, the foster
homes policy, and so forth), Beatrice Culleton seems mostly interested
in spelling the divergent definitions of History and its damaging functions, and she raises fundamental issues: what is History, can there be
two forms of History? Who produces them, who learns them, whom do
they benefit?

In the novel History defines one sister against the other. It builds the
identity of the first one (Cheryl), whereas the second one (April) builds
her identity against it. Like a wall, it gradually separates, irremediably,
those who were meant to be a single flesh and mind. The story of these
two Métis sisters removed from their home because their parents were
alcoholic forms one of the most tragic contemporary Native novels. We
know they were sent to various foster homes, some hospitable, some
repulsive and repressive. When April, the narrator, discovers who her
parents actually were and what they did, she opts out of Métis values and
culture and chooses to identify with the other Canadians. Her climbing
the social ladder of mainline society is made manifest by her constantly
changing houses and landing a wonderfully rich husband who owns an
enormous mansion. From greedy Cinderella she turns into a poor prisoner of the Toronto palace, seeing the outside world and its treacheries
(those of her husband and mother-in-law) only through the window.
Her social ascent is diametrically opposed to that of her sister Cheryl,
who slowly descends into the hell of prostitution, alcohol, abuse.

The only thread of hope Cheryl retains is her passion for the history
of the Métis and her desire to make it known. The first radical shock
came to her after April turned ten. Cheryl was finally able to visit her at
one of her foster homes and offered her a book on Louis Riel. Instead
of being happy, April later narrates how she "crinkled [her] nose in dis-
taste." For indeed she had internalized the official Canadian version of
her Métis past in the history class at school: to her Riel was a no-good.
One sees here clearly how history is written by conquerors and how its
biased teaching participates in the control of the minds because what
teachers say is endowed with authority and truth. April at this stage re-

mains in utter darkness and refuses the prodding of her younger sister toward the light. She can but recite by heart the propaganda she had to ingest: "I knew all about Riel. He was a rebel who had been hanged for treason. Worse he had been a crazy half-breed. I had learned about his folly in history. Also I had read about Indians and the various methods of tortures they had put the missionaries through. No wonder they were known as savages. So, anything to do with Indians, I despised" (44–45). In the same paragraph April explains how she was afraid that her school comrades may discover she was one of those Métis: "I remember how relieved I was that no one in my class knew of my heritage when we were going through that period in Canadian history." Official History, when it is badly taught, instills shame in those people whose ancestors did not write it. Only someone like Cheryl could dare challenge such a version of the Riel Rebellion, yet this would bring her trouble: when the teacher reads "to the class how the Indians scalped, tortured and massacred brave white explorers and missionaries, Cheryl's anger began to build. All of a sudden, she had loudly exclaimed, 'this is all a bunch of lies.'" The teacher then claims: "There are not lies; this is history. These things happened whether you like it or not" (57). We then recall how History was defined as "the truth," whereas Myth became "lies." Later Cheryl would remark that "history should be an unbiased representation of the facts" (84).

It is the very attempt of Cheryl to share the true history of Riel with her sister, a true account that made her proud of such a legacy, which spells the first dent in the so-far-perfect relation between the sisters. From their osmosis as near twins they grow more and more estranged. April fears that Cheryl's affirmation of her identity as a Métis will hinder her own affirmation, or pretense, to be white: "How was I going to pass for a white person when I had a Métis sister?" (49). And, totally unaware of the impact of her enthusiasm for Riel on her unreceptive sister, Cheryl carries on a wonderful epistolary relation with her, a pitiful attempt at bridging their physical remoteness, constantly enriched by details of Métis history (75, 77, 84, 95). Such emphasis produces the opposite result; April shrinks before Métis history: "To preoccupy my mind I read Cheryl's essay on Riel and the Red River Insurrection. But reading her essay didn't help. Knowing the other side, the Métis side, didn't make me feel any better. It just reinforced my belief that if I could assimilate myself into white society, I wouldn't have to live like this for the rest of my life" (85). Cheryl, however, cannot be said to be solely concerned with her own Métis history, for she is fascinated also by the events taking place outside, in particular the assassination of Kennedy in 1963, which also shocked April. On this particular point, thus, the two sisters react in the same way. Yet Cheryl cannot but add a piece on Riel to her thoughts on Kennedy and thus loses ground in the struggle to reach her sister's soul.

A Métis herself from Manitoba, Beatrice Culleton knew firsthand the fate of her people, a fate far worse than that of the Canadian First Nations. It is rather strange indeed to know that it would only be in September 2003 that the Supreme Court of Canada handed down the history-making *Powley* decision granting the Métis their aboriginal rights. In her novel the thirst to understand this history and to convince her sister that this is what matters most for the present and the future keeps Cheryl alive, but only for some fugitive time. Not able to share her conviction with April, whom she considered her true half, she commits suicide. It is when her sister reads her diary that she comes to terms with her own culture and can suddenly call the Métis "her people." It is therefore thanks to the act of writing down her personal history, her own tragic chronicles, that she can act upon the conscience of April, who had blinded herself to such enlightenment. Memories of her own past surge up, the personal joining the sisterly and the communal.

The conflict Culleton stages in *In Search of April Raintree* is not so much between Myth and History as between official History, biased and mind colonizing, produced and imposed by the government and its supporting majority, and the History written by the other party, without the knowledge of which minority members cannot mature and integrate as full citizens of mainline society. History should enhance identity, not bastardize it.

The second strategy chosen by a fair number of Native novelists uses History somewhat differently; this strategy implies grounding the diegesis in the actual historical events that have disrupted Native societies: the Conquest, treaties, Removal, the reservation system, Allotment, Termination, Relocation. This is a way for postcolonial writers (and all writers willing to make whatever statement about the past) to reappropriate their own history, to define it from their perspective, that of the victims, by refusing to have it written by the victors exclusively. These novelists do not negate the "official" version of History, they do not necessarily subvert it, but they want to exhibit what the tragedies of the past have provoked on their own people and to inscribe them forever in their books. It is the strategy of the now canonical works of John Joseph Mathews (the discovery of oil for the Osage in Sundown [1934]), D'Arcy McNickle (the imprisoning on reservations in The Surrounded [1936] or the desecration of land and the stealing of sacred objects in Wind from an Enemy Sky [1978]), N. Scott Momaday (fighting in white wars and Relocation in House Made of Dawn [1983]), Leslie Marmon Silko (fighting also in white wars in Ceremony [1977]), James Welch (the end of the golden age of the Blackfeet in Fools Crow [1986]), Linda Hogan (the murders of oil-rich Osage in Mean Spirit [1990]), and of more recent works such as LeAnne Howe's Shell Shaker in which the recourse to History is given a new twist.[1]

Shell Shaker won the American Book Award in 2002 and was nominated for the French prize Médicis Étranger in 2004. The plot fuses historical eras, past conundrums surfacing up constantly to be reexperienced and solved at last at the end of the twentieth century. They are all based on authentic events centered on the opposition in the eighteenth century between the tribal faction allied with the French and the one allied with the British. The latter would betray the whole tribe then and again in the twentieth century by working closely with the Italian mafia and the IRA.

As in House Made of Dawn, all the chapters bear a precise date and place, between 1738 and 1991. The first chapter is set in Yanàbi Town, the original district of the tribe, on September 22, 1738, during the autumn equinox, the second in Durant, Oklahoma, again on September 22, but in 1991. These two dates seal the history of the Choctaw. They had first met the Spaniards (Hernando de Soto is referred to many times in the story), then, because they lived in what was to become Louisiana, they became the allies of the French, later those of the British. The internecine war ended with the victory of the pro-French group, a short-lived one at that, since France lost all its colonies in North America in 1763. In 1805 the Choctaw started to cede property to the Spaniards and the Americans through various treaties. In 1820 they swapped some lands against others in Indian Territory, but most stayed in Mississippi until the infamous Treaty of Dancing Rabbit Creek that gave them the privilege of being the first tribe to be deported forcibly in application of the 1830 Removal Act.

The novel opens on the rivalry between the tribe and its neighbors, the Chickasaw, who had allied with the British. Red Shoes, the warrior chief of the Choctaw, has lost the respect of his people. He has two wives: the Chickasaw one is assassinated, and the other wife, Anoleta, is accused of having killed her out of jealousy. Because she belongs to the Choctaw clan of the peacemakers, her mother, Shakbatina, offers herself as the sacrificial victim to maintain peace between the two peoples. The first chapter is narrated through her voice. She knows her essence will live through her daughters and their descendants, and she hurries to teach them what they will need. In particular, she advises Anoleta to ask their French friend Bienville (the actual French explorer and governor) to continue to harass Red Shoes and the English. The reader experiences Shakbatina's ritualistic murder from the inside. After the horrible pain of the blow that shatters her head, she feels peace when she enters in the other world and is welcome by Hashtali, Mother Porcupine, the Creator of the Choctaw. This motherly trickster solves the plot in the twentieth century. Founding myth, past and present, combine constantly to allow the younger generations to understand their origins and prepare their future.

Even though the novel bears on the rupture brought about by the European Conquest, Howe does not hold it to be the only traumatizing event. She often states that, even before the arrival of the whites, the tribes had fought among themselves. Red Shoes, who is reincarnated as McAlester, is the guilty one because he betrayed twice his own people out of greed. To restore harmony a new victim must be found, and it cannot just be an innocent woman like Shakbatina. Indeed, the historical Red Shoes was actually murdered by his own tribe in 1747. Yet the murder did not eliminate his negative influence, and it would only be in 1991 that the combined action of strong women would finally eradicate his power. He is at this point found assassinated in his own office, his mistress, Auda, at his side, covered in blood. One understands she is the reincarnation of Anoleta. History repeats itself: Auda's mother, Susan Billy (the reincarnation of Shakbatina), is taken to prison, and, because of all the secrets Auda shared with McAlester on the mafia's and the IRA's involvement in the tribe's companies, the enemies of the Billy family plot to dispose of her. Her daughter Auda receives visions or dreams that emanate from the eighteenth century, and her person is but the avatar of her female ancestors having been reincarnated a final time to bring the cleansing ritual to its completion. At the same time the sisters and their mother become one: "The world that had separated them vanished. . . . at last they are of one mind" (108–9).

Like all the authors who ground their fiction in History, Howe conducted extensive research in archival documents, in the archival documents called the Choctaw stations notably, and history books whose references are dutifully given in the end. She takes History seriously and does not intend to subvert it; rather, she plans to correct it. It is the material thanks to which her heroines can dispel their nightmares. The major one, Auda, is indeed herself a historian who published *The Eighteenth-Century Choctaws*. In one key passage for my analysis, in the chapter entitled "Penance," she discusses the power of history with her lawyer and friend, Gore Battiste (probably an echo himself of Jean Baptiste Bienville). It turns out that he worked at the Oklahoma Historical Society as an archivist and thus discovered the entanglements between the Indians, Al Capone, and other crooks. History and chronicles form the best weapons against rumors and falsehood. Later Auda argues for the absolute necessity of understanding History correctly: "It occurs to her that most Indians in Oklahoma, including him, don't consider the details of their tribal history as she and Red did. Though there was a difference. She wrote about Choctaw history as a way to correct the misinformation about the tribe, Red saw their history as a means to an end. . . . 'Red's excuse for everything he did was based on Americans' treatment of Indians.'" To which Gore replies: "So we're absolved by history?" (112–13). Unlike McAlister, the two friends do not feel history (that of Conquest) should absolve the Natives, or anyone else for this matter, and allow them to behave immorally. Later in the same chapter, Auda searches for a small rabbit, not incidentally a French one, to whom she gave the name of the famous friend of the Choctaw who fascinates her: Jean Baptiste le Moyne, sieur de Bienville, whose life is summarized in the text (121). The rabbit echoes, of course, both the treaty that displaced the Choctaw and one of the tribe's tricksters, History and Myth fusing to help Auda solve the problems of her community at the end of the twentieth century. The rabbit's being French recalls the friendship between France and the "good" Choctaw and should prove a good omen for the future. For Howe History—that is, in the case of Indians, the history of their dispossession—cannot justify the treachery of individual Indians against the others. Rather, History can help us understand that the present is but the result of ancient actions. Healing can proceed from the knowledge revealed by the chronicles that are open accounts of the past. Subversion is not necessary; only a proper interpretation of what they tell us is required. Moreover, History cannot operate alone: it wants the benevolent assistance of mythic protectors, of tricksters, either the rabbit or Mother Porcupine, who actually act upon the chronological sequence of events to give them a specific direction, within the human sphere and in the contemporary world that some would have us believe to be totally cut from the magic world of mythic time.

LeAnne Howe then moves a step further than her contemporaries. By insisting on the power of Choctaw women to solve the conundrum that weakened the tribe and in the long run provoked the tragedy of its deportation, she wants to minimize the impact of the European Conquest, which is radically at odds with the accusation generally leveled by Natives. She has said that in reality European intruders had no power at all over the Choctaws: "The foreigners especially the French are colonizing NOTHING. They are trying to hang on by their toenails to keep their place in the New World. Without our Choctaw support, they have no one of any consequence to protect them. We Choctaw are a major population or confederacy at this time who supports them. The French members are thin compared to ours. . . . The French do not win any war here. . . . Fire power means very little."[2] Such a denial of the impact of the Europeans on the plight of the Choctaw is intriguing. Historically, if the French indeed lost ground pretty quickly, their presence in Louisiana did not go without major consequences for the Mississippi Basin tribal relations. As for the Anglo-Saxons, they have dictated the fate of the tribes from their early arrival until today. One sees here the radically different perspective of a novelist who is convinced that her fiction can redress the course of official History by endowing it with a new understanding: the Choctaw were responsible for their fate, and today, with their new consciousness added to the ever operative trickster help, they can again self-define their future.

The third stance toward History presented here is Gerald Vizenor's. He is the writer who has most vigorously attacked the intrusion of History into the mythic time and space of the Natives, both in his essays and histories and in the "mixed-media history book" entitled *The People Named the Chippewa* that can be seen as staging the struggle between Chronos, the Greek god of time, the father of History and chronology, and Naanabozho, the timeless trickster of the Anishinabeg. For Vizenor it is Myth that spells the truth because it can be reinterpreted, reoriented, to serve didactic purpose. Here, as in various works, Vizenor denounces also Writing that is intimately linked to History. Both are the enemies of the oral tradition that constantly recreates the world. For Vizenor writing freezes the word as it freezes events, as it chronicles the present to turn it into the past. Thus, Writing and History kill Myth, and it is the duty of artists to subvert them.

As I argued at the beginning of this essay, written historical records give a linear vision of time, moving from one beginning, a specific event that will serve as a time marker, and evolving into the future that some groups (those belonging to the biblical tradition) interpret as leading to a definite end, whereas mythic time is cyclical and never-ending. To explain his point, Vizenor quotes a long passage from Frederick Turner's *Beyond Geography: The Western Spirit against the Wilderness* (1980):

> The traders and their employers could tolerate the wilderness only in the hope that eventually they could make enough money to leave it behind. . . . Here they would establish a post and make it known that they stood ready to supply the needs of the resident tribes in return for pelts taken in trapping and hunting. . . . Here again we encounter the clash between history and myth, with the whites, driven to enormous technological superiority, producing a vast array of seductive items for peoples of the globe whose spiritual contentments had kept their own technologies at comparatively simple levels. (*People* 24)

Further, Vizenor denounces anthropological and historical inventions and states:

> Traditional tribal people imagine their social patterns and places on the earth, whereas anthropologists and historians invent tribal cultures and end mythic time. . . . The Anishinaabeg have been invented by ethnocentric methodologists who wear the professional cloaks of missionaries, ethnologists, anthropologists, and historians . . . [they] have been invented, separated from their imaginative recollections, which has allowed a material and linguistic colonization of tribal families. (27)

To qualify such assertions, however, one must add that History is not just a mechanical recording of activities, for it is anything but a definitely scientific and objective rendering of how human or natural events occur.

On the contrary, as I claimed earlier, history is a subjective discourse on events that more often than not expresses the interpretation the winners give to the turn of events. This is clearly why several other Native writers object not to History per se but to the process that "makes history." This is clearly the case of Beatrice Culleton's novel, which is structured along these parameters.

In his book Vizenor strangely wavers between two interpretations. After telling us that historians have invented and misrepresented his people, he still chooses extracts from their books (either those written by mixed-bloods or by whites) to tell us their history, and it is impossible for the reader to decide whether those quotations are to be taken ironically or not. His own book is thus a fascinating collage of extracts from "official" books of history and his own imaginative re-creation of the past, not so much against the deadly archival records as *around them*, in a process that he names "Narrative histories." One of the most forceful chapters is entitled "Shadows at La Pointe." It is a moving passage in which Vizenor poetically reactualizes the mythic past of his people. It stages two little girls on the shore of Lake Superior looking at the trees meeting the water, "an invitation to follow the sun over the old trade post to a new world of adventures" (*People* 37). The edenic old days are, however, already intruded upon by History embodied in the trade post, painted red, as if it pretended to be "red skinned" to attract the Natives better and deliver them into the world of the incomers, often into their red-light districts through the fur trade. The two girls narrate their own personal and tribal histories, which are inseparable: "I have nothing more to write. I might say that I have almost consumed the history of my life. Well, I believe this is the end of my story" (39). The passage moves from the mythic image of the pure wilderness of the lake to History that creeps in irremediably into the Garden of Eden that Manitoulin Island constitutes for the Anishinabeg.

The end product, the text, raises another issue. If, as Vizenor says, Writing is the accomplice of History, for without it no frozen records of live events could be made, what are we to think of a *printed book* on the history of the Chippewa? The differences between The *People Named the*

Chippewa and canonical history textbooks may be not so radical after all. By narrating on the printed page the distant or recent events that befell the Chippewa/Anishinabeg, this provocative book displays some of the ambiguities a Native "writer" gets intertwined in when he "makes history" while condemning the very concept at the root of this process.[3] Moreover, one may argue that the Westerners have dwelled in Myth as much as the Natives. Granted, Vizenor and all Native authors consider their writing as the continuation under another medium of the oral tradition, but such a continuum occurs in other cultures as well, and notably in the West, where writing derives also from the oral tradition. Even for Westerners it is a fine line that separates History from Myth; clearly, for example, much of the history of the European colonization of North America belongs to the mythified narrative genre that successive generations of historians constantly seek to correct, not realizing that they too are weaving their newly imagined versions of what took place, or that they suppose to have taken place, into their fastidious reading of archives. We can see how this operates in the passage in which Vizenor has the young girls on Manitoulin Island talk about their teacher: "She worked ever so hard to teach us how to read and write . . . [she] promised that we could establish in the wilderness a new civilization with books" (*People* 44). Since they go precisely to the mission school, the Christian religion is part of the teaching. Through this ironic allusion to the design of civilizing the wilderness with books, Vizenor is obviously alluding to the Bible, or Scriptures, the epitome of Writing that reinforced colonization because it was so often associated with the sword.

Yet one may argue that (even if some of its adepts refuse to accept it) the Bible is the written version of ancient myths. The new civilization the colonists introduced was just as much grounded in myth as the cultures they sought to transform. Furthermore, this new civilization was the American utopia: the settlers, particularly in their Puritan version, were convinced that, now that they had left History and its evils in Europe, they could start a new cycle, a new Eden, better than that of the Natives because it would be economically productive and based on The Book. This new cycle would reiterate that of the Hebrews reaching Canaan. American History incorporates the cyclical time of Myth because the Westerners have definitely not abandoned the cradle of Myth either. The struggle might not be then so much between History (as Euro-American) against Myth (as Native) as between two mythic interpretations of the world.

Pursuing his own vision of this competition, Vizenor would later adopt a more resolutely satirical stance in his short histories or novels, thanks to the comical subversion of official History through reversals and exaggerations, as, for example, in The Heirs of Columbus (1991), a novel that transforms entirely the character and mission of the man he calls the inventor of the Indians. Vizenor joins here the numerous postcolonial writers throughout the world who, as a major political tool, are fond of reversing (humorously or not) the meaning of official and linear History by turning the dispossessed into the winners and by summoning up new cycles (Thomas King's Green Grass, Running Water [1993] being a good example in Native North America). Nevertheless, Vizenor's originality does not solely rest here. Beyond these developments, which one could call "intra-tribal," he is the only Native American writer (to my knowledge) who has carried the quest for a newer understanding of History far beyond the mere Natives-against-Westerners arena onto the broader stage of world History. This was first staged in Griever, an American Monkey King in China (1987) and more recently in Hiroshima Bugi (2003). His analysis of socialist China and of imperial Japan has retained the same mocking perspective that allows us to decipher official history and decode the petty and pseudo myths that contemporary politics have churned out for passive societies to feed on. Like The People Named the Chippewa, these two texts blend fiction with nonfiction, high Myth with History, and elaborate a profound mythic thought fit for our times and our global community.

What conclusions can be drawn on the function of History in the three works I have presented? The first and most obvious point is that In Search of April Raintree and Shell Shaker seek to prove the importance of knowing the history of one's family and tribe in order to make it one's own and move forward. Once the heroes/readers possess their history, they become stronger and ready to fight for their rights. Even Vizenor, who in *The People Named the Chippewa* blames the history-making process, thinks that it is important to know the records given that he publishes them himself. Plotting History in fiction turns into a means of empowerment.

Beatrice Culleton offers, however, a pessimistic version of this: granted, April stops having to search for herself when she at last accepts the history of the Métis and of her family, but the sister who knew best this history, Cheryl, commits suicide because she can't help this history of dispossession and abuse from repeating itself (she has become an alcoholic like her parents). The sister who can survive is the one, April, who flees the constant reenactment of this collective and private history and only accepts it intellectually once she is physically removed from it. Not incidentally, it is in the foothills of the Rockies, very far from the background of her first novel, that Culleton sets *In the Shadow of Evil* (2000), her second novel, and evil is here the personal and social history of the heroine (Christine, who is an alter ego of April) catching up with her to try to destroy her. Although she triumphs over it in the end, the book remains grim.

The second point is that, in spite of the assaults of History against it, Myth has resisted and continues to thrive. This is particularly visible in Vizenor's work and in *Shell Shaker*, which intimately integrate historical events, visible as such, into the mythic frame inherited from ancestors and alleviate the travails of their protagonists thanks to the ever-present benevolent tricksters. Even if Culleton's craft is less easily decoded as being mythic, it is also deeply rooted in ancient narratives, notably that of the antagonistic and/or complementary Twins. As I have shown in *Le Mythe et la plume*, this literary strategy has been adopted by a great variety of Native writers to such an extent that it is to my mind one of their major characteristics. One then realizes that, through the weaving of historical and mythic time, such authors reorient, more than simply subvert, the meaning of History toward a new understanding of the protagonists' function in the world. Tragedies such as the many sufferings undergone by the colonized Natives (deaths, loss of parents, physical and psychological injuries, territorial and cultural dispossession) are to be read as the cyclical reenactment of mythic and didactic stories centered around initiatory suffering and healing. The violence they undergo gets interpreted as a necessary step in the heroes' quest to succeed in their initiation rituals and gain experience. The Native readers (as well as non-Native readers) may at last understand that their own hardships are neither new nor unique and that they should follow the model offered them in traditional stories. From this, however, we may infer another conclusion: if all the tragedies experienced by the Natives have always existed in mythic plots, can we still accuse the Euro-American colonizers of the destruction of Native communities and cultures, or should they be identified as the mere opponents encountered in any universal quest narrative and over which the heroes must triumph? Would History, so paramount for Westerners, simply revert to playing but a puny part in Native narratives and cultures? This seems to be at least the very message of LeAnne Howe, who, as we have seen, refuses to accept the historical version of the French or the English colonizers as powerful explorers and administrators and forcefully claims that the Choctaw have the key to their past and future in their own hands.

We then move here toward a possibly different function of History, my third contention. We may indeed wonder whether such mythic reenactments do not somehow anesthetize the will of readers to operate radical changes in the current social and political system at large that would entice them "to make history" in their turn. If practically all the hurdles encountered by the protagonists, yesterday and today, are in the end perceived as embedded in a timeless structure, the traumatizing impact of imported History may seem to be somewhat lessened. In the major novels of the Native American Renaissance (along with *House Made of Dawn*, readers might also think of James Welch's *Winter in the Blood* [1974], *The Death of Jim Loney* [1979], *The Indian Lawyer* [1990], Paula Gunn Allen's *The Woman Who Owned the Shadows* [1983], Leslie Marmon Silko's *Ceremony*), instead of potentially leading to active and open political rebellion against the domineering society, the alienation of Native protagonists is subsumed into the mythical *mal être* of the searching heroes. Even among the novels of the following generation, few advise political action outside the Native community. Silko's *Almanac of the Dead* (1991) may be counted as a rare one, and, as we have seen, Vizenor's *Griever* and *Hiroshima Bugi* are unique in their interest in politics at large. Louis Owens did work in this direction as well in *The Sharpest Sight* (1992), which, adhering to the *roman noir* mode, blamed the plight of the protagonists on the American economic superstructure, but he too enshrined the tragedy in Myth (Greek and Choctaw) and concluded it on a ritual Native healing ceremony. Characters feel empowered to claim their rights, as I noted earlier, but they do not have a major political agenda, whereas this could be expected from postcolonial authors. It is not enough to counter my argument by protesting that Native Americans have not yet reached a true "postcolonial" status. Rather, I would contend that this lack of activism derives from the fact that Native writers share more than they are willing to admit the same acceptance of the general political consensus as non–Native American writers, who, even when they denounce corruption and exploitation, never really dare offer a major political upheaval as the solution to social or ethnic inequalities. The way in which the potentially explosive plots of two of the rare novels that engage in such a debate, Welch's *The Indian Lawyer* and Sherman Alexie's *Indian Killer* (1998), peter out without a clear political message or resolution testifies to this.

What, then, unites the writers presented here is their acting like the persona of Betty Louise Bell, who in *Faces in the Moon* (1994) threatens the librarian of the Oklahoma Historical Society (the epitome of the very taken/given/reduced Indian territory and of Writing and History forced upon the Natives) with the weapon they fear most, an Indian woman with a pen in her hand. Their pens have learned to write what the schools of the invaders taught: History. It will not be imposed any longer but, rather, possessed and shared so that the narratives may again be polyphonic and polysemous, in order to cooperate on a par with what never left the people, Myth. Thus, even those novels and stories that exhibit a preoccupation with the science of History display the basic difference between history textbooks and fiction (in general, not just the one I am dealing with here). When, as I argued earlier on, historians must refuse to see man as governed by God or the gods, fiction writers invite the gods back into the text in order to guide and rescue the characters from the mistakes that have been recorded precisely as history. The mission of the Native novelists is therefore different from that of Native historians, who started as early as the nineteenth century to publish their own versions of the past. Writers have far more freedom to shape their message, and therefore may have more power too, for they can remain more faithful to the narrative tradition of their ancestral culture. This is why they revel in the fabulous gift that fiction grants them, which is to metaphorize History back into Myth.

Notes

1. I have developed my analysis of the interaction between historical time and cyclical time in my book *House Made of Dawn*.

2. Extract from an e-mail letter Howe exchanged in April 2005 with Ryad Bensouyad.

3. I have addressed some of these issues in my essay "Naanabozho contre Chronos ou les ambiguïtés de l'histoire chez Vizenor."

Works Cited

Ashcroft, Bill, Gareth Griffiths, and Helen Tiffin. *The Empire Writes Back: Theory and Practice in Post-Colonial Literatures*. London: Routledge, 1989.

Bell, Betty Louise. *Faces in the Moon*. Norman: University of Oklahoma Press, 1994.

Bensouyad, Ryad. "A Brief Account on Choctaw Experience with the White Man from the Early Contact until 1907, through LeAnne Howe's *Shell Shaker*." Master's thesis, Université Bordeaux 3, UFR Pays Anglophones, June 2005.

Châtelet, François. *La Naissance de l'histoire*. Paris: Éditions de Minuit, 1962.

Howe, LeAnne. *Shell Shaker*. San Francisco: aunt lute books, 2001.

Momaday, N. Scott. *House Made of Dawn*. New York: Harper and Row, 1968.

Mosionier, Beatrice Culleton. *In Search of April Raintree*. 1983. Reprint. Winnipeg: Peguis Publishers, 1992.

———. *In the Shadow of Evil*. Penticton, B.C.: Theytus Books, 2000.

Owens, Louis. *Other Destinies: Understanding the American Indian Novel*. Norman: University of Oklahoma Press, 1992.

Rigal-Cellard, Bernadette. *House Made of Dawn*. Paris: Didier Érudition, 1997. (In English.)

———. *Le Mythe et la plume. La Littérature des Indiens d'Amérique du Nord*. Paris: Éditions du Rocher, 2004.

———. "Naanabozho contre Chronos ou les ambiguïtés de l'histoire chez Vizenor." *Annales du CRAA* (Talence: MSHA) 14 (1989): 19–31.

Vizenor, Gerald. *The People Named the Chippewa: Narrative Histories*. Minneapolis: University of Minnesota Press, 1984.

———. *Griever, an American Monkey King in China: A Novel*. Urbana: Illinois State University Press, 1986.

———. *The Heirs of Columbus*. Hanover NH: Wesleyan University Press / University Press of New England, 1991.

———. *Hiroshima Bugi*. Lincoln: University of Nebraska Press, 2003.

3 Transculturality and Transdifference

The Case of Native America

For a number of years cultural theory has discussed multiculturality no longer exclusively as a condition of selected nation-states such as Canada and the United States but as a global phenomenon.[1] Indigenous peoples have not made it, however, to the center of the debates on multiculturalism, nor do they figure prominently in postcolonial theory or any other branch of cultural studies, including general discussions of interculturality and transculturality. They remain doubly marginalized because their claims to land, language, ethnogenetic survival, or even sovereignty are often at odds with the interests not only of the respective dominant society but also of other parts of the population that have immigrated or been forced to immigrate over a period of hundreds or more years. They remain the object of ethnographers and cultural specialists such as those in Native American Studies.[2] And yet their problems might shed light on processes of intercultural contact elsewhere and add significant aspects to theories derived from multi-immigration societies. This is particularly obvious in the case of the indigenous peoples of the Americas, whose interaction with European and other intruders extends back for half a millennium.

Here I shall focus on two concepts of cultural and individual identity formation that were formulated in the context of European discussions of processes of inter-, trans-, and multicultural contact and negotiation, transculturality and transdifference, and shall apply them to Native America. The former concept has a long history. In its original meaning the term *transculturación*, as coined by Fernando Ortiz in 1940, referred to processes of the mutual deculturation and acculturation of African and European cultural components that were involved in the colonial and postcolonial formation of a Cuban identity. According to Ortiz, they did not result in any kind of *mestizaje* but in a rhizomatic interconnectedness and overlapping of old components that facilitated the rise of new ones and resulted in a dynamic and heterogeneous society. The term *transculturality* is sometimes used in a general sense of denoting the interpenetration of cultural components in situations of intercultural exchange, particularly in the current period of globalization. Wolfgang Welsch has raised it to a general theory of contemporary culture and identity, and it is this concept that shall be discussed here.[3]

Welsch takes issue with the eighteenth-century concept of cultures as hermetic spheres, which was made into a general model by Johann Gottfried Herder. It is characterized by "social homogenization, ethnic consolidation and intercultural delimitation" ("Transculturality" 194). Each of these central elements has become questionable in modern societies that are diversified, ethnically mixed, and in constant exchange with others. The Herderian "sphere premis[e] and the purity precept ... render impossible a mutual understanding between cultures" (195). According to Welsch, modern cultures and individuals are shaped by transculturality, whose functioning he explains with respect to the following five aspects: (a) the external networks connecting the individual cultures; (b) the hybridization of cultures by the importation of cultural components from abroad, a phenomenon that as an effect of globalization nowadays shapes all walks of life but has already been at work in the high culture of modernism; (c) the disappearance of the self-other dichotomy because of the mutual penetration of cultures; (d) the transcultural formation not only of societies but also of individuals; and (e) the separation of cultural and national identity ("Auf dem Weg" 323–28).

While *transculturality* is a term exclusively used in cultural studies, the second concept under discussion, *transdifference*, has a different and much wider range of reference. Although the term originated in a doctoral program on cultural hermeneutics at the University of Erlangen, it can be applied in other fields of knowledge as well.

> The term *transdifference* refers to phenomena of a co-presence of different or even oppositional properties, affiliations or elements of semantic and epistemological meaning construction, where this co-presence is regarded or experienced as cognitively or affectively dissonant, full of tension, and undissolvable. Phenomena of transdifference, for instance socio-cultural affiliations, personality components or linguistic and other symbolic predications, are encountered by individuals and groups and negotiated in their respective symbolic order. As a descriptive term transdifference allows the presentation and analysis of such phenomena in the context of the production of meaning that transcend the range of models of binary difference. (Breinig and Lösch, "Transdifference" 105)

Where the negotiation of identities across cultural boundaries is concerned, transdifference "refers to moments of contradiction, tension and undecidability that run counter to the logic of inclusion and exclusion" (Breinig and Lösch, "Introduction" 25). In particular, it can be applied to persons and groups of plural ethnic or other affiliation. In contrast to models of *mestizaje*, creolization, or, indeed, transculturation, it does not refer to cultural synthesis, to an overcoming of difference. And, in contrast to Homi Bhabha's concept of hybridity, it does not refer to an ongoing and basically Derridean deconstruction of difference. Quite the opposite: difference, as Heidegger has pointed out in his short study on *Identity and Difference*, is a precondition of Being and certainly of any system of meaning. Therefore, we see difference such as the distinction of self and other as indispensable and inevitable in the reduction of world complexity, which, in Niklas Luhmann's theory, is what the creation of meaning and thus of cultural systems is all about. Binary thinking, difference and sameness, are essential for living with contingency. Contingency will not go away, however, although we may repress or disregard it by applying binary categories. And transdifference concerns that area of thought and experience that we try to exclude by binary differentiation.

The phenomena referred to by the term *transdifference* are commonplace and well-known both in the context of cultural affiliations and beyond. In a sense transdifference is banal, and it is only our uneasiness vis-à-vis cognitive dissonance, ambivalence, and all those phenomena that are in the way of a reduction of contingency, and hence the production of meaning, that makes us cut it out. The concept of transculturality is equally commonplace if we mean by it the mutual interaction and interpenetration of cultural systems in general terms. Thus, transdifference and transculturation are not mutually exclusive but complementary.

This is already evident in Ortiz's text on the transculturation of Cuban society. I harp on the specific postcolonial origin of the term *transculturality* in order to point out the problematic implications of Welsch's usage, which is at the same time one-sided because it privileges the present and generalizing because it claims global validity. His message of the disappearance of otherness reveals a misunderstanding of the processes of cultural exchange as they have gone on for thousands of years, and it is a misunderstanding going back to a Western model of globalization optimistically seen as a positive de-alienizing process. In view of contemporary concepts of cultures as open systems of knowledge, meaning production, and social practice, Welsch's fight against the vestiges of Herder's model of cultures as hermetic spheres looks quixotic where it concerns the level of theory. Only when we turn to the popular debate regarding multiculturality and the mass immigration by, say, people from Muslim countries do we find old notions of cultural and at the same time national purity dominating people's minds, and it is here that transculturality in Welsch's sense might appear as a hopeful alternative. Even his more recent presentations of his theory show traces of a confusion of old versus new conditions of culture, on the one hand, and old versus new theories of culture, on the other. But transculturality is neither new nor remarkable: cultures are and have always been relational because, in their respective sum total of components, they differ from other such systems, but they overlap, are interconnected in myriad ways, and are constantly evolving in a process of change that is both autopoietic and extra-induced. As a theory of the benefits of contemporary processes of global exchange, however, transculturality is in danger of becoming a theory of acculturation to the culture of those in power—that is, the West.

In response to his critics Welsch has acknowledged that transculturality has been a common feature of societies for ages, but he nevertheless privileges the present. His most radical statement is the following:

> Henceforward there is no longer anything absolutely foreign. Everything is within reach. Accordingly, there is no longer anything exclusively "own" either. Authenticity has become folklore, it is ownness simulated for others—to whom the indigene himself belongs. To be sure, there is still a regional-culture rhetoric, but it is largely simulatory and aesthetic; in substance everything is transculturally determined. Today in a culture's internal relations—among its different ways of life—there exists as much foreignness as in its external relations with other cultures. ("Transculturality" 199)

Let us therefore examine how far the concept of transculturality can help us describe and explain the state of Native America, past and present—a field of cultural interaction that has been going on for almost five hundred years. I will begin with one of the wittiest and most complex self-positionings by any contemporary Native American author, the Anishinabe Gordon Henry:

> I am not:
>   postmodern or modern; a sign, or a signifier, between signifieds; surreal or existential; neo-traditional or beat; transcendental or metaphysical; confessional, shaman, warrior, or sun priest; trickster, nationalist, exile, or anthropocentric; psycho-dramatizer, or dishwasher safe, microwaveable, sunday supplement collector plate; sellout, or shade; or shadow chaser; or orphan boy,

pop icon, trapper, trader, weaver, stone carver, powwow investor;
or an angel looking backward. ("Entries" 165)

He goes on like this for another page and a half of terms, metaphors,
stereotypical projections, and ascriptions. What looks like a monstrous
disclaimer, however, ends like this:

> No I am none of these.
> These are just some of my relatives. Some of them are buried
> between memories of falling leaves; some live as we speak; some
> of them are on the road; some have traveled many roads: some of
> them not good, some of them red, some of them not red, many
> of them red, not good, many of them good not red, many of them
> both or neither. Still they are my relations and for them I am thank-
> ful. (167)

The family, the key factor of traditional tribal identification, has
turned into a network of relations transcending ethnic and cultural borders that seem to locate the author as a postmodern intellectual in a
context of transculturality—that is, to make him a member of the set of
external networks of cultures characteristic of contemporary societies,
according to Welsch. Henry's text also conforms to Welsch's postulates
with respect to hybridity because it shows the marks of a blending, or
intermingling, of cultural components.[4] Yet, while the external linking
of cultures and the formation of all kinds of hybridity are commonplace
phenomena in the age of globalization (as they were before), Welsch's
claim that "henceforward there is no longer anything absolutely foreign," the disappearance, that is, of the difference between in-group
and out-group, remains questionable. As will be seen, Native American identity concepts such as Gordon Henry's may serve as evidence not
only of the transcultural formation of individual identities but also of
the limits of such transculturality.

By its multiple references to contemporary Western intellectual discourses, Henry's self-portrait bears witness to processes of transcul-

turation that affect Native Americans just as much as other populations. What seems even more striking, however, are his confusing and sometimes contradictory claims of belonging and non-belonging, his references to inclusion and exclusion. His claim that he is not one of those with bi- or plurilateral attachments—"a sign, or signifier, between signifieds"—is counterbalanced by his emphasis on family relations, albeit in a generalized sense of *family*. The phenomenon of concurrent but conflicting affiliations, the simultaneous applicability and nonapplicability of identity components points less in the direction of a transcultural disappearance of borders than in that of transdifference.

Transdifference, as will be shown, does not only apply to a synchronic copresence of discordant affiliations but also to the diachronic process of identity formation in which one situation of transdifference (and, potentially, the repression of transdifference in the effort to homogenize the cultural system) is succeeded and, as it were, overwritten by the next, in a long palimpsestic chain. Many Native American texts—for instance, most novels by Gerald Vizenor—evoke this palimpsestic process. In Henry's essay the synchronic and the diachronic palimpsest sides of identity formation are impressively demonstrated by the four sections that in combination form a series of overwritings of the autobiographical self. In the first part, "THE FIRST DOOR: I AS NOT I," the essay starts out with the enumeration of alternative, copresent, and in their combination transdifference-engendering, intercultural categories of belonging, profession, and other identity groups. The diachronic side is presented in a series of biographical remembrances in the long poem of "THE SECOND DOOR: I AS TRAVELER I," and in the evocation of stages of the writer's development in "THE THIRD DOOR: I AS ALTER I—AN AUTOBIOGRAPHICAL META-TALE ON WRITING." The situative, present-tense "FOURTH DOOR: I AS STILL OPEN I—FROM SPAIN, 1994" takes the subject out of its past contexts into the present and future as imagined. That is to say, the four parts form a chain of rewriting the speaker's identity that in this sense is a palimpsest in its own right. One of the rejected and then re-embraced alternative identity couples in the first part is "a presence

in absence, an absence in presence, intense" (166), an almost Derridean description of the alternatives of the self as traces. And the whole
text abounds in references to writing and rewriting, just as the stages of
Henry's education are presented as overwritings and his development
as a writer appears in the shape of a series of poems and other short
texts. There is no idealization: "There was a past I couldn't live in, a
past of languages and words I never learned, a past of words my father
couldn't share" (176). But Henry can sum up the process of intercultural
identity formation and knowledge acquisition in an affirmative manner:
"These ways of seeing and understanding helped me to recognize the
stories in all things; these ways of seeing helped me to try and see the
cumulative past in the being present" (179). Autobiography, then, is
seen as palimpsestic growth, a series of reinscriptions of situations of
transdifference.[5]

Today's Native America is a collectivity of people whose existence is
simultaneously shaped by colonialism, postcolonialism, and neocolo-
nialism. The high percentage of persons with mixed, Native and non-
Native, heritage makes the question of individual and cultural identity
even more complicated. The history of Native American and European
interaction since the beginning of contact provides an outstanding example of transculturality as mutual interpenetration of cultures. While
Europeans traditionally conceived of indigenous peoples as static and
incapable of change, Native Americans adopted numerous elements
of European culture right from the start and integrated them into their
tribal system, so much so that, for instance, the widespread belief among
the Navajos that the horse and the sheep have been part of their lifestyle
since the creation of the world can make us marvel at the integrative
power of cultural memory. On the other hand, as is equally well-known,
none of the settler communities would have survived without the adoption of indigenous food plants, hunting skills, meteorological knowledge, and medicinal lore. If we apply Pierre Bourdieu's categories, we
can say that both sides achieved gains of capital—that the various forms
of economic, cultural, and symbolic capital circulated between the two

populations.[6] It is important to remember that transculturation always also means trans-capitalization.

On the whole the increasing asymmetry of power distribution during the colonial and particularly the postcolonial period has made the investments in transculturation more and more one-sided. Euro-American society depended less and less on cultural transfer from the indigenous peoples while these populations faced an enormous pressure to acculturate to European cultural norms or else face extinction. Cultural theory, and that of transculturality in particular, often speaks of a mutual negotiation of cultural components. But in fact, like in other marketplaces, there are winners and losers. Transculturality requires egalitarian means of resource management, or else it turns into a model of one-sided acculturation only thinly veiled by notions of a globalization of goods and cultural knowledge. There is a good deal of historical irony in the fact that Native food crops that were part of the tribal cultural systems and have helped the West survive the period of industrialization are now undergoing genetic engineering and thus becoming patentable non-Native economic capital.

In the case of Native Americans the history of cultural contact proved that, if they were to avoid genocide, there only remained the alternative of ethnocide, and it is one of the miracles of Native history that so much of their cultures survived this onslaught. How dominant acculturation models have been from the start can be seen in particular in the field of pedagogy. Education always meant European education. The practice of sending Native American children to white (usually missionary) schools started in colonial times. The best-known case is Eleazar Wheelock's Indian Charity School in Connecticut, which was moved to Hanover, New Hampshire, in 1770. As James Axtell has pointed out, Wheelock's missionary goals were to make the Indians adopt European norms of cleanliness, industry, self-control, and obedience and to learn how to read and write so that could they be turned into good Protestant Christians. But this was not an end in itself. I quote Wheelock: "For if they receive the gospel, they will soon betake themselves to agriculture for their support, and so will need but a very small part, comparatively, of the lands which they now claim" (quoted in Axtell 99), lands that would then be free for white colonists—cultural capital thus turning into economic value. Wheelock expected his male students to become teachers or missionaries, the girls were supposed to become housewives, teachers, or seamstresses—European clothing being expected to be in much demand. As messengers bringing British culture to their native villages, the students would embody transculturation as acculturation. "In other words, education has been the mechanism by which colonialism has sought to render itself effectively permanent, creating the conditions by which the colonized could be made essentially *self*-colonizing, eternally subjugated in psychic and intellectual terms and thus eternally self-subordinating in economic and political terms" (Noriega 374). One notices the complete convergence of the various levels of culture: religious, theoretical and practical, textual and material.

The school had to be located as far as possible away from territory still occupied by Native communities in order to remove the students from the tolerant, nonrepressive way that Native societies educated their children. With amazing frankness Wheelock wrote: "Here, I can correct, & punish them as I please" (quoted in Axtell 100). He was highly irritated by the resistance he met with particularly from the Iroquois against his pedagogical methods, which were based on corporeal punishment and hard labor on the school's farm. Indian chiefs and elders were well aware of the cost of transculturation as acculturation. One of them, the Seneca chief Cornplanter, replied to Benjamin Franklin's praise of (European) learning with a statement of cultural relativism:

> You, who are wise, must know that different Nations have different Conceptions of things; and you will therefore not take it amiss, if our ideas of Education happen not to be the same as yours. We have had some experience of it; Several of our young people were formerly brought up at the Colleges of the Northern Provinces; they were instructed in all your Sciences; but, when they came back to us, they were . . . neither fit for Hunters, Warriors, nor Counsellors; they were totally good for nothing. We are however not

the less oblig'd by your kind Offer, tho' we decline in accepting it; and to show our grateful Sense of it, if the Gentlemen of Virginia will send us a Dozen of their Sons, we will take great Care of their Education, instruct them in all we know, and make *Men* of them. (Quoted in Noriega 376)

Yet an acceptance of relativity, and hence the convertibility of cultural capital, remained inconceivable for most Europeans and Euro-Americans; elements of tolerant Indian education found their way only into very few (if any) experimental Western schools of the twentieth century. Thus, the Indian boarding schools that were established by the state or the churches during the nineteenth century and remained in operation well beyond the middle of the twentieth continued Wheelock's model. Native children were now sent there even against their and their parents' wishes. The brutality of the reeducation program at the Carlisle Industrial Indian School, for instance, is notorious. The Lakota Lame Deer who had suffered this traumatizing treatment and told about it in 1972, commented on recent developments:

The schools are better now than they were in my time. . . . The teachers understand the kids a little better, use more psychology and less stick. But in these fine new buildings Indian children still commit suicide, because they are lonely among all that noise and activity . . . . These schools are just boxes filled with homesick children. The schools leave a scar. We enter them confused and bewildered and we leave them the same way. When we enter the school we at least know that we are Indians. We come out half red and half white, not knowing what we are. (Lame Deer and Erdoes 24–25)

The aim of these Indian schools was to strengthen the children's individuality and weaken the communities of family and tribe, as did the Relocation policy after World War II. What was strengthened in most students, however, was the fear of failure so common among Native American young people even today. And, if the famous Indian writers' festival "Returning the Gift" celebrates at least the acquisition of written languages, Gordon Henry, in a poem that is part of his identity definition, has this to say about his memories of Indian schools and the compulsory acquisition of written English:

I am a traveler:
in the hands of sisters
in Catholic services,
in schools where the mist
takes the shapes of children
and eats lives whole and complete
in cursive and the arrangement of
letters.
(167)

This overwriting of native cultures has not resulted in a total and permanent erasure, however, but a kind of palimpsest. In Klaus Lösch's words:

From a diachronic perspective, systems of meaning can . . . be aptly described as palimpsests: what has been excluded can never be erased, but only overwritten by what has been selected. And the traces of the repressed are therefore present and the repressed alternatives can be reconstructed. Expanding the metaphor of palimpsest in dynamic terms, we propose to call the reproduction of systems of meaning a palimpsestic process: in the cycles of reproduction the excluded has to be re-inscribed and overwritten again and again in order to ban its destabilizing threat. This iterative moment produces transdifference, since it reintroduces world complexity by necessarily referring to other possibilities to validate its selection. To a degree, systems of meanings, or cultures, do not only carry suppressed seeds of transdifference with them but permanently reproduce moments of transdifference. This means that transdifference can never be completely controlled; even repressed transdifferences can be reconstructed from the palimpsestic cultural text in progress and can be used by individuals and/or subgroups as a starting point for interrogating the consistency and the truth claims of the symbolic order, thus serving as seeds of resistance, as it were, to rigid patterns of inclusion and exclusion and the concomitant normative pressures. (Breinig and Lösch, "Transdifference" 110)

That is to say that Native Americans have not only retained elements of their cultural heritage but have acquired the whole of Western culture, whether by (forced or voluntary) education, intermarriage, or other sources such as the media. At the same time, the various historical periods of transdifference-creating interaction that both sides have gone through have become part of the palimpsestic reproduction of all the cultures involved and are therefore part and parcel of any production of meaning. To demand a return to traditional culture-plus-education as quite a few essentialists do would amount to denying indigenous cultures the faculty of change and development. But to define the poles of transdifference in the contemporary situation of enormous variety of political and subject positions among the Native community between claims of Indian sovereignty and an acceptance of total assimilation is a Sisyphean task. The Cherokee educator Marvin Buzzard comments:

We have convinced ourselves that there is a tremendous tension between white and Indian values. We've been sold the notion, not just by the larger society, but by ourselves, that Indians are noncompetitive, that they don't care about money, that if they don't own anything, that is an expression of their "Indianness." This sort of thing is both racist and romantic, and it abets a lot of the self-destructive behavior that is out there. It tells us, in effect, that we have to decide between "being Indian" and being able to provide for our families, that unless you're suffering, you're not really an Indian. I doubt that Crazy Horse rode around in rags. . . . Any notion that we can, or should, live in isolation from contact with whites is absurd. (Quoted in Bordewich 299–300)

The metaphor of the gift of writing refers to much of what enables Natives to survive in the modern world. Native students have benefited from the Euro-American education they have received—and some, for instance the Indian intellectuals who teach at American universities, have benefited a lot. They have become part of the palimpsest of contemporary Native America that is not completely transculturated but represents transdifference as an often painful but also often creative condition.

To accept this situation requires the acknowledgment that the tribal pole of identification continues to be as relevant as that of the dominant society. As recently as 1989, the success rate of those indigenous students who attended a tribal college before they entered a "regular" university was forty times higher than for those coming directly from high school because the tribal colleges and schools make traditional types of knowledge appear as valuable (Bordewich 275). Thus, the continued underfunding of tribal colleges perpetuates an acculturative agenda and contributes to the destructiveness of the bicultural situation. Raymond Fogelson has pointed out that Native American identity constructions are still divided, full of contradictions, full of transdifferent personality features. Notwithstanding the omnipresent processes of transculturation, the loss of tribal languages, and the fact that very many American Indians are of mixed descent, the element of strangeness, the awareness of difference, remains. Indigenous authenticity has not simply become folklore and simulation, as Welsch sees it, but it remains a goal for many Native people. Male students still tend to fantasize themselves in the roles of traditional tribal warriors and leaders. Whatever their actual blood quantum may be, they tend to claim a much purer Native genealogy than can be proved. Fogelson describes contemporary problems of identity construction among young Native Americans for whom a biological essentialism seems more adequate than N. Scott Momaday's famous dictum in "The Man Made of Words" that "an Indian is an idea that a given man has of himself" (162):

Thus, in a particular situation a Native American's ideal identity might be that of a full-blood, a feared identity might be a Wannabee, a "real" identity is a person having three-eighth's blood quantum, and a claimed identity is a person with a nine-sixteenths degree of Indian blood. However, identity components are rarely so ordinal or quantifiable. A group of protesting Native Americans might see their ideal identity as that of traditional warriors, have a feared identity as self-serving "radishes," a "real" identity as a disenfranchised minority fighting for their rights, and a claimed identity, claimed by black T-shirts with a distinctive logo, as active members of the American Indian Movement (AIM). (Fogelson 41)

Whether they are Navajo shepherds or San Jose computer specialists, Native Americans experience not only transculturation but a constant reproduction of transdifference. Many new developments have been described in Fergus M. Bordewich's *Killing the White Man's Indian: Reinventing Native Americans at the End of the Twentieth Century*. It remains to be seen if the economic capital provided by the "New Buffalo," the casinos on Indian reservation land, can be turned into cultural capital.

Transcultural change and the persistence of transdifferent pluri-affiliation are best reflected in Native American literary texts, and most often by writers of mixed ancestry such as Gerald Vizenor, whose "postindian" is a more adequate conceptual and linguistic embodiment of transdifference than David Hollinger's notion of "postethnicity." In *Mixedblood Messages* Louis Owens attacks Lakota Elizabeth Cook-Lynn's essentialist notion of "tribal realism" and argues for the creative or at least unavoidable doubleness of place and spatial movement, of family (clan, tribe) and the individual adrift in society at large, of cultural loss and gain, of the past and the future. Whereas the classics of the so-called Native American Renaissance such as Momaday's *House Made of Dawn* and Silko's *Ceremony* emphasized the healing potential of a return into a tribal community, a contemporary Native American protagonist such as that of Sherman Alexie's short story "The Toughest Indian in the World" embodies successful transculturation into the dominant postindustrial society but is suddenly and in a kind of Joycean epiphany shaken and made aware of his in-between position when an Indian hitchhiker he takes along puts not only his heterosexuality in doubt but also his notions of toughness and heroic manliness. When the end shows him walking on bare feet in the direction of his tribal place of origin, this does not amount to a permanent return, given that the narrative stance remains unaltered, but to a recognition of the continued strength of his Native ties.

Transculturality refers to phenomena of transition. In the collective history of Native and European Americans such transcultural transitions have been going on for five hundred years, but this has resulted in one situation of transdifference after the other. Authors such as Vizenor, Owens, Henry, and Alexie, in their respective and highly diverging ways, have represented the essence of *transdifference* not to do away with difference nor to folklorize it in a model of transcultural harmony-in-diversity but to make us experience the tensions resulting from a simultaneous validity of conflicting or at least diverging elements, the persistence of strangeness and difference in a society in which—I rephrase Welsch—there will always be something absolutely foreign. Only when we acknowledge the ongoing copresence of transcultural and transdifferent phenomena can we adequately grasp the meaning of survival for contemporary Native American cultures and individuals.

Notes

1. See the essays collected in David Bennett, ed., *Multicultural States*.

2. Thus, Karsten Fitz's valuable study *Negotiating History and Culture: Transculturation in Contemporary Native American Fiction* analyzes phenomena of transculturation as they are represented in American Indian literature but has to depend on postcolonial and other cultural theories that were developed in the context of non-Native societies. The problem is competently addressed in Elvira Pulitano, *Toward a Native American Critical Theory*.

3. Welsch has presented his theory in several publications. Where it is possible I quote from the English version, "Transculturality—the Puzzling Form of Cultures Today," but I also refer to the later and extended German version, "Auf dem Weg zu transkulturellen Gesellschaften."

4. I will skip Welsch's point about the separation of national and cultural identity because a discussion would require a differentiated set of definitions of *nation*, nationhood being claimed by many Native American tribes.

5. Henry's novel *The Light People* is a series of mutually explanatory narratives and in this way has a palimpsestic structure, too. One scene makes this particularly obvious. The central character (comparatively speaking) opens an old cabinet that belonged to his grandparents: "Oskinaway looked and reached further into the empty space. Then he saw words and pulled back the plastic on the shelving. There were layers upon layers of brittle yellow newspaper, each layer older than the layer before. He read parts of each layer until he reached the paper covering the wood. He read the words: they were parts of *The Progress*, a turn-of-the-century reservation newspaper. . . . He pieced the brittle fragments together into whole paragraphs on the table. Then he worked the larger pieces into two-page-spreads" (192–93). It turns out that these are allotment records, telling documents of intercultural negotiations.

6. In Bourdieu's terminology *cultural capital* refers to forms of knowledge. Particularly in his later publications, *symbolic capital* means "prestige, reputation, fame, etc., which is the form assumed by [the other] kinds of capital when they are perceived and recognized as legitimate" (*Language and Symbolic Power* 230).

Works Cited

Alexie, Sherman. "The Toughest Indian in the World." *The Toughest Indian in the World*. New York: Grove Press, 2000. 21–34.

Axtell, James. *The European and the Indian: Essays in the Ethnohistory of Colonial North America*. Oxford: Oxford University Press, 1981.

Bennett, David, ed. *Multicultural States: Rethinking Difference and Identity*. London: Routledge, 1998.

Bhabha, Homi K. *The Location of Culture*. London: Routledge, 1994.

Bordewich, Fergus M. *Killing the White Man's Indian: Reinventing Native Americans at the End of the Twentieth Century*. New York: Doubleday, 1996.

Bourdieu, Pierre. *Language and Symbolic Power*. Ed. John B. Thompson. Trans. G. Raymond and M. Adamson. Cambridge: Harvard University Press, 1991.

Breinig, Helmbrecht, and Klaus Lösch. "Introduction: Difference and Transdifference." In *Multiculturalism in Contemporary Societies: Perspectives on Dif-*

ference and Transdifference. Ed. Helmbrecht Breinig, Jürgen Gebhardt, Klaus Lösch. Erlangen: Universitätsbund, 2002. 11–36.

———. "Transdifference." *Journal for the Study of British Cultures* 13.2 (2006): 105–22. Special issue: *Theorizing Cultural Difference and Transdifference.* Ed. Doris Feldmann, Ina Habermann, and Dunja Mohr.

Fitz, Karsten. *Negotiating History and Culture: Transculturation in Contemporary Native American Fiction.* Frankfurt: Peter Lang, 2001.

Fogelson, Raymond D. "Perspectives on Native American Identity." In *Studying Native America: Problems and Prospects.* Ed. Russell Thornton. Madison: University of Wisconsin Press, 1998. 40–59.

Heidegger, Martin. *Identity and Difference.* Bilingual ed. Trans. Joan Stambaugh. New York: Harper and Row, 1969.

Henry, Gordon. *The Light People.* Norman: University of Oklahoma Press, 1994.

———. "Entries into the Autobiographical I." In *Here First: Autobiographical Essays by Native American Writers.* Ed. Arnold Krupat and Brian Swann. New York: Modern Library, 2000. 164–81.

Hollinger, David A. *Postethnic America: Beyond Multiculturalism.* New York: Basic Books, 1995.

Lame Deer, John (Fire), and Richard Erdoes. *Lame Deer: Seeker of Visions.* New York: Pocket Books, 1976.

Luhmann, Niklas. *Soziologische Aufklärung: Aufsätze zur Theorie sozialer Systeme,* vol. 1. Opladen: Westdeutscher Verlag, 1970.

Momaday, N. Scott. *House Made of Dawn.* New York: Harper and Row, 1968.

———. "The Man Made of Words." In *The Remembered Earth: An Anthology of Contemporary Native American Literature.* Ed. Geary Hobson. Albuquerque: University of New Mexico Press, 1981. 162–73.

Noriega, Jorge. "American Indian Education in the United States: Indoctrination for Subordination to Colonialism." In *The State of Native America: Genocide, Colonization, and Resistance.* Ed. M. Annette Jaimes. Boston: South End Press, 1992. 371–402.

Ortiz, Fernando. *Contrapunteo cubano del tabaco y el azúcar.* Barcelona: Ariel, 1973.

Owens, Louis. *Mixedblood Messages: Literature, Film, Family, Place.* Norman: University of Oklahoma Press, 1998.

Pulitano, Elvira. *Toward a Native American Critical Theory.* Lincoln: University of Nebraska Press, 2003.

Welsch, Wolfgang. "Transculturality—the Puzzling Form of Cultures Today." In *Spaces of Culture: City, Nation, World.* Ed. Mike Featherstone and Scott Lash. London: Sage, 1999. 194–213.

———. "Auf dem Weg zu transkulturellen Gesellschaften." *Paragrana: Internationale Zeitschrift für Anthropologie* 10 (2001): 254–84.

2. FROM EARLY FICTION
TO RECENT DIRECTIONS

4 American Indian Novels of the 1930s

John Joseph Mathews's Sundown and
D'Arcy McNickle's Surrounded

John Joseph Mathews's Sundown and D'Arcy McNickle's The Surrounded were published in 1934 and 1936, respectively, and were favorably if not widely noticed but—not unlike many other valuable books that appeared during the Depression years—very soon afterward sank into oblivion, to resurface only in the late 1970s, in the wake of the interest aroused by the novels of a younger generation of American Indian writers. Yet, since their reissue, they do not seem to have reached a very large readership beyond the one ensured by their adoption as textbooks in Native American Studies university programs, nor have they yet obtained the amount of critical recognition they deserve, both being works to be counted—by any of the current criteria of evaluation—among the most significant American novels of the 1930s.[1] What has been pointed out, however, most limpidly by Louis Owens (the first, to my knowledge, to pair them off for discussion), is their importance in the history of the subgenre to which they belong. In Other Destinies: Understanding the American Indian Novel (1992) Owens opened the chapter devoted to Mathews and McNickle by stating: "With the publication of Sundown in 1934 . . . John Joseph Mathews introduced the modern American Indian novel, laying out the pattern for novels by Indian writers that would be confirmed two years later when D'Arcy McNickle published The Surrounded and again and again in succeeding decades" (49).

The pattern Owens referred to is the one that both writers must have found most suitable to carry out their intention of exploring what it was like being an Indian in contemporary America and of doing so through a strict adherence to the codes of realism. One only needs to turn to the handful of novels written by Indian authors before 1934—works in which (excepting Mourning Dove's *Cogewea* [1927]) Indian concerns have to be culled from under the trappings of the love cum adventure kind of popular frontier romance—to realize that it is indeed with Mathews and McNickle that the American Indian novel comes of age. And how very viable was the pattern they discovered—each unaware, at the start, of the other's endeavor[2]—is proved by the fact that not only did the pattern reappear in the novels that launched the Native American Literary Renaissance but also continued to shape the majority of American Indian novels well into the 1980s.[3]

Before focusing on *Sundown* and *The Surrounded* in order to recognize the elements of the pattern that they actualize as well as each novel's markedly different ways and aims in doing it, let us pause to see how Mathews and McNickle went about the task of casting their stories into the innovative mold of realism.

Mathews (1894–1979), the son of a one-fourth-degree Osage who had made it so good with his trading post as to become the founder of a local bank, belonged to one of the more prosperous families in the Osage Nation, which in turn presented the very uncharacteristic picture of a wealthy Indian tribe—wealthy even before the royalties from the oil extracted from their former reservation lands in the northeastern corner of Oklahoma made the Osage, for several years during the 1920s, literally "the richest people in the world."[4] Although the Mathews family did not take part in the tribe's ceremonial and social life (their descent from an Osage female ancestor excluded them from the patrilinear clan system), they "maintained an active interest in Osage culture" and also "strong personal ties with the traditional Osages" (Bailey 207), notwithstanding the constant frictions between the progress-minded mixed-bloods and the conservative full-bloods over tribal policies. Aside from horseback riding over the prairie, hunting and visiting the old chiefs' camps, Mathews's education was, however, a typically white American one. From a public school he went to college, and in 1920, after serving as a pilot in World War I on the French front, he graduated from the University of Oklahoma with a degree in geology. To round out his education he moved to Europe—to Oxford (where he read for a bachelor's degree in natural science) and then to Geneva (where he earned an International Relations Certificate). Not needing to find a job because his share of oil royalties made him financially independent (and would keep him so for his entire life), from 1924 until around 1929 he led the leisurely life of an American expatriate, traveling around Europe and hunting in North Africa.

In the fall of 1925 twenty-one-year-old McNickle—the grandson of Métis (Cree and French) who had escaped from Canada after the quelling of the "Riel rebellion" in 1885 and found shelter on the Reservation of the Five Confederate Tribes in western Montana—also came to Europe, but his stay was much shorter and certainly not as pleasurable as Mathews's. His avowed aim was to complete the studies he had not finished at Montana State University with an Oxford BA degree, but he was also asserting his determination to put as much distance as possible between himself and what at seventy (three years before his death in 1977) he still remembered as "a hell of a society to grow up in."[5] He was running away from a milieu rife with prejudice against Indians and mixed-bloods as well as from painful boyhood memories: the wrangling between his Méti mother and his Irish-descended father, the ensuing disruption of his family, and the years of strict regimentation in faraway Oregon at one of those boarding schools created for the purpose of detribalizing young Indians and irreversibly making them into "civilized," "regular" Americans. But he was also fleeing toward places that promised richer intellectual stimulation to a young man already bent on becoming a writer. By selling the land he had been allotted thanks to his adoption into the Flathead tribe, McNickle did not succeed, however, in securing enough money to support himself until graduation, and he had to content himself with spending a few months in shy loneliness on the fringe of Oxonian student life and a few more in Paris, for a whiff of la vie artistique among other expatriates. Back in the States by early summer 1926, he settled in New York. Ahead of him were the ten years during which, while eking out a living mainly in odd jobs in the publishing field, he wrote and untiringly kept revising his first novel. But also—as the go-getting and getting-ahead imperatives rampaging in the late 1920s and, then, the economic and social ravages of the Depression disenchanted him with mainstream America—he came to a definition of his own set of values, which would henceforth inform his life choices and work. In an entry of his diary for 1932 he wrote: "In my first job, selling automobiles, I went through a seven months' daily betrayal of my birthright in opposition. Everything I was called upon to do was a violation of instinct and desire. . . . instincts, right or wrong, cannot be abandoned without seriously impairing integrity, out of which rise self-possession, confidence, the very ability to act and think." For McNickle heeding his own instincts involved, first of all, facing and trying to make sense of the unpleasant past he had thus far repressed. Although he would not return to "the scenes from which [he] had fled," much later (and only for one short visit) he did reestablish ties with his mother, which he had severed on leaving Montana, and he returned to using, as a reminder of his tribal affiliation, the family name he had renounced for that of his mother's second husband.[6] More important, he began to read eagerly about the Indians and the history of the West. It is through his writings, however—when "The Hungry Generations" is compared with *The Surrounded*—that one can best gauge his acceptance of the Indian side of his identity and how profound his commitment had become to the responsibilities it entailed.[7]

McNickle's reclamation of his Indianness verifies the definition Momaday was to give of the Indian as "an idea which a given man has of himself" ("Man Made of Words" 97). And so does Mathews's. As he recalled some forty years later, it had been the behavior of Kabyle tribesmen in the North African desert that made him suddenly feel homesick and wonder, "What am I doing here? Why don't I go back and take some interest in my people , . . . the Osages?" (quoted in Logsdon 71), and so decide to go back home. This may sound like a romantic dramatization of fact, especially in the light of the interlude Mathews had in California as a real estate businessman before reaching Oklahoma, soon after the 1929 Wall Street crash. But there is no doubt that his identification with the Osages motivated the wholehearted concern with the preservation of their cultural heritage that Mathews was to manifest ever after, not only as a writer, dealing with Osage land, history, and life in four of his five published books, but also as a politically active tribesman, defending the implementation of the Indian Reorganization Act against Oklahoma state legislators and sparing no efforts to establish an Osage Tribal Museum he himself had conceived as "an instrument of cultural reinforcement" (Wilson 281).

Mathews's and McNickle's (re-)awakened consciousness of themselves as Indians was a very important agent of realism in the making of *Sundown* and *The Surrounded*. That both writers drew largely and circumstantially on their own experiences—from the topographical precision in which fictional Kihekah and St. Xavier match Pawhuska, Oklahoma, and St. Ignatius, Montana, to (as it has been amply noticed) a great deal of character traits and story incidents—is hardly uncommon in the writing of novels. What bears stressing is the two authors' own personal investment in the stories they tell.[8] One of the disastrous aftermaths of the oil boom that must have distressed Mathews upon returning home was the sight of so many of his contemporaries among the Osage rentiers aimlessly wasting their lives (when not losing them through all sorts of excesses). Through Chal Windzer's story not only could he review what his own bicultural life had been since feelings of "fear and bittersweetness, and exotic yearning" (*Osages* viii–ix) had characterized his earliest perceptions of the Osages; he could also meditate on what his life, too, might have become had he not succeeded in leaving behind the aimlessness of his years abroad, had he not been able to follow that "racial instinct" that Chal feels guilty about and keeps repressing in *Sundown* (136). As for McNickle, the very process of writing his novel was essential for him to mirror and test, at the same time, his own changing attitude toward the Indians, as he transformed—revision after revision—the Archilde Leon of "The Hungry Generations," who sees his Indian forebears as fatalistic, helpless savages and settles down as a happily assimilated, thrifty farmer soon to marry the white American girl of his dreams, into the Archilde of *The Surrounded*, who is irresistibly drawn back into Indianness by the "pull[s]" exerted on him by the land and his people (16, 233).⁹ Furthermore, by having the novel end with Archilde ominously entrapped on the reservation, McNickle found a realistically appropriate answer to a question that, as Parker suggests, he was likely to have often brooded on: "What happened to those boys he had known at school who did stay at home? . . . There was no future there for the young men who remained. . . . He himself had escaped, but he knew that if he had gone back to the reservation" (*Singing* 46–47), he too would have become, like Archilde, one of the surrounded.

Realism, however, was not simply an effect of the autobiographical matrix of the two novels. It was also the mode that Mathews and Mc-Nickle must have felt could best authenticate their representation of the Indian at a time when this was being monopolized by Euro-American culture. Even before the last Indian resistance to the westward march of "progress" had been put out, ethnographers, anthropologists, and historians had hastened to record the features of tribal cultures believed to be doomed to an imminent demise by their "primitivism," but their work had too often resulted in a falsifying reduction of the object of study within the conceptual frames of the investigator's culture. How aware Mathews was of this practice we do not know. We do know, however, that, as soon as he was back in Oklahoma, he started gathering information about the Osage past from tribal elders, who were as anxious as he was to prevent its falling into oblivion. The knowledge he thus obtained, while only marginally used in his earlier works (*Wah'Kon-Tah, Sundown*, and *Talking to the Moon*), became his main resource, along with written historical records, for *The Osages: Children of the Middle Waters* (1961), his magnum opus and a pioneering achievement for both its reliance on the oral tradition and presentation of a particular tribal history from an Indian viewpoint. McNickle likewise declared his "distrust[ing] and fe[eling] antagonized by . . . those 'translations' one finds of Indian poetry in which the 'translator' has made the Indian singer over into a kind of sonneteer or at worst a *verse lyricist*,"¹⁰ and at about the same time he was subtly reworking the anthropologists' dulling transcriptions of the traditional stories he was using in chapter 6 of The Surrounded into "speakerly texts," capable of suggesting the interactive effects of traditional storytelling strategies.[11]

Furthermore, Indian subject matter had figured conspicuously in the American novel of recent years, a field of special interest, presumably, to the two would-be Indian novelists. Whether Mathews and McNickle knew Willa Cather's rendering of her enraptured discovery of southwestern cultures in The Professor's House (1925) and Death Comes for the Archbishop (1927) or Edna Ferber's lurid view of peyote religion in her best-selling Cimarron (1930), they are more than likely to have read Oliver LaFarge's Laughing Boy (1929), which was awarded a Pulitzer Prize in 1929. This novel by a young Harvard anthropology graduate told a story that, no matter how believable in the context of a very strong and still unadulterated traditional culture such as the Navajos' in the year 1915, certainly did not tally with their own experiences in Osage or Salish country. And on reading its finale—with Slim Girl, who is "re-made" an Indian after death, through the funeral rite performed by Laughing Boy and Laughing Boy's smooth readjustment to Navajo ceremonial life and seamless reentry into tribal life rhythms—they might well have felt challenged to write stories dealing with the difficulties arising from accepting one's Indian heritage and choosing to live an Indian life in which conditions had been irrevocably shaped by the advent of the white man.

But, once the challenge posed by Euro-American representations of the Indian had been accepted, Mathews and McNickle still had to make sure that their novels would not be rejected by American publishers and readers, whom they could safely assume to be unprepared for their innovative treatment of Indian realities. It was probably to avoid such a risk that extensive segments of their narratives came to be shaped so as to recall the reassuring features of kinds of fiction that had been in vogue for the past ten years (such as the novel about college life, the one about World War I veterans, the one about expatriation) or popular for a longer time (such as the western and the detective novel). While it is interesting that both writers resorted to the same strategy of acclimatization, it must also be pointed out that both practiced it with a subversive twist—witness the biting satire of collegiate fatuousness pervading chapters 7 to 9 of Sundown, the deprecation of the wasteful inanity of expatriate artists' lives in the section of "The Hungry Generations" set in Paris, or, in The Surrounded, elements of western fiction used to highlight not the epic grandeur but the moral rawness and violence of frontier society, along with a detective plot resulting in a bungling enforcement of the law rather than the achievement of truth and justice.

Neither Sundown nor The Surrounded, however, is a "novel of protest" of the sort that was being written in the 1930s: in dealing with the Euro-Americans' treatment of the Indians and the land, with the Euro-American version of history, with Euro-American prejudices and cultural values, Mathews and McNickle do not rely primarily on loud denunciation. In fact, the heterodiegetic narrators of their stories resort very sparingly to direct comments of an ideological import. In Sundown they are very few, and they are very short (as when the oil derricks sprawling over the prairie are compared to "some unnatural growth from the diseased tissues of the earth" or the "ugliness" spread all over by the white man is attributed to his alienation from the land [62, 90]). In The Surrounded narratorial pronouncements are hardly more frequent, although they are usually more extensive and delivered in a tone ranging from bitter irony to sarcasm. Such is the case, for instance, in the passage exposing the mismanagement of the Indian Service (151–52); the one denouncing the interferences of missionaries and government with the dances, that essential expression of the Indian spirit (203–5); and the ones contrasting Euro-American and Indian lifeways and values to point out their radical difference (171–73, 195–96). Mathews's and McNickle's narrative strategy is subtler. They prefer indirection, calling for more active interpretive cooperation on the part of the reader.

Thus, in Sundown imagery and irony are very effective indirect ways to convey a narratorial ideology that in the light of Mathews's other writings can only be identified with the authorial one. A number of vivid descriptions record the onslaught made by "civilization" on the environment and question the dubious nature of a "progress" whose march has lasted no longer than the colonial-like exploitation of the oil fields. As for irony, it is the dominant tone in the presentation of the protagonist's mixed-blood father: a declaimer of Byron's *Childe Harold* who has named his son "Challenge" because "he shall be a challenge to the disinheritors of his people" (4), John Windzer has a conceited sense of his own importance as one of the mixed-bloods' party favoring "Progress" at all costs and despises the full-bloods for their resistance to the allotment of Osage land but does not suspect that "in reality allotment was forced upon the tribe by people outside the reservation who had no particular interest in the welfare of the tribe" (49). Irony also colors the ways—romantic misrepresentation, condescension, obtuse incomprehension leading to scorn, sheer dishonesty—in which whites relate to Indians, and, in a text that uses speech (both reported and transposed) to characterize and differentiate social and ethnic groups, irony is unmistakable in the ungrammatical English of the sort of whites, supposedly the bearers of civilization, who swoop on the Osages to partake of their riches. Irony also suffuses the narrating of the mixed-bloods' enthusiastic expectation of "the indefinite glory" that was sure to come with the oil wells (85), of the climate of illegality, corruption, and violence at the peak of the oil boom, and, once this is over, of the general senseless hope for a return to flush times. But no narratorial irony is shed on the full-bloods: not on Chal's taciturn mother, who clings to tribal ethos, distrusts the white man's talk, and sees through her husband's delusions and her son's aimlessness and vacillations; not on Watching Eagle, who, in his speech to the tribesmen gathered in the sweat lodge, upbraids the young ones for taking a "bad road . . . , thinking it is the white man's road" (271), but is also firmly convinced that the Osages will be able "to keep [their] place on earth" in the face of the frenzied and disruptive changes forced on them by Euro-American culture (275), especially after the discovery of massive mineral resources under their land. The same conviction was held by Mathews at the end of *Wah'kon-Tah*.

Also in *The Surrounded* imagery is ideologically charged, as, for instance, in the description of St. Xavier's "Townsite" and "Indiantown" (35–36), through which the narrator silently invites the reader to ponder the sad outcome of the Christianization and colonization of the Salish. But it is to the characters that the core of the ideological function is assigned. Hence, the frequent recourse to meta- or pseudo-diegetic segments and also the very frequent (and masterful) use of an indirect free style to render the mulling over to which the characters are given because, in the fictional world of this novel, interpersonal communication is not easy even between members of the same race or the same family. Thus, it is mostly through transposed inner speech that the young protagonist comes to an ever clearer awareness of why what he had meant to be a final leave-taking from his people and his land is turning into an ineluctable homecoming. And that technique is also amply employed as a merchant on the verge of bankruptcy, one of the first missionaries among the Salish, Max (Archilde's Spanish father), Catharine (Archilde's Indian mother), and her kin Modeste revolve, one after another and each according to his or her experience, mind-set, and insight, the same question that Catharine, bewildered at the discord in her family and the "confusion, dread and emptiness" all around, asks herself at the beginning of the novel: "What had come about since the day of the planting of the cross?" (22).

What has come about at Sniél-emen is the inevitable failure attending any encounter between two different cultures in which one imposes its models and values with no consideration for those of the other—a failure representative of what has happened anywhere else in the Americas, or in any of the other "New Worlds," whenever an indigenous culture has had to endure the shock of the modern Western one. The cumulative effect of those five elder characters' musings amounts, therefore, to a stringent indictment not only of the conquest of the West (all the weightier when the character who pronounces it is not one of its victims but one of its promoters or one of its presumed beneficiaries) but of colonization as a worldwide phenomenon. Indian cultures do possess, however, an intrinsic vitality, as the meditations and, of course, the actions of both Catharine and Modeste unmistakably prove. Modeste successfully relies on tribal wisdom to cure young Mike's sickness, and he has been going back to "the old things" since the day when not Christian prayers but the help of "his guardian spirit" saved him from death (211). Catharine, notwithstanding the "great happiness" promised by the missionaries (21), has never come to the Salish, has faithfully stuck to Christian observance, but she too abjures Christianity when she believes absolution is impossible for the mortal sin she has committed, and it is only after spontaneously submitting to whipping (that is, to the traditional Salish way to expiate a serious crime) that she recovers her peace and the way to the Indian paradise, the only one she now desires.

Modeste's and Catharine's behavior is not a nostalgic escape into the past, a running away from harsh realities that would be as sterile as Archilde's young nephews' flights to the mountains where they think they can live forever, hunting and fishing. As Modeste well knows, the old times "are dead and won't come back" (70). But the old-time values are not dead as long as a Salish keeps finding in them inner peace, moral sustenance, and a compensation for all that the new order has taken away. By choosing to go back to "the old things", Modeste (whose version of the coming of the missionaries sparks the process through which Archilde arrives at a full acceptance of his Indian identity) and Catharine (whose recantation of Christianity Archilde salutes as "the triumph of one against many; . . . the resurrection of the spirit" [272]) validate the journey back into Indianness made by Archilde. The parallelism between the stories of the two Salish elders and that of the young mixed-blood protagonist embodies an essential aspect of McNickle's ideology: the conviction that, "despite what seemed on the surface to be a massive and rapid breakdown in Indian cultures across the continent, an essential core of cultural integrity was being maintained" (Ortiz 633). This view was to inform McNickle's subsequent anthropological-historical works as well as his activity at the BIA.

But this is not the only aspect of authorial ideology embodied in *The Surrounded*: McNickle was also a strong advocate of self-determination for the Indians, and the stories of Archilde, Catharine, and Modeste affirm the Indians' right and capability to decide by themselves what is good as well as what is good for them. In particular, Archilde sounds like the perfect spokesman of the author's ideas when, taught by his own deeds about the uselessness of unsolicited helpfulness, he reflects that "all ideas were damn fool until they were understood and believed; and it was useless to wish them on to anybody else until the other person had come to them in the same way—by understanding and believing" (247).

The interweaving of the story of the protagonist with the history of the nation he descends from—which is such a crucial feature of *The Surrounded* but can be seen in *Sundown* as well, inasmuch as Chal's disorientation is compounded by the dizzying changes the Osages are going through—is one of the elements of the pattern Owens referred to and the only one to work in both novels in a homologous way.

Another element of the pattern will come into view when the protagonist's story is segmented in three phases: (1) the protagonist's growing up in an Indian milieu that has already felt the pressures and interferences of Euro-American culture; (2) his (spontaneous or enforced) immersion into the strange and unsavory (even when one is successful) world made by Euro-Americans; (3) his physical and/or spiritual journey back into or at least toward Indianness. *Sundown* and *The Surrounded* actualize it quite differently: while the former deals with the three phases chronologically (so as to achieve a "saturated," and most convincing, representation of Chal's incapacity to overcome his irresoluteness), the latter (like a number of novels from the 1970s onward) treats phases 1 and 2 analeptically, to concentrate on phase 3 (so as to follow Archilde closely in his gradual change of heart and mind in regard to his Indian heritage and identity).

But the most important element of the pattern is, no doubt, a certain type of protagonist: a young man (only in a few novels a young woman), intelligent, sensitive, reflective, and endowed with a keen capacity of observation and, in some instances, with a fine sense of humor, who is the negation of hard-to-die Euro-American stereotypes, since he is neither "vanishing" nor "dumb," neither incapable of understanding (and judging) the white man's ways nor unable (if allowed) to steer his own life. But he suffers from a "dissonance" due to his having to live in two different worlds (Hogan 123), the native and the Euro-American, to neither of which he can fully belong. His condition is a double marginality, all the more evident and painful when, as is the case in most novels, he is a half- or mixed-blood, often looked at askance by both Indians and whites. It is a condition that may engender depression, confusion, a sense of inadequacy and ineptitude, verbal inarticulateness, and from which he seeks a way out through the definition of *who he is*. His story centers therefore on the possibility of achieving a more secure sense of his own identity.

The protagonists of *Sundown* and *The Surrounded* do share most, if not all, of these traits, but their stories unfold in opposite directions. If it were appropriate to consider the two novels as *Bildungsromane*, one might say that *Sundown* presents Chal's failed Indian *Bildung* and *The Surrounded* Archilde's successful one. Put another way, while Archilde experiences a transformation so profound that it might be equated to a kind of conversion, no real transformation takes place in Chal.

Nowhere in the novel is Chal seen to be able to reconcile—and give stable order to—the impulses coming from within his Indian self and the values and models of behavior proposed by the Euro-American world. The adult is prefigured in the child who plays at being a panther, a red-tailed hawk, a coyote, and, interchangeably, an American general of the Revolution, who is in turn frightened and fascinated, overawed and disgusted, by white people and who, while very proud of the warlike and oratorical deeds of Osage chiefs, thinks (under the influence of his father's talk) that the full-bloods "must be 'mean' or something" (46). As an adolescent, Chal feels "that dreamy joy of living, as when he was a little boy" (69), only when he is away from the booming little town where the noises of "Progress" have already overtopped and silenced the sounds of the natural world, riding "his pony at a dead run across the prairie" or "looking at sunsets, and having the desire to make songs about everything he [sees]" (69, 71–72). "One day he strip[s] off his clothes and dance[s] in a storm and [sings] a war song" (70); another time ("he did it only once" [72]) he paints his face, but he feels ashamed of the things he likes to do during his solitary outings on the prairie—as he also starts feeling "vicarious shame" for the way his old full-blood playmates behave (68).

Later, too, when at the university, Chal may choose to leave the bustle of the campus behind and walk to the river, where he abandons himself to hours of ecstatic, dreamy contemplation and to singing, if that "racial instinct" comes to him (136), but at the end of the day "he [is] disappointed with himself and he fe[els] that he ha[s] somehow reverted . . . , that he [is] out of step, . . . that he [is] hopeless" (138). The phrase "out of step" rings in Chal's mind whenever he is afraid of not being able to measure up to what is expected of him by the white brothers at his fraternity, those "men [who are] the representatives of civilization" (89, 100). At the same time, Chal is embarrassed by being "slapped on the back . . . the obvious insincerities . . . the effusiveness of the brothers" (95–96), and there are many other things about the white students that he cannot explain, such as their spirit of competition, their egotism, and their sense of humor hinging so much on something so natural as "mating" (139), but in all cases he hides his discomfort and censors his thoughts. He worries about the darkness of his skin, which, he fears, "set[s] him off from other people" (117), and, being angry with himself for his shyness in society, he curses every "drop of God damn Indian blood in [his] veins" (160). Later, as a cadet in the air service, he will go as far in denying his identity as to let the woman he is having an affair with believe that he is Spanish. More and more he finds solace in his fantasies, imagining himself as he knows he is not and will never be, whether a football champion or a war hero honored by the whole tribe or a successful businessman. Being "civilized" means, he feels, that one "ought to be doing something" (162): the phrase "doing something" recurs (245, 262, 279), variously modulated, as Chal toys with the idea, but what that "something" might be never becomes less than vague.

Enlisting is an extemporaneous decision that Chal makes as the idea of war has just awakened "a deep, hereditary emotion" in him, although flying "in the air, like a bird" is going to fulfill one of his childhood dreams (166). Flying at night, thousands of feet above the earth, gives him "a feeling of superiority, and he [keeps] thinking of the millions of people below him as white men. When he bec[omes] conscious that he [is] thinking of them as white men he smile[s] to himself" (218): by being a pilot (having succeeded where many of his white comrades had failed), by having a white mistress, Chal acquires the self-assurance he has always lacked, "and he fe[els] that he ha[s] begun to be gilded by that desirable thing which he call[s] civilization. He was becoming a man among civilized men" (230).

But when, at the end of the war, he returns to Kihekah and finds himself in the welter of "the Great Frenzy," what begins for him is a journey not toward a more secure identity but toward a state that substantiates the title of the novel. Month after month, year after year, Chal simply "[doesn't] know what to do with himself" (262), and his "guess[ing] that he must have two dignities, one tellin' him to do something, and one tellin' him not to do anything" (263), is one indication that his mind is as divided and contradictory as ever. When he escorts two white girls to a social dance, he is annoyed with them, because he knows that they are going to take it as a mere tourist attraction, but also "with himself because in some vague way he fe[els] that he [is] not worthy" of the spirit of the dance (253). Soon he has the desire to join the dancers, "as usual": "He had always felt that by joining them he could express that thing that came over him at times; that something which had to be expressed, but which he couldn't possibly put into words or actions" (257), but once again he knows that he will not be able to do it. His emotion reaches a pitch when the singers intone the song of his ancestors, but, when they end, he is embarrassed because the girls have seen him making the customary gift to the singers.

Because Chal's admiration for his father has been shaken at the time of the latter's political discomfiture and because his mother has mostly been for him a background presence, dearly sweet but turned still to the tribal past, he has never had creditable elder figures to make him prize Osage cultural values and traditions. He has such an opportunity when he takes part in the sweat lodge ritual and can listen to Watching Eagle clearly discriminating between the people's good road and the white man's false road and as clearly affirming: "We are Indian, we are not white men" (274). However desultory his comprehension of the chief's words, the ceremony has a restorative and moving effect on him, leav-

ing him "in a sort of pleasant trance" (279), but only two days later he
is ready to dismiss his emotions as silly sentimentalism and the Osage
beliefs as unpractical, mystical things. By now he is in a state of inebria-
tion most of the time: if at the beginning he drank "with a vindictive
feeling" for the unhappiness caused him by the defilement produced
by the oil wells on places dear to his childhood memories (251), now
he drinks because he thinks that "there [isn't] anything else to do anyway" and because alcohol feeds his daydreaming (264). He is flush with
whiskey the night that, after leaving a drunken and promiscuous party,
he madly races his red roadster through the prairie, possessed by an
urge "to express himself in some bodily action." But when he gets out
of the car among the blackjacks, his solitary frantic dancing and wild
singing are of no avail to free "that terrific emotion which [is] dammed
up" inside him (296). When he wakes up at dawn, he is seen for the first
time at odds with the animal world, whose voices strike him as strange,
hostile, and jarring.

In the last scene of the novel Chal has just come home from a two-
week binge at a gangster's hangout, and, when his mother hints that
going back to flying would be a good thing for him, he gets angry with
her because "she ha[s] been looking into his heart" (310), as she has
always done, but immediately resorts to what the reader knows to have
been his tactics for a long time: "to have a purpose, and that a practical
one, to hide his purposelessness" (170). "There isn't anything to flyin'
anymore," he retorts, proclaiming that he will be going instead to law
school "and take law—I'm gonna be a great orator." His mother, who
sees in front of her not so much "a swaggering young man" but "a little boy in breech clout and moccasins," makes the firmness of the purpose that has "occurred to him [just] the moment before" appear very
doubtful (311). To further suggest the standstill that Chal's life has been
all along, as he falls into a stuporous sleep, the leaf shadows play on
his silk shirt exactly like "the leaf shadows [that had danced] over his
bronze body" when he was a child (11). Around him the natural world
keeps tending, unperturbed, to its business, whatever it may be.

In The Surrounded the attentive reader will not miss the recurrence of words that underlie Archilde's transformation. One is *pull*, referring the first time to natural sounds and odors: "nothing that could be touched, yet hav[ing] strength and substance" (16), they are what has caused him to come back home for what he believes will be his last visit; much later, the "pull" on him is exerted, instead, by human beings, as Archilde is struck by the desolation and emptiness of the life the Salish are leading (233). And there is also the pairing *entwined/intertwined*: in the same passage in which *pull* occurs for the first time, are the images of the land that Archilde feels "entwine" themselves "into one's life" (16); when he is at his dying mother's bedside, he realizes that "people grew into each other, became intertwined, . . . grew together like creeping vines" (258), and his subsequent thoughts and actions reflect that realization: he has recovered his place within the nation and knows that now, for good or bad, "he too belong[s] to the story of Sniél-emen" (275). And there are, finally, two pairs of opposites, *not real / real* and *meaningful/meaningless*. To Archilde, just back from the whites' world, the old people, their habits and views, are "not real"; they belong, like the buffaloes, to an age that is "gone, dead" (62-63). But they start to become real when he pays attention to the story of the Salish he has heard so many times before without listening and "for the first time he really [sees] it happen" (74). The opposition *real / not real* plays once again in Archilde's mind on the Fourth of July: as he watches the women who are preparing the boys for the dance, he is struck by the religious precision of their gestures and thinks that "[for] these people it was real" (215), but, when he leaves the lodge and sees the dancing ground exposed to the desecrating irreverence of the white audience, he feels that "there was nothing real in the scene" (216). The care with which his mother prepares her grandson for the dance is full of meaning, while, after this revelation, the decor, music, and dances at the Farmers' Hall cannot but appear "meaningless" (225). Likewise, working as an advance notice of Catharine's recantation, which he will presently apprehend, the cross formed by the window frame stares at him "meaninglessly" (257).

In the transformation of Archilde's journey from the one *away from* Indianness that he had intended into the one *into* Indianness that he makes, the first important step is his experience of a storytelling event intently attended to for the first time in his life, which softens in him "some stiffness, some pride" (74), and makes him begin to understand and be moved by what the old people have gone through. His transformation is fostered by acts of imagination and memory: on the fatal hunting trip, traveling in the mountains becomes for Archilde a "trying to go backward in time" (116), as he imagines what those places might have been like for his ancestors, hunting not for pleasure but for survival; the story of "Coyote and the Flint" leaves "a spark of gay remembrances in his mind" (66), and so do the pleasant times he spent with his mother as a little boy, while of the years spent at the mission school it is "darkness and heaviness of spirit" that he remembers (103).

The recognition and acceptance of the Indian side of himself is, at the beginning at least, an unconscious process. It is true that, after the first postponement of his leaving, all the subsequent ones are motivated by a chain of fatalities and by the load of responsibilities that Archilde feels thrown on his shoulders. But, at a deeper and truer level, what nails him at Sniél-emen is the "pull," as irresistible as, at first, unconscious, to regain his place among the Salish. Hence, his regret that "whatever he did, . . . he remained on the outside of [his relatives'] problems. He had grown away from them" (193).

In proceeding from "the outside" to "the inside" of the Salish world, Archilde is helped by what he learns about their history and culture—pondering Modeste's story, grasping the equation between "fear" and "sickness" at the base of Modeste's cure for Mike, feeling the religious aura in the preparations for the dance. It is here that, for the first time, "for a moment, almost, he [is] no longer an *outsider*, so close [does] he feel to those ministering hands" (215–16; emphasis mine). This sense of communion, shattered by what shocks him around the dancing ground ("The idea was of a spectacle, a kind of low-class circus where people came to buy peanuts and look at freaks" [216]), comes back to him even though—again—"for a moment" only, while watching Mike dance, "he fe[els] everything Mike fe[els]" (218), the body's delight, the music, and a liberating self-confidence. But, finally, that very evening, in the "unaccountable security" of his mother's tepee, Archilde comes to feel the Salish "*move in his blood*. . . . It was all quite near, quite a part of him; *it was his necessity*, for the first time" (222; emphases mine).

From this point on, the bond between Archilde and his people is indissoluble (even if he realizes, this is not going to make his leaving any easier). Now "he [doesn't] know why, but he [cannot] help himself" from looking around and noticing their "misery and hopelessness" and trying to be of some help (232). Unrequested, he gives money to a deaf and half-blind old woman and tries to save a skeletal mare, to which "he [has] to show kindness in spite of herself" (240). His failure leaves him confused, but he appears to have learned his lesson when he has to decide whether to force his nephews to go back to school and concludes that one's views must not be imposed on anybody who does not understand them. "All they [ask]", he reflects, "[is] to be left alone" (247)—a reflection that might encompass colonization and Christianization as well as the various Indian policies devised without taking the time to know what the Indians thought of them.

The feeling that his "people move in his blood" deepens in Archilde when, looking at his dying mother, he realizes that "people [grow] together like creeping vines" and, after she is dead, that "others were also bound to her" (258, 261). His sense of "intertwinedness" culminates when he takes care of all who have gathered to mourn Catharine; now he feels "near to these people" as never before (269). "The distance he ha[s] travelled since a year ago, when he returned for what he had intended as a last visit" (272), the narrator stresses, is marked by the pride Archilde feels for his mother's strength in abjuring Christianity. But it is also marked by his now being concerned not only about his own future but about that of his nephews, who—like all Indians—are entitled to "something better" than what Euro-American society has so far offered them (275).

Archilde's story does not end, however, on the affirmative note of an Indian identity regained. Had it done so, the requirements of realism that must have induced McNickle to reject the pat and reassuring ending of "The Hungry Generations" would not have been properly satisfied. At the conclusion of his journey Archilde knows that by now "he too belong[s] to the story of Sniél-emen" (275), and this is made clear by the novel's ending: surrounded by law officers suspecting him of the game warden's murder, Archilde leaves the scene in shackles, bound to appear before a judge that he will be at pains to convince of his innocence. Just before being arrested, he was telling the Indian girl who, distrustful of the whites' justice, had dragged him in a desperate flight: "You can't run away nowadays, Elise" (287). The same words are uttered by the Indian agent in the last scene, when Archilde's nephews launch yet another of their vain attempts to escape from "civilization." But they are uttered with an eloquent amplification: "It's too damn bad *you people* never learn that you can't run away" (296–97; emphasis mine), which underlies the confinement Archilde has come to share with the Salish, an entrapment that is not just physical and geographical but economic and cultural as well.

Through Archilde and Elise, who, divided by the impossibility of a meaningful communication, remain "as far apart as two worlds bobbing along side by side" even at the moment of lovemaking (290), the novel's ending presents an image of "rift" that recalls and confirms the manifold and lacerating fissures characterizing Sniél-emen—from the mutual incomprehension of the respective cultures dividing the Salish and the Euro-Americans to all the other conflicts stemming from this one, like the dissensions between husband and wife, parents and children, in the Leon family or between generations among the Salish.

The foregoing contrastive overview of *Sundown* and *The Surrounded* ought to have brought into light, I trust, three more elements of the pattern (or, maybe, paradigm) that Mathews and McNickle actualized and, so to say, bequeathed to the novelists of younger generations. One is the all-important role elders can play in acquainting or reacquainting the protagonist with the features of traditional culture. (The parental figures of the novels of the 1930s tend to be replaced by grandparental ones in those written in more recent decades.) The second element is the emphasis on imagination, memory, and dreams, given that it is through the protagonist's own remembering and imagining as well as his responding to his elders' memories that he may (re-)connect not only with his early Indian experiences but also with tribal history and old-time lifeways and thus come to a sense of belonging in an ongoing cultural continuum. (Similar effects may also be produced by dreams.) The third element consists in typical events that may help the protagonist's progress in the (re-)discovery and (re-)articulation of his Indian identity, such as listening to the stories of "long ago," performing in or just assisting at dances or other ceremonial functions, feeling in communion with the land and all forms of life it contains, feeling the impulse to sing one's wonder and delight at being alive in a world of beauty.

There is one element of the pattern that neither Mathews nor McNickle activated, and that is the (more or less overt) mythological framework: cosmo- and anthropogenic tribal myths that contain and prefigure all possible subsequent happenings, including therefore the disorder the protagonist suffers from—a disorder whose cure is offered by the rituals these myths established. Making mythology the "informing structural principle" of the novels was to be the more recent writers' major contribution to the pattern (Owens, *Other Destinies* 257).

Notes

1. Studies of Mathews's work add up to sections of Warrior's monograph (1995) and less than a dozen essay-length contributions. McNickle has comparatively fared much better, with two monographs (Purdy, *Word Ways*; and Parker, *Singing*), a collection of essays edited by Purdy (*Legacy*), and a score of shorter contributions.

2. McNickle started working on the project that was to become *The Surrounded* toward the end of the 1920s and, as Purdy (*Word Ways* 67) surmises, he might have read Mathews's *Wah'kon-Tah*, which came out in 1932 to become a national best-seller. But during the last revisions of his novel McNickle might have read *Sundown* too: interesting similarities of detail emerge when one compares the episodes of the Indian dance and the ball at Farmers' Hall in *The Surrounded* with passages from *Sundown* (32, 254 ff., 282 and 292–94). (In this essay I refer to reprint editions of the two novels.)

3. I am referring, of course, to N. Scott Momaday's *House Made of Dawn*

(1968), James Welch's *Winter in the Blood* (1974), and Leslie Marmon Silko's *Ceremony* (1977). None of these authors, it is worth noticing, was likely to have read either *Sundown* or *The Surrounded*, which had not yet been reprinted at the time. Vizenor's *Darkness in Saint Louis Bearheart* (1978), for instance, is a significant departure from the pattern of realism I am trying to define.

4. Although Mathews's life has been limned by Terry P. Wilson ("Osage Oxonian") and McNickle's painstakingly documented and engagingly told by Dorothy Parker (*Singing*), it is useful here to start with a review of those aspects of the two writers' experiences that appear to have had some bearing on the making of the two novels.

5. Letter to Robert Bigart, October 15, 1974 (McNickle Papers, Newberry Library), as quoted in Parker, *Singing* 16.

6. Entry for August 11, 1932 (McNickle Papers, Newberry Library), as quoted in Hans, "Re-Visions" 182.

7. It is the only extant early version of the novel. Its holograph is among the McNickle Papers at the Newberry Library.

8. McNickle's credo at the time he was completing his novel was that "if writing does not emerge naturally from one's experiences it can serve no purpose" (letter to William Gates, March 25, 1934, McNickle Papers, Newberry Library), as quoted in Purdy, *Word Ways* 20.

9. "The Hungry Generations" clearly suggests that at the time of its composition McNickle was still sharing the quite popular social Darwinist view that assimilation was the only way Indians could avoid becoming "the vanishing race."

10. Letter to William Gates, July 26, 1934, (McNickle Papers, Newberry Library), as quoted in Purdy, *Word Ways* 53.

11. "Speakerly text" is Henry Louis Gates Jr.'s term for a written text "whose rhetorical strategy is designed to represent an oral tradition and to produce the illusion of oral narration" (181). Purdy offers a careful analysis of McNickle's strategies to recapture the effectiveness of Indian verbal arts in the storytelling event of *The Surrounded* (*Word Ways* 51 ff.) Phillip E. Doss and William Brown also devote essays to this topic (in Purdy, *Legacy* 53–84).

Works Cited

Bailey, Garrick. "John Joseph Mathews." In *American Indian Intellectuals*. Ed. Margot Liberty. St. Paul MN: West, 1978. 205–16.

Brown, William. "*The Surrounded:* Listening between the Lines of Inherited Stories." In *The Legacy of D'Arcy McNickle Writer, Historian, Activist.* Ed. John L. Purdy. Norman: University of Oklahoma Press, 1996. 69–84.

Cather, Willa. *The Professor's House.* New York: Knopf, 1925.

———. *Death Comes for the Archbishop.* New York: Knopf, 1927.

Doss, Phillip E. "Elements of Traditional Oral Narratives in *The Surrounded.*" In *The Legacy of D'Arcy McNickle Writer, Historian, Activist.* Ed. John L. Purdy. Norman: University of Oklahoma Press, 1996. 53–68.

Gates, Henry Louis, Jr. *Black Literature and Literary Theory.* New York: Oxford University Press, 1988.

Hans, Birgit. "Re-Visions: An Early Version of *The Surrounded.*" *Studies in American Indian Literatures* 4.2–3 (1992): 181–96.

Hogan, Linda. "To Take Care of Life." In *Survival This Way: Interviews with American Indian Poets.* Ed. Joseph Bruchac. Tucson: University of Arizona Press, 1987. 119–33.

LaFarge, Oliver. *Laughing Boy.* 1929. Reprint. New York: Signet Books, 1971.

Logsdon, Guy. "John Joseph Mathews—A Conversation." *Nimrod* 16 (April 1972): 70–75.

Mathews, John Joseph. *Wah'kon-Tah: The Osage and the White Man's Road.* Norman: University of Oklahoma Press, 1932.

———. *Talking to the Moon: Wildlife Adventures on the Plains and Prairies of Osage Country.* Norman: University of Oklahoma Press, 1945.

———. *The Osages: Children of the Middle Waters.* Norman: University of Oklahoma Press, 1961.

McNickle, D'Arcy. "The Hungry Generations" (early MS version of *The Surrounded*). McNickle Papers, Newberry Library, Chicago, n.d.

———. *The Surrounded.* 1936. Reprint, with intro. Lawrence W. Towner. Albuquerque: University of New Mexico Press, 1978.

Momaday, N. Scott. *House Made of Dawn.* New York: Harper and Row, 1968.

———. "The Man Made of Words." In *Literature of the American Indians: Views and Interpretations: A Gathering of Indian Memories, Symbolic Contexts, and Literary Criticism.* Ed. Abraham Chapman. New York: New American Library, 1975. 96–110.

Mourning Dove [Hum-Ishu-Ma]. *Cogewea, the Half-Blood: A Depiction of the Great Montana Cattle Range.* With notes and biographical sketch by Lucullus Virgil McWhorter. 1927. Reprint, with intro. Dexter Fisher. Lincoln: University of Nebraska Press, 1981.

Ortiz, Alfonso. "Obituary: D'Arcy McNickle, 1904-1977." *American Anthropologist* 81 (1979): 632–36.

Owens, Louis. *Other Destinies: Understanding the American Indian Novel.* Norman: University of Oklahoma Press, 1992.

Parker, Dorothy. *Singing an Indian Song: A Biography of D'Arcy McNickle.* Lincoln: University of Nebraska Press, 1992.

Purdy, John L. *Word Ways: The Novels of D'Arcy McNickle.* Tucson: University of Arizona Press, 1990.

———, ed. *The Legacy of D'Arcy McNickle: Writer, Historian, Activist.* Norman: University of Oklahoma Press, 1996.

Silko, Leslie Marmon. *Ceremony.* New York: Viking Press, 1977.

Warrior, Robert Allen. *Tribal Secrets: Recovering American Indian Intellectual Traditions.* Minneapolis: University of Minnesota Press, 1995.

Welch, James. *Winter in the Blood.* New York: Harper and Row, 1974.

Wilson, Terry P. "Osage Oxonian: The Heritage of John Joseph Mathews." *Chronicles of Oklahoma* 59.3 (1981): 264–93.

5 Transatlantic Crossings

New Directions in the Contemporary Native American Novel

How much are Native Americans part of the project of American identity? How have Native American novels contributed to it, particularly in the context of recent debates over multiculturalism? Considering the growing popularity of Native American literature in Europe, how far have Europeans become an implied audience? How "American" or "cosmopolitan" are Native American novels? These are the questions that led me to look at some recent novels by Native American authors. I was also curious about whether we can detect certain trends or new directions in Native American works of fiction. I will argue that many recent novels explore transcultural connections and point to the instability of ethnic and national identities by tracing affinities (including transatlantic ones) between people beyond culture, ethnicity, and nationality. Although I will, especially in part 1, resort to groupings and generalizations that might ignore the particularities of authors and texts, I nevertheless see all of the Native American authors discussed here as highly individual writers with their own distinct styles and issues. What they (might) have in common are certain concerns connected to Native American histories and experiences.

"Classic" Paths

War experiences (especially in World War II), assimilation, relocation and their consequences for Indian lives as well as Indian counterstrategies for cultural and personal survival and self-determination had been central to the novels of the "classic" Native American Renaissance—N. Scott Momaday's *House Made of Dawn* (1968), James Welch's *Winter in the Blood* (1974), and Leslie Marmon Silko's *Ceremony* (1977). These literary works commented critically on and simultaneously drew creative energy from "Western," or "Euro-American," traditions. Although not all readers did (or were willing to) acknowledge it, these novels destroyed the cozy idea of an alternative "pure" "Indian" counter-identity (albeit suggesting vague symbolic "returns") and insisted instead on sketching complex, if troubled, "mixed" identities between "Indian" and "white" worlds—a hybridity also reflected in the aesthetic models drawn from tribal oral literatures, storytelling and folk traditions, European classic mythology, as well as (Euro-)American literary traditions. This was, for instance, manifested in Momaday's engagement with Euro-American modernism, which suggests that the American tradition in itself reflects the influence of an "indigenous" America. Native American novels drew attention to the issue of mixed and relational identities (as Louis Owens has convincingly shown in *Other Destinies*) and questioned American myths of innocence and "newness" by pointing to a multi-layered American past (articulated at times in the form of complicated "re-memberings" by Momaday's and Silko's protagonists). At the same time they rearticulated the American "myth of regeneration," to use Richard Slotkin's term, by constructing narrative paths to cultural and psychological regeneration (for example, in the creation stories integrated in *Ceremony*). They also opened perspectives on global networks and responsibilities in their protagonists' visions of a connectedness that transcends geographic and cultural boundaries.

Native American novels have thus, since the 1960s, contributed to contemporary debates on American identity in the context of diversity by, for instance, resisting the depiction of Native Americans as victims, by insisting on the positive qualities of a hybrid existence, and by (re)establishing the importance and adaptiveness of the tribal heritage in a modern world. As the number of Native American novelists increased by the 1980s, individual authors chose to work in specific new directions. Women writers such as Paula Gunn Allen, in *The Woman*

Who Owned the Shadows (1983), and Janet Campbell Hale, in *The Jailing of Cecelia Capture* (1985), explored the female side of the Indian quest for survival and identity. In *Fools Crow* (1986) James Welch reconstructed the traditional world of a young Blackfoot man in the 1860s and 1870s by immersing himself and the reader into the linguistic, terminological, and philosophical bases of nineteenth-century Blackfoot culture. Linda Hogan's *Mean Spirit* (1990) added another slice of anthropological-historical reconstruction by focusing on gendered Osage experiences in Oklahoma in the early twentieth century. Hogan's first novel already pointed to the engagement with environmental issues that would become central in her later novel, *Power* (1998).

While some of these novelists focused on the perspectives of individual protagonists, others integrated a multiplicity of narrators, voices, and viewpoints into their fictional worlds. This was especially the case in the first series of novels by Louise Erdrich—*Love Medicine* (1984), *The Beet Queen* (1986), *Tracks* (1988), and *The Bingo Palace* (1994)—and, to a certain degree, those of Michael Dorris in *A Yellow Raft in Blue Water* (1987) and *Cloud Chamber* (1997). Again, this was not specifically "Native American" but reflected the strong influence of Euro-American modernist writers, particularly William Faulkner. This being said, the reference to a Faulknerian "influence" cannot capture the creative energy with which Erdrich devises and peoples a world of her own—a world of interrelated families and stories that all comment on one another, contradict each other, and create distinct, equally valid versions of the "truth." Unlike earlier Native American works, her novels provide no comforting tribal ceremonies or rituals for their protagonists.

In fact, it is often difficult to distinguish between what is "white" and what is "Indian" in Erdrich's fictional world—its denizens are all so mixed up in terms of descent, lifestyle, worldviews, and religious beliefs. What also shines through Erdrich's narratives is a trickster humor that threaded its way through some of the earlier novels (in the figure of Momaday's Tosamah or in the bizarre, surreal events in Welch's first novel) but which finds a much more programmatic articulation in the works of Gerald Vizenor, Thomas King, and the late Louis Owens. All of these writers challenge concepts of the "pure" "Indian" by creating "crossblood" or "postindian" fictions (Vizenor 1994). Moreover, they question the possibility of gaining Native counter-truths, underlining this point of view in their use of subversive humor, parody, and satire. Especially Owens's novels and criticism are informed by a critical focus on mixed-blood identity and hybridized narratives and are situated within academic debates on postmodernity, on the post- or neocolonial situation, on transcultural identities, hybridity, and the borderlands, as well as on the New Age revival of interest in Native Americans (see Georgi-Findlay 2003; Pulitano 2004).

"New" Routes

Which are, then, the "new" directions in the Native American novel? Many of the trends suggested here are probably continuations of issues and concerns that had already been there, albeit on the margins, in earlier Native writing. This applies, for instance, to the use of trickster humor and play in the Native engagement with the Western Judeo-Christian tradition. Whether we take Louis Owens's novel *The Sharpest Sight* (1992) or Thomas King's *Green Grass, Running Water* (1993), Native oral traditions and storytelling enter into a competition with the white variant of storytelling—the Bible and literature—a contest that Momaday had already dramatized in *House Made of Dawn*. In this competition the Western tradition invariably loses out (which would, on a superficial level, suggest the superiority of Native traditions). Its writers may tell great stories, but they are not aware of—or they distrust—the impact their storytelling has on the real world. Or they are too obsessed with mastering and controlling the world and take themselves too seriously (see Owens, *Sharpest Sight*). And yet, while some Native American writers (such as Allen, Hogan, and Cook-Lynn) seem to assume the existence of a deep, unbridgeable chasm between "white" and "Native" worldviews, Owens and King portray cultural conflict more playfully as a necessary result of cultural diversity and interaction. The conflict of perspectives may thus be productive, despite problematic asymmetries of power that may impede cultural dialogue.

A new direction taken especially by Louis Owens has been the critical, albeit humorous, engagement with the celebration, commodification, and marketing of the "authentic" Indian in American and European popular culture (for example, in movies such as *Dances with Wolves*, New Age retreats, ethno-tourism, and German hobbyists playing Indians). Especially his last novel, *Dark River* (1999), questions the desirability of revisionist versions of Indian-white history and of politically correct embraces of Native America that welcome Indians as another colorful piece in the mosaic of multicultural America. The marketing of Native American culture is also examined critically by Evelina Zuni Lucero in *Night Sky, Morning Star* (2000).

If Owens and others challenge stereotypes of "the Indian," they may continue work begun by earlier Native writers. At the same time, the images that Native writers have to engage with today are qualitatively new. Based on politically correct assumptions of tolerance and multicultural harmony, today's (American *and European*) New Age images of Native Americans are extremely benign. Yet they are still essentially paternalistic, reflecting white people's claim to the right of knowing, defining, and imitating authentic Indians and making it infinitely problematic for Native people to learn and know who they are. In this respect Owens challenges both American liberal visions of multiculturalism and European images alike. The latter traditionally tend to focus on Indians as tragic victims, fixed in the past and positively antimodern, and are often used to criticize white American society as intolerant, materialist, and violent. Yet, as Owens seems to suggest in the direction of Europeans, their images of Indians completely leech out the complexities of Native existence in contemporary America. In contrast, Owens's mixed-bloods are at the same time victims and perpetrators, cowboys and Indians, invaders and invaded, rejecting the plots assigned to them.

Like Vizenor, Owens challenges earlier literary representations of a potentially stable Indian identity by questioning whether in today's postmodern media culture any person, and particularly one with Native ancestors, may even be able to define who they are. Aren't all positions one takes, he suggests, just poses? At the same time, he aims to somehow anchor his protagonists by giving them and us as readers a sense of how identity (as an ongoing narrative) may be rooted in a place and a particular history. What may also be new about Native American literature are certain debates among the writers themselves. According to Owens and others, for example, the dangers of ethno-tourism may even lurk in Native American literature itself. Thus, the popular works of Sherman Alexie are criticized by other Native American writers for their exaggerated depictions of eccentric, drunk, asocial, or psychopathic Indians, which presumably perpetuate stereotypical images and function well to sell Indian literature (Owens, *Mixedblood Messages* 75–76). But, then, what is new about the debates? We may all remember Silko's critique of Erdrich's novel *The Beet Queen* ("Here's an Odd Artifact" 1986). Also, Owens's focus on mixed-blood Indians (in fact, his own identity as a mixed-blood) has fed suspicions (by Cook-Lynn, among others) that he was doing Indian literature a disservice (Owens, *Mixedblood Messages* 151–66). "Authenticity" still seems to be an issue within Native American writing.

But one can also find themes in recent Native American writing that had not been explored before. One of them is the (mostly involuntary) Native encounter with Europe that is described in Leslie Silko's *Gardens in the Dunes* (1999) and James Welch's *Heartsong of Charging Elk* (2000). The second theme is a focus on late-nineteenth-, early-twentieth-century cultural history and a more intense exploration of the transatlantic encounter occurring in an immigrant context. This is the case especially in Louise Erdrich's contribution to the literature of the American Dream, *The Master Butchers Singing Club* (2003). A third focus is laid on a more intense questioning of culturally constructed gender roles, which occurs in a particularly striking manner in Louise Erdrich's *Last Report on the Miracles at Little No Horse* (2001).

Transatlantic and Transcultural Connections

Gardens in the Dunes is a historical novel that moves between the two diametrically opposed worlds of Native American peoples in the Southwest and of American and European upper-class culture in the late nineteenth century. Both worlds meet when Indigo—a girl from the Sand Lizard tribe, desert people who appear odd to their Indian neighbors—encounters the couple Hattie and Edward Palmer. In a manner reminiscent of Henry James, Silko uses this couple to sketch the intellectual horizons of late Victorian America, defined by religious dogmas and rebellions, the belief in science and progress, connectedness to European history and culture, and medical concepts of sexuality and the female mind. Especially Hattie strains at the confines of female education by studying early church history. In this American upper-class world (East and West) Native Americans appear, if at all, on the margins—for example, as objects of ethno-tourist interest on tours to the West. Silko uses the story of Indigo and her three-generation family of women to write Indians into the history of the late-nineteenth-century American West. It is a history of loss, displacement, and brutality at the hands of "aliens," "strangers," or "invaders" (17), which becomes especially dramatic because it is told from the perspective of a young innocent girl. At the same time, the history of Native Americans is embedded in a larger, multicultural history of interaction between whites, blacks, Mexicans, and Indians.

But Silko also uses Indigo's story to show how the Native American presence can touch upon the lives of Eastern Americans. Indigo, who has witnessed a Ghost Dance and has internalized the messages of this Native American version of Christianity, hopes that by involuntarily journeying to Europe she will meet a real-life Jesus who is also traveling east. This Native reading of Christianity is a mirror version of Hattie's Gnostic interpretation of Christianity as female inspired. Indigo's presence changes Hattie's outlook on her environment, confronting her with parts of American history previously unknown to her. Indigo also destroys any idea of a common pan-Indian culture. But what connects Silko's characters beyond their local and cultural roots is their common interest in and reliance upon plants and gardens. Plants, Silko suggests, are the universal, transcultural elements defining a global web of cultures. At the same time, if plants and their cultivation have been central unifying forces in world history (underlying migrations, colonizations, and conflicts), the views cast upon them also distinguish cultures from each other. If gardens *are* a form of culture, they also express cultural differences and specific worldviews. Thus, in Silko's novel people are characterized by the way they look at gardens and plants.

The first garden we encounter is a desert garden that had given the Sand Lizard people food and sanctuary in hard times. This is the garden that had provided refuge to Indigo's family and in which she had learned to understand plants as sources of sustenance and spiritual well-being. In contrast, for the gentleman-scholar, botanist, and explorer Edward, gardens are parts of a research laboratory. Plants are "specimens." As Silko describes Edward's expeditions and business ventures, she draws attention to the fact that by the end of the nineteenth century the collection and smuggling of certain plants had become a lucrative business, amounting to biological theft. For Edward's sister gardens are fashionable expressions of upper-class identity. Thus, she uproots and destroys her Renaissance garden to transform it into an English landscape garden. To Hattie, however, gardens are sources of aesthetic pleasure and physical regeneration.

On their travels to England and Italy, Indigo, Hattie, and Edward encounter two more types of gardens. What is Silko trying to do here? I think that she aims to trace the transatlantic connections that link Old Europe to Old (Native) America. The first garden is tended by Hattie's Aunt Bronwyn, an unconventional American exile—as she quips, "whatever an American is" (244)—in Bath, England. While her visitors exhibit the typical "American" admiration for eighteenth-century buildings, she is interested in a much older Europe of Celtic mythology that, as Indigo's reaction to her stories suggests, triggers a certain recognition in the Sand Lizard girl. Aunt Bronwyn's cloister garden is structured along the four corners of the world and their respective plants and thus tells the story of the global travel and exchange of plants to which, as she explains, Native America has made a major contribution (245–46).

The second garden is tended by a female Italian professor and includes stone figures of pagan origin. Although Edward insists that these archaeological artifacts belong in a museum, not a garden, and deems them unfit for the eyes of a child, their sexual explicitness leaves a sensual impression upon the couple. Old Europe, Silko's Italian scenes suggest, appreciates sensual pleasures, including those of food and wine, to a degree that is uncomfortable to more puritanical Americans. In contrast, Indigo's socialization (Silko describes her and her people's attitude toward sexuality as rather uninhibited) and her reaction to some of the Old European stone figures (snakes and bears) suggest an affinity between the sensibilities of pre-Christian Europe and Native America, an affinity that eludes Hattie and Edward (305). Old Europe thus is made to function positively as a contrastive foil to white America.

Silko's plot, although it ties Indigo and Hattie's stories so tightly together, eventually has the two characters live in two separate gardens (Hattie goes to live with Aunt Bronwyn) that, despite the affinities described earlier, remain far apart and cannot coexist. Does she suggest that plants can flourish in foreign environments but people cannot?

The story of James Welch's protagonist ultimately seems to suggest quite the opposite. Charging Elk is an Oglala Sioux who in 1889 had traveled with Buffalo Bill's Wild West Show to Europe to perform as a "wild Indian," which, according to contemporary Euro-American standards, he is. As a non-reservation Lakota with little schooling, he is unfamiliar with America's dominant language and culture. After a riding accident he is left by the troupe to fend for himself in Marseille, France, an even more unfamiliar environment whose workings he has to understand in order to survive and find a way home. From a cultural studies perspective Welch's fictional twist is brilliant: he has his protagonist "read culture" in the most basic sense. Charging Elk has to rely on the careful reading of signs without apparent meaning: what should he make of the display of a Christmas crèche in a show window? or of the fishmongers yelling at their customers at the market? Continuing a technique he had begun using in *Fools Crow*, Welch writes from the perspective of the speaker of a Plains Indian language who needs to describe the unfamiliar with familiar terms (Welch, *Heartsong* 2000).

The fact that an American should be stranded in a French hospital in 1889 should not cause alarm because the United States is represented by a vice-consul. Yet Welch's plot takes an ironic and tragic turn because the young man who introduces himself as "American Lakota" to the vice-consul "couldn't speak the language of his own country" (14, 88). Welch plays on the insecurities concerning the citizenship status of Native Americans: if, on the basis of treaties, "Indian tribes were their own nations within the United States," could the Indian be a citizen of the United States? At the same time, the vice-consul muses, "the individuals were wards of the government and as such were entitled to diplomatic representation in foreign countries" (85). If the American vice-consul's attitude toward the Indian is marked by indifference, the French authorities' position is even more extreme: because the Indian doesn't have any citizenship papers, he doesn't exist. Caught in bureaucratic red tape, the "vanishing Indian" subsequently vanishes in Marseille, left to fend for himself. Charging Elk becomes the quintessential ingénue in a culture that simultaneously celebrates and excludes him.

Welch's France does not evoke the same affinity in the Native American as Silko's Italy did. The entertainer Charging Elk is proud to "display the old ways," however "fake" the display seems, and he feels that "the French appreciated the Indians and seemed genuinely sympathetic" (55). But he will find that the French fascination with Indians is confined to the context of entertainment and show. While the French "looked at them with awe" when the Indian performers "walked the streets of Paris in their fancy clothes" (45), beyond this context he is perceived as different and foreign. People eye him "with suspicion, even with hostility, just as the Americans did" (55). In France the Native American "who had not thought of himself in terms of color" soon learns to define himself as part of the colored others, together with "the Arabs or the *nègres*" (213). The working-class neighborhood of Le Panier, with its "many tongues, mostly North African and Levantine," reminds him most of his own Lakota village (205).

Even those who aim to help Charging Elk seem to be motivated less by a genuine interest in the man than by moral self-righteousness. The young journalist St-Cyr "had come to think of the creature in the cell as an animal that had been cornered. And in a way, he cared more for the animal than the man" (110–11). In the end, by committing a murder, Charging Elk confirms the fears and stereotypes surrounding his Indianness. His case becomes a media sensation and a stage on which ideas about the Indian could be aired: he was a poor child of nature who "did not have the mental capacity to understand the rules of a civilized society" or "an illegal immigrant who should have been deported long ago" (343). St-Cyr uses the case to portray Charging Elk as a victim "of the American and French governments" and to confirm his ideas of Americans as "arrogant and demanding," as "the new Romans . . . who came to Massilia with their big ships and demands for tribute" (355, 316). In the same way the demonstrations organized by students to demand Charging Elk's freedom are ultimately staged to support the students' antigovernment protests (357–60). The Indian is instrumentalized in the service of French people's own political issues. Thus, while Silko had used Europe as a positive contrast to white America, Welch exposes the way Europeans use Indians to criticize America and in the process create positive self-images that mask the realities of racial exclusiveness in their societies.

Like Louis Owens, Welch describes the transatlantic relationship as based on images, effects, and thus on misunderstandings. For one Frenchwoman, Buffalo Bill's Wild West Show is the yardstick by which she measures a whole country: "The Americans seemed to think that violence was just a way of life. The announcer had said as much. But it was not the French way" (120). Welch thus plays upon a long tradition of anti-Americanism in Europe that is often used for purposes of self-definition.

Ironically, Charging Elk's status as a member of a separate nation will free him again after many years at La Tombe penitentiary: he is classified as a political prisoner, pardoned, and released (388). He becomes a French citizen and marries a Frenchwoman (432). When his chance to return home finally arrives, sixteen years after his accident, he refuses. Although Welch does not elaborate much on Charging Elk's decision, he seems to suggest that the choice is informed more by the alienation and distance from the former home than the warmth of the new one.

Perhaps he insinuates that at the end of the day European hostility and stereotyping are the lesser evil, compared to American political and legal discrimination? On the other hand, as Elizabeth Archuleta has noted, in his protagonist's inability to connect with his Indian heritage, Welch continues his earlier theme of Native American "isolation, alienation, and separation from an 'Indian' world" (185). In the end it is personal affection and responsibility that connect people, not culture.

In Erdrich's novel *The Master Butchers Singing Club* the transatlantic encounter initially takes place in an immigrant context. As the author addresses the German part of her mixed-blood heritage, she aims to explore transatlantic issues from the immigrant perspective. The novel begins with young German Fidelis Waldvogel's return from World War I in 1918 and with his marriage to Eva, the pregnant fiancée of his best friend fallen in the war. Erdrich imbues him with traits she describes as particularly German: one of those born "in the phenomenon of strength"—perhaps "of that old Germanic stock who roamed the forests and hung their god from the tree of life"—he had learned to kill efficiently during the war, a skill also central to his trade as a butcher (5). In Fidelis's story Erdrich explores the American dream and its disappointments. This producer of food is literally drawn to America by a slice of bread (which, once he has arrived at his destination, he will never taste). Intrigued by the evenness and fine texture of this mass-produced bread, "an artifact from some place that must adhere to an impossibly rigid order" (7), he is convinced that he should follow this bread to its source (it had been sent from Seattle). His father's sausages, which pay his train ticket to the West, however, only take him to Argus, North Dakota, the place that readers of Erdrich's novels *The Beet Queen* and *Tales of Burning Love* are familiar with. Food and another traditional German predilection, singing, will continue to be at the center of the butcher's life. His new country, "where Germans were Germans regardless of their regional origins" (8), amazes him with the goodwill of its people, "but then, he reminded himself, they were neither starving in the main nor recently and thoroughly defeated and detested outside their diminished borders" (11). The Waldvogel household is defined as German by its efficiency, orderliness, and frugality as well as by its comfortable bathroom (35). Eva's household is described as "based on order, rich baking scents, cleanliness, and life" (41). She misses and is proud of "Old World Quality" (95). And she is very much concerned with appearances. In contrast, her garden "was everything raw and wild that Eva's house was not" (108)—due to an indescribable need rather than to a German preference (Germans like their gardens orderly, like their households).

Erdrich's Argus is a small-town America inhabited by people of immigrant stock (with the Polish-American Delphine Watzka and her alcoholic father, Roy, as characters forming a circle with the Waldvogel family), with a few peripatetic Indians (Cyprian Lazarre and Step-and-a-Half, both Metis of Ojibwe descent) interspersed throughout. Erdrich's characters are not divided by the extreme cultural contrasts that feature so prominently in Silko's and Welch's novels. There might be tensions, as the one between Fidelis and Cyprian, who had fought in the war in Europe on opposite sides. When Fidelis learns that Cyprian is a Native American, the revelation confirms Fidelis's sense of the man's difference: "So that was it! . . . He had always known there was *something* about the man. And he hadn't caught it. . . . It came to him. An Indian. Cyprian was an Indian. That's all it was, all along, that uneasy feeling. Somehow he'd known and not known, the man was different. Thinking of Cyprian as an Indian now made things all right" (213). The reader is aware that Fidelis is deluding himself because what stands between the two men is their common love for Delphine. And the reader also knows that Fidelis's sense of the other man's difference might derive from the fact that Cyprian is homosexual. Cyprian finally leaves Delphine to travel the country, performing in a traveling vaudeville act with a Jewish man. On his only return to Argus he explains to Delphine: "Well, he's a lot like me. . . . He made it over here from Lithuania and he's a Jew. I was a real curiosity to him at first." In fact, both are curiosities to each other: the Jew had never met an Indian; the Indian had never known a Jew. The latter did know about Indians and "believed we were one of the lost tribes of Israel doomed to wander, too, like his people. Always to be on the edge of things" (317).

Erdrich captures the dynamics of human relationships, the tensions of everyday life, the simple pleasures, and the difficulties of coping with tragedies and loss. Human character, she seems to suggest, is only superficially defined by culture. For her characters, who are often of mistaken or unknown parentage, ethnicity or cultural identity can serve only, if at all, as unstable, unreliable fictions. Instead, they receive love and strength in however shaped surrogate families.

Even belonging to a national culture, Erdrich suggests, denotes only an impermanent status. Thus, Franz, Eva's first son born in Germany, will be defined by a "proud, easygoing American temperament perfectly transparent and opaque at the same time" (86). In contrast, his brothers, Erich and Emil, born and raised in Argus and then transplanted at a young age to a Germany that was turning to national socialism and war, struggled hard to be German and fought against Americans in the war. Erich's identity becomes thoroughly confused when he is captured by GIs after the German defeat and is transported to a POW camp not too far from his former American home. He refuses to meet his father because, "in a fierce crush of training and in the years of his formation, he had become in his deepest person thoroughly German. Or what he thought of as German. . . . Erich's fanaticism was that of the culturally insecure" (352). Is he an American playing a German or the other way round? In the end the only trait that identifies him as his father's son is his singing.

I have wondered about the role of the singing club, indeed a powerful German tradition. In Erdrich's novel singing is a form of expression for men who cannot articulate their feelings otherwise. The singing of Fidelis's club and of his sons is in the end interwoven with Step-and-a-Half's memories of the songs of the Ghost Dancers who perished in the hail of army bullets (387). If for Silko gardens define universal humanity, something that people share regardless of their country of origin, something that travels with people, for Erdrich it is singing: "Our songs travel the earth. We sing to one another. Not a single note is ever lost and no song is original" (388).

Music also plays a central role in *The Last Report on the Miracles at Little*

No Horse. But here it is interwoven with a focus on religious and spiritual experience in the intercultural context of a Catholic mission among the Ojibwe in the early twentieth century. Erdrich explores these issues through her main character, the German-American Agnes DeWitt, who had taken her temporary vows as Sister Cecilia and had to leave the convent on account of the passion that gripped her upon playing the piano. After having lost her German lover and portions of her memory to a bank robber's bullet, and after she is swept north by a devastating flood, Agnes disguises herself as Father Damien Modeste in order to pursue the religious work among the Ojibwe that he was sent to do but couldn't—because he drowned in the flood en route to his Indian mission in North Dakota.

In the course of her/his life as a male priest at the Ojibwe settlement of Little No Horse, Agnes/Damien collects evidence of the "spiritual transactions" supposedly performed by Sister Leopolda / Pauline Puyat, the Catholic nun who had traumatized Marie Lazarre in *Love Medicine*. Damien's reports to the pope (only answered after her/his death) and to the priest who investigates Leopolda's sainthood reveal an increasing insecurity concerning the nature of sainthood and conversion and a gradual turn toward a hybrid faith that incorporates Ojibwe concepts of the sacred. Or is it an insecure faith incorporated into an Ojibwe religious experience that is comfortable with mixtures?

Agnes's life on the reservation confronts her with a place suffering from hunger, disease, land loss, and internal feuds. But her encounter with Ojibwe culture also takes place on a deeply spiritual level, for which she seems to harbor a particular affinity. Only the Ojibwe can really explain her eccentricities and her visitations—she has known God in a man's body and is visited by Satan/death in the form of a black dog who speaks German (308). Melanie Wittmier has noted that in Erdrich's novel the use of German is intended to "symbolize lack of communication and verbal skills" (241). Indeed, Agnes DeWitt's relationship with the farmer Berndt Vogel, which had relied on German, had been curiously devoid of communication. Only among the Ojibwe will she be able to find a language with which to communicate and describe herself.

Again, Erdrich explores the nature of identity as a fabrication by constructing fictions of fatherhood and motherhood. But this time she draws specific attention to the constructed character of gendered forms of identity. Agnes as Damien lives "the great lie that was her life—the true lie, she considered it, the most sincere lie a person could ever tell" (61). What is gendered identity, she suggests, other than a performance? "Both Sister Cecilia and then Agnes were as heavily manufactured of gesture and pose as was Father Damien" (76). The way Agnes sees it, her life had been a series of transformations even before she arrived on the reservation. Now she has not only slipped into Damien's clothes but has entered a new life: "She decided to miss Agnes as she would a beloved sister, to make of Father Damien her creation" (77). The love she shares and consummates with Father Gregory Wekkle in the secrecy of her priest's cabin is doomed when the young man asks her to give up her disguise and marry him: "I cannot leave who I am" (206), she answers, convinced that she is as much a male priest as a woman. Erdrich supports the convincing nature of this synthesis by referring alternately to Agnes (if the private person is meant) and Damien (if the public person is meant).

Ironically, the woman living as a man is slow to realize that her disguise never fooled Father Damien's Indian flock, who were socialized in a culture in which gender transformations have a secure place (64). As the tricksterish old man Nanapush explains, the Ojibwe know about "woman-acting" men and "man-acting" women but see nothing special in them (232). Even the noun in the Ojibwe language is, as Agnes finds, "unprejudiced by gender distinctions" (257).

Moreover, the priest who had wanted to nurture the Ojibwe finds that he in turn is in need of being sustained and healed by them (214). Toward the end of Agnes's life Damien reports to the Holy Father that he has "discovered an unlikely truth that may interest your Holiness. The ordinary as well as esoteric forms of worship engaged in by the Ojibwe are sound, even compatible with the teachings of Christ" (49). The heaven she longs for is inhabited by Ojibwe and Catholics (211), and she realizes that there "is no one I want to visit except in the Ojibwe heaven, and so at this late age I'm going to convert . . . and become at long last the pagan that I always was at heart before I was Cecilia" (310). Agnes's story replicates that of the young Jesuit who had taken a chessboard with him to convince his Indian flock of the white man's intellectual superiority—and who ironically finds that he is beaten and bested at the game by the supposedly underdeveloped savage mind (229–30). The difference lies in the relationship that Agnes establishes with the Ojibwe, a relationship based on true exchange and affection. What finally motivates Agnes to keep up her disguise, to renounce the pleasures of physical love in the full knowledge that conversion provides doubtful benefits to the Ojibwe? Erdrich suggests that she is driven by a deep sense of responsibility and love. Agnes is "forced by the end to clean up after the effects of what [she] helped to destroy" (239). She is also impelled by the intricate ties between belief and identity: "All that I am is based upon belief" (314). Only her "job of becoming Father Damien had allowed the budding eccentricities of Agnes to attain full flower" (344).

All four of the novels I focus on here explore the boundaries of culture by pointing to transcultural connections and the instability of ethnic and national identities. While Silko and Welch thematize these issues around the transatlantic encounter between Old (Native) America and Old Europe, Erdrich turns to the non-Native immigrant experience, religious experience, and gender issues to trace affinities between people beyond culture, ethnicity, and nationality. All of them contribute creatively to the interrogation of what is "American" by emphasizing the "cosmopolitan" character of hybrid Native and non-Native American lives, whether in the context of transatlantic journeys, immigration, or religious missions. Europe and Europeans have become important subjects for these Native writers. While Owens critically interrogates Europeans' images of Indians, Silko uses Europe as a positive, contrastive foil in order to explore the failures of white America. In contrast, Welch explores the way Europeans use Indians to express their criticism of or ambivalence toward America, masking the realities of racial exclusion in their own societies, while Erdrich tries to explore the transatlantic encounter and the American Dream from the perspective of the European immigrant.

Works Cited

Allen, Paula Gunn. *The Woman Who Owned the Shadows*. San Francisco: Spinsters Ink, 1983.

Archuleta, Elizabeth. "The Heartsong of Charging Elk." *World Literature Today* 75.1 (Winter 2001): 185.

Dorris, Michael. *A Yellow Raft in Blue Water*. New York: Henry Holt, 1987.

———. *Cloud Chamber: A Novel*. New York: Scribner, 1997.

Erdrich, Louise. *Love Medicine: A Novel*. New York: Holt, Rinehart and Winston, 1984.

———. *The Beet Queen: A Novel*. New York: Henry Holt, 1986.

———. *Tracks: A Novel*. London: Hamish Hamilton, 1988.

———. *The Bingo Palace*. New York: HarperCollins, 1994.

———. *Tales of Burning Love*. New York: HarperCollins, 1996.

———. *The Last Report on the Miracles at Little No Horse*. New York: HarperCollins, 2001.

———. *The Master Butchers Singing Club*. New York: HarperCollins, 2003.

Georgi-Findlay, Brigitte. "Mixedblood Messages: Louis Owens' Fiction and Criticism." In *Imaginary (Re-)Locations: Tradition, Modernity, and the Market in Contemporary Native American Literature and Culture*. Ed. Helmbrecht Breinig. Tübingen: Stauffenburg, 2003. 149–66.

Hale, Janet Campbell. *The Jailing of Cecelia Capture*. New York: Random House, 1985.

Hogan, Linda. *Mean Spirit: A Novel*. New York: Atheneum, 1990.

———. *Power*. New York: Norton. 1998.

King, Thomas. *Green Grass, Running Water*. Boston: Houghton Mifflin, 1993.

Lucero, Evelina Zuni. *Night Sky, Morning Star*. Tucson: University of Arizona Press, 2000.

Momaday, N. Scott. *House Made of Dawn*. New York: Harper and Row, 1968.

Owens, Louis. *Other Destinies: Understanding the American Indian Novel*. Norman: University of Oklahoma Press, 1992.

———. *The Sharpest Sight*. Norman: University of Oklahoma Press, 1992.

———. *Mixedblood Messages: Literature, Film, Family, Place*. Norman: University of Oklahoma Press, 1998.

———. *Dark River: A Novel*. Norman: University of Oklahoma Press, 1999.

Pulitano, Elvira. "Crossreading Texts, Crossreading Identity: Hybridity, Diaspora, and Transculturation in Louis Owens's *Mixedblood Messages*." In

Louis Owens: Literary Reflections on His Life and Work. Ed. Jacquelyn Kilpatrick. Norman: University of Oklahoma Press, 2004. 79–102.

Silko, Leslie Marmon. *Ceremony.* New York: Viking Press, 1977.

———. "Here's an Odd Artifact for the Fairy-Tale Shelf." *Impact Magazine Review of Books, Albuquerque Journal,* October 7, 1986, 10–11.

———. *Gardens in the Dunes: A Novel.* New York: Simon and Schuster, 1999.

Slotkin, Richard. *Regeneration through Violence: The Mythology of the American Frontier, 1600-1860.* Middletown CT: Wesleyan University Press, 1973.

Vizenor, Gerald. *Manifest Manners: Postindian Warriors of Survivance.* Hanover NH: Wesleyan University Press, 1994.

Welch, James. *Winter in the Blood.* New York: Harper and Row, 1974.

———. *Fools Crow.* New York: Viking Press, 1986.

———. *The Heartsong of Charging Elk: A Novel.* New York: Doubleday, 2000.

Wittmier, Melanie. Review of *The Last Report on the Miracles at Little No Horse* by Louise Erdrich. *Explicator* 60.4 (Summer 2002): 241–43.

3. TRAUMA, MEMORY, AND NARRATIVES OF HEALING

6 Of Time and Trauma

The Possibilities for Narrative in Paula Gunn Allen's *The Woman Who Owned the Shadows*

In the introduction to her 1998 essay "Contemporary Two-Spirit Identity in the Fiction of Paula Gunn Allen and Beth Brant" Tara Prince-Hughes observes that for Native American writers the "struggle for identity has required writers to engage actively and dispute dominant Western fictions of 'Indianness' and to express the fragmentation experienced by people of mixed ancestry" (9). In this essay I want to address the way in which Paula Gunn Allen, in *The Woman Who Owned the Shadows* (1983), actively engages and disputes dominant Western fictions of "trauma" in a Native American context. In a central sequence of episodes in the novel Allen depicts her protagonist, Ephanie, undergoing Western-style therapy in the attempt to heal her alienated condition. Eventually, Ephanie comes to reject psychotherapy because at the point when she leaves her therapist she finds herself in a more alienated and fragile state than ever. Western approaches to the healing of trauma are powerless to help Ephanie; in this novel, however, Paula Gunn Allen offers us not only an alternative vision of healing but also a different way of viewing and understanding trauma itself.

This essay considers the contested thematics of trauma, in Paula Gunn Allen's novel, in terms of the treatment of time. The connection between time and trauma is crucial to the Western understanding of trauma presented by influential theorists such as Ruth Leys and Cathy Caruth. I want to use trauma theory to approach the question of the representational capacities of language within the context of a trauma that is both racial and gendered, historical and personal. In particular, I want to question the issue of trauma as characterized by Caruth's concept of "belated temporality" in relation to the ways in which Allen depicts the destruction of subjectivity within trauma and the implications of this representation for the construction of a temporal narrative of self. I want to introduce in this context Allen's insight into an alternative approach to trauma: the idea that in fact trauma is unrepresentable in narrative terms because the destruction of the traumatized "I" renders the linear history of trauma unrecuperable.

Let me begin by acknowledging that trauma may seem to be an inappropriate approach to Allen's work (especially given the negative representation of psychotherapy in the novel) and, indeed, to Native American literature in general. As Hartwig Isernhagen observes in his essay in the present volume, Native American literature can be distinguished from African-American writing (to take one fairly arbitrary example of American "minority" literature) in that Native writers have avoided "trauma narrative" as a designation for their work, and critics of Native American literature have tended to follow this lead ("They Have Stories"). Writers such as Paula Gunn Allen emphasize the status of their texts as healing narratives, and it is in these terms that Allen describes her project in The Woman Who Owned the Shadows in the essay "Whose Dream Is This Anyway? Remythologization and Self-definition in Contemporary American Indian Fiction" (Sacred Hoop 98–100). At the same time that Allen approaches the issue of Native experience from the perspective of a woman-centered Keres-Pueblo cultural tradition, however, she offers a revisionary perspective on the whole contemporary discourse of trauma. A monolithic view of trauma, such as seems to be emerging from the contemporary orthodoxy surrounding trauma studies, cannot offer this revisionary approach. But a sensitive, tribally informed approach, such as Allen's novel represents, can uncover for us a larger truth about identity de/formation under conditions of trauma.

Of Time and Trauma

In most dominant theoretical accounts of trauma there are two moments in the chronology of psychic trauma: the original traumatic event and its belated emergence as a symptom. Ruth Leys explains:

> The idea is that, owing to the emotions of terror and surprise caused by certain events, the mind is split or dissociated: it is unable to register the wound to the psyche because the ordinary mechanisms of awareness and cognition are destroyed. As a result, the victim is unable to recollect and integrate the hurtful experience in normal consciousness; instead, she is haunted or possessed by intrusive traumatic memories. The experience of the trauma, fixed or frozen in time, refuses to be represented as past, but is perpetually reexperienced in a painful, dissociated, traumatic present. (2)

In these terms trauma is defined by a belated temporality; trauma resides in the repetition of an earlier event that is forgotten or repressed and so is neither recalled nor known as traumatic, except in the repetition of symptoms or traumatic memories. But these repetitions are not identical, and, because each repetition is not self-identical, there opens the potential for analysis. Through the analysis of difference within a pattern of repetition the original traumatic event can be isolated, revealed, and treated.

This description of the chronology of trauma offers the field of trauma literature as a rich ground for literary analysis, representing as it does the symptoms of trauma in an essentially narrative form. Indeed, the prominent trauma theorist Cathy Caruth argues in the essay "Unclaimed Experience: Trauma and the Possibility of History" that trauma offers literary criticism a resolution of the problem of referentiality and consequent "political and ethical paralysis" posed by some critics of poststructuralist or "deconstructive" approaches. Caruth argues that trauma describes "an overwhelming experience of sudden, or catastrophic, events, in which the response to the event occurs in the often delayed, and uncontrolled repetitive occurrence of hallucinations and other intrusive phenomena" (181). She identifies the figure of the shell-shocked soldier, whose traumatic experience of violent and massive death is received in a benumbed state but is relived in years of nightmares, as the iconic representation of modern trauma. Such an example offers Caruth the opportunity to argue that the representation of trauma is not strictly referential, that it is necessarily indirect, symbolic, and so subject to interpretation. More important for my approach to the issue of time and trauma is her construction of trauma as a linear narrative process: trauma as belated repetition is trauma as an unfolding linear history. Caruth claims: "Through the notion of trauma . . . we can understand that a rethinking of reference is not aimed at eliminating history, but at resituating it in our understanding, that is, of precisely permitting *history* to arise where *immediate understanding* may not" (182). This history that arises does so as a result of cumulative understanding derived from the repetition of the traumatic event. This is a convenient way of opening the field of historical understanding to literary analysis by insisting upon the narrative and referentially indeterminate nature of historical understanding. This theory weakens, however, in the presence of texts such as Paula Gunn Allen's novel, which, while obviously documenting the consequences of trauma in the life history of the protagonist, Ephanie, does not disclose any single sudden or catastrophic event. Caruth's paradigmatic case of trauma, the soldier haunted by his wartime experience, or indeed the other examples of traumatic event that she cites—"rape, child abuse, auto and industrial accidents, and so on" (182)—finds no counterpart in Allen's trauma narrative. While, it is true, Ephanie's story does describe the pattern of forgetting and return that Caruth sees as the essential pattern of trauma, the trauma itself cannot be located in any single event. What are we to make of this? At this point we, as readers, must read the novel against the theoretical grain and question the universal applicability of the theoretical concept of "belated repetition" as characteristic of trauma in every case.

It seems to me that we must exercise some skepticism toward theoretical models, especially in relation to such contentious issues as post-traumatic stress disorder and recovered memory (and false memory syndrome). Particularly, we should explore alternative accounts of the relations between time, trauma, and memory. One such alternative theory is presented in the essay "Symptoms of Discursivity: Experience, Memory, and Trauma." Here Ernst Van Alphen argues persuasively against the assumption made by Caruth that experience somehow precedes trauma. If we return briefly to Caruth's definition of trauma as "an overwhelming experience of sudden, or catastrophic events," we find her arguing that experience precedes response, a response that may come years after the event or experience. Van Alphen, in contrast, argues not that trauma is an experience of particular kinds of events but that trauma in fact destroys experience. His view of experience is based on the understanding that, in order to come into existence, experience must be discursively constructed: "Experience depends on discourse to come about; forms of experience do not just depend on the event or history that is being experienced, but also on the discourse in which the event is expressed/thought/conceptualized" (24).

Experience and, by extension, the subjectivity constituted by that experience are thus discursive constructions: "subjects are the effect of the discursive processing of their experiences" (Van Alphen 25). There is no contradiction between Van Alphen and Caruth in terms of the understanding of subjectivity and experience as discursive constructions. Where the two theorists part company is in relation to when experience can be said to have taken place and how this experience is retrospectively constructed as memory. Caruth presents experience as the foundation of trauma and that to which traumatic memories return the victim. This "foundational" view of experience is criticized by Van Alphen from the outset when he observes of the status of experience in historical analysis that "experience is put forward as true or self-evident, as uncontestable [sic], and as an originary point of explanation" (24). For Van Alphen, in contrast, the foundation, or "originary point of explanation," for trauma lies in some sensation to which we cannot have access because it cannot be transformed discursively into experience and so cannot be articulated, even to the victim of the trauma. This is the trauma, for Van Alphen, but not for theorists such as Caruth and Leys, who, following Freud, posit the knowledge of trauma at some subsequent moment and the trauma itself in the repetition of the traumatic event.

Van Alphen's account of the relations between experience and subjectivity is important for his understanding of traumatic memory, in which memory is seen as the retrieval not of the past itself but of the discursive experience of the past. Memory is a special category of experience, and, in the terms Van Alphen presents, traumatic memory is impossible. Trauma is a case of what he calls "failed experience" and so of "failed memorialization" of that experience, which eludes discursive representation. Incidentally, we might note here that Freud, in *Dora: An Analysis of a Case of Hysteria*, observes that a characteristic of hysteria is the inability to tell coherent stories as a consequence of what has been repressed (30–31). In Van Alphen's argument trauma itself lies in the impossibility of experiencing, and so remembering, an event that resists all discursive formulation.

The concept of the unrepresentability of trauma takes on a new significance in this perspective. When Van Alphen refers to the unrepresentability of the Holocaust, for example, he does not mean the impropriety of representing the Holocaust under certain circumstances; rather, he means that survivors of this historical trauma find it impossible to narrate their traumatic memories because the trauma itself has destroyed the discursive basis for the construction of experience and the memory of that experience. Van Alphen explains:

> The difficulty of telling the past of the Holocaust should not be located in the extremity of the events itself, but rather in the process and mechanisms of experience and its representation. . . . I presume . . . that in principle representation does offer the possibility of giving expression to extreme experiences. The issue, however, is that representation itself is historically variable. Sometimes there are situations or events—and the Holocaust is prototypical for such situations—that are the occasion of "experiences" that can-

not be expressed in the terms that language (or, more broadly, the symbolic order) offers *at that moment*. (26)

This is precisely the problematic situation in which Allen's traumatized protagonist finds herself.

For Ephanie her suffering is focused upon the impossibility and continual frustration of failing to make herself understood to others and, often, even to herself. She does not possess a vocabulary sufficient to the construction of her experience, and, consequently, she loses the sense of her own self, her own subjectivity, as a construction of experience that would be prerequisite for the articulation of that experience. The absence of a coherent and self-consistent subject of/in the narrative accounts for the radical fragmentation that characterizes the language of the text. In the section entitled "Shaking, She Makes It Matter," for example, the narrator attempts to represent the nameless fear that haunts and periodically paralyzes Ephanie: "Fear. Bloody fingers pressing her temples. Her breastbone. Her gut. I will not be afraid. Fear, the destroyer. Even I know there is nothing really frightening here. The red carpet. The stereo. Dusty records. Table, dark brown. The sun in the window. Going out. The lamps. Coming on. Turning them on, Ephanie" (6). The language of this passage stresses not only discontinuity but also the primacy of sensation. The fragmentation of sentences emphasizes a lack of causal connections in favor of sensations such as color (red, dark brown), light (the sun, the lamps), and the body (breastbone, guts, temples). These sensations do not cohere into experience, which makes sensations explicable and communicable. Ephanie does not have at her disposal forms of representation that enable her to "have" experiences in a way that can be understood and communicated. The events of her life cannot become experience in the forms of articulation available to her. Instead, she has sensation that is without meaning, or experience that is sensation constructed according to an inauthentic discourse that she perceives to be inauthentic.

It is this failure of discourse that itself constitutes trauma rather than functioning as a symptom of traumatic experience. In Van Alphen's words and in his example of Holocaust survivors:

The problem of Holocaust survivors is precisely that the lived events could not be experienced because language did not provide the terms and positions in which to experience them; thus they are defined as *traumatic*. The Holocaust has been so traumatic for many, precisely because it could not be experienced, because a distance from it in language or representation was not possible. In this view, experience is the result or product of a discursive process. Thus, the problem of Holocaust experiences can be formulated as the stalling of this discursive process. Because of this stalling the experience cannot come about. (27)

This gives rise to a further revision of assumptions about traumatic memory and the chronology of trauma. The problem of unrepresentability is not an issue subsequent to the traumatic event but is constitutive of the trauma itself: "the later representational problems are a continuation of the impossibility during the event itself of experiencing the Holocaust in the terms of the symbolic order then available" (27). This description of trauma as constituted by the denial of subjectivity that occurs at the same moment that the traumatic event refuses to be articulated as experience contradicts the view of theorists such as Cathy Caruth that trauma is characterized by a "belated temporality" that is subsequent to the traumatic event and which reappears in the form of hysterical symptoms and the pathological repetition of the trauma. It is, however, an accurate description of the trauma depicted in *The Woman Who Owned the Shadows*.

On Trauma Narrative and Narrative Symbolism

As I remarked earlier, Allen's narrative is uniquely marked by the absence of any single traumatic event in the depiction of Ephanie's suffering. Rather than seek to articulate and bring to meaning some specific failed experience, to use Van Alphen's term, the narrative emphasizes time, recollection, and memory and the idea of circling, or repetition. These repetitions are not the hysterical symptoms of trauma in the sense that Caruth describes the insistent repetition of the singular traumatic moment. These repeated motifs appear in the narrative, as it is told by an omniscient third-person narrator, and these motifs tell a story of Ephanie that is distinct from the story Ephanie would tell about herself. At times this narrator reports Ephanie's own first-person voice, but this occurs only in moments of intense introspection, when meaning dissolves back into raw uninterpretable sensation. The narrative remains insistently focalized through Ephanie, but there remains a disjunction between the narrator's voice and that of Ephanie, who is alienated from everything and everyone: including herself. In this way the narrative structure seeks to represent Ephanie's trauma as something that resists conceptualization, that remains stubbornly in a condition of sensation rather than experience, in the absence of sufficient discursive forms to transform these sensations into experience. Allen's narrative style presses language to convey trauma in its full unspeakable horror by resisting any normalizing literary style that would reduce the alien and terrifying nature of trauma.

The Woman Who Owned the Shadows is an example of the way in which literature can preserve the authenticity of trauma as an experience that takes place in a liminal space outside the normal contexts of experience and meaning. The significance of trauma as unspeakable horror is, in the view of theorists such as Cathy Caruth and Walter Benn Michaels, articulated as pure horror when the referential function of language is pressed beyond its limits. Then, in the words of Benn Michaels, we have access to "not the normalizing knowledge of the horror but the horror itself" (8). In a literary context trauma can be witnessed without being fully comprehended because "language is capable of bearing witness only by a failure of witnessing or representation" (Leys 268). The peculiar epistemology of trauma resides in the special authority attributed to the survivor, who, alone, is qualified to articulate the trauma he or she has experienced. But, when the victim cannot clearly articulate that trauma as experience, then the very attempt to articulate this failed experience pushes the representational limits of literary language. This is precisely what Allen achieves in this narrative: the depiction not of a story of trauma but the trauma in all its unintelligibility. What critics such as Elizabeth Hanson have condemned as the unnecessary repetition of mundane events and activities is in fact the recording of sensation that cannot be transformed into a state of meaning. Similarly, the radical fragmentation of the narrative, into four major parts and more than seventy sections of unequal length, underscores the absence of any coherent paradigm or logical structure into which this story could fit. The fragments that constitute the narrative stress the impropriety of linear narrative as a form that could contain and "tell" this story. Ephanie's trauma does not conform to a neat repetition of a singular, originary event, and the narrative does not lead in any simple way toward the idea of healing the trauma.

What does unite these fragments is the pattern of symbolic repetition through which key images accumulate significance that finally becomes a language capable of transforming Ephanie's life into a condition of meaning and "experience." The narrative charts this progress from a state of failed experience to experience that can be articulated and so offers the prospect of healing. We should recall that Ernst Van Alphen stresses the historical variability of representation when he points out that "there are situations or events . . . that are the occasion of 'experiences' that cannot be expressed in the terms that language (or, more broadly, the symbolic order) offers *at that moment*" (26). What Paula Gunn Allen depicts is the gradual historical shift from a moment when no appropriate language is available to a later moment when the structure of the symbolic order is such that these situations and events can be articulated as traumatic experiences.

This shift, which is a chronological one, takes place through the symbolic subtext of the narrative. In memories, dreams, and visions a series of key symbols is established and developed throughout the narrative: flying or jumping, the imagery of shadows, and the image of Grandmother Spider. But memory also brings recollections of loss, abandonment, and violation. These images come together in the conclusion of the narrative, converging in a vision that provides Ephanie with the explanatory paradigm she needs to transform her life into meaningful experience. Images of flying or jumping are associated with betrayal and abandonment in the early part of the narrative, but in the section "She Remembers Something" what Ephanie recalls is the tribal story of Sky Woman, who is betrayed by her husband as he pushes her through a hole in the sky so that she falls through the void. This, however, is a creation story in which birds break the woman's fall and place her gently on the back of Grandmother Turtle, upon whose back they have spread the mud from which the earth grows. At this point in her development Ephanie names the tree that is uprooted to reveal the hole through which Sky Woman falls a "death tree" (38). When the same story is repeated later, in the section "In the Shadows She Sang, Remembering," Ephanie sees this fall as a fortunate and creative one and the woman as someone "who entered a new world and upon it planted her seed. Who gave the sun and moon their light. Who from death made life" (191). This is the knowledge that Ephanie has resisted, the vision attached to this story and the symbolism of falling: "She understood at last that everything was connected. Everything was related. Nothing came in that did not go out. Nothing was that did not live nestled within everything else. And this was how the stories went, what they had been for. To fit a life into. To make sense" (191; my emph.).

This knowledge is unpalatable for Ephanie because, in order to remember the stories that communicate this understanding, she must remember her own fall, her literal fall from the apple tree in her mother's garden. This tree opens not a hole in the sky but a hole in Ephanie's life as she learns from the experience fear and self-doubt. After this fall, which breaks her ribs and punctures her lung, Ephanie no longer trusts her own body, and so she learns a passive femininity, forgetting how she once trusted her own judgment and vision. "'I abandoned myself,' she said. 'I left me'" (204). Ephanie falls into a world symbolized by shadows, signifying this fear, confusion, abandonment, and betrayal. The imagery of shadows, which of course lends the narrative its title, signifies the loss of control that characterizes Ephanie's life. She calls herself "Shadow Woman" and the city where she seeks refuge the "Shadow Place" (36, 58). Gradually, the accretion of significance around the image of shadows becomes the focus of Ephanie's growing need for knowledge. It is the "shadow sister," Grandmother Spider, who assists Ephanie in pursuing this knowledge, which is the recollection of knowledge she had and forgot. Early in the narrative the image of the spider is associated with memory and assumes the status of a guardian of historical memory. Indeed, Ephanie is hostile toward spiders during the long period when she does not want to remember. But the figure of the spider acquires additional meaning as a witness to the death-dealing brought by white people; the spider even witnesses Ephanie's attempt at suicide. It is as a figure waiting for the people finally to come to peace that the spider takes on its most powerful significance. In Ephanie's vision of the convergence of all creation, past and present, it is the Spider Grandmother who tells her: "'Little sister, you have jumped. You have fallen. You have been brave, but you have misunderstood. So you have learned. How to jump. How to fall. How to learn. How to understand'" (211). In this way, necessarily through complex strategies of symbolic indirection, the narrative describes its transformation of Ephanie's "failed" traumatic experience into meaningful experience.

On the Possibility of Representing Collective Trauma

Jeffrey K. Olick, in his essay "Collective Memory: The Two Cultures" (1999), addresses the issue of the collectivity of remembering, which takes place in and through language, narrative, and dialogue, arguing that "it is not merely that individuals remember in language, coding their experiences as language and recalling them in it. Language itself can be viewed as a memory system" (343). This is not a new argument; as Olick points out, Mikhail Bakhtin, in *Problems of Dostoevsky's Poetics* (1963), claims that each speech act contains a "memory trace" linking it to the utterances that have preceded it. Linguistic events make sense through a complex interplay of recollection and innovation. The historical development of linguistic usage takes place through genres. Each genre "lives in the present, but always remembers its past, its beginning. Genre is a representative of creative memory in the process of literary development" (Bakhtin, qtd. by Olick, 343). If collective memory is contained in some way in literary forms or genres, we must ask, then, whether the collective recollection of traumatic memory can be contained also in literary form. If personal trauma can be articulated in symbolic form, as opposed to the form of conventional linear narrative, what form is required, or indeed possible, for the articulation of collective trauma? Can the trauma of an entire community be brought into the condition of meaning that would create a collective experience of trauma?

Olick describes trauma as the disruption of "the legitimating narrative[s] that we as individuals produce for us as a collectivity" (345). Trauma lies in the inability of the victim to make sense of the traumatic event because no existing language, system of moral values, or explanatory paradigm is sufficient. This creates complications for any view of the inheritance of trauma or for the construction of collective traumatic memories. Olick continues:

> While we may speak of the residue of individual traumas, insofar as parents or grandparents imparted to their offspring stories of their experiences, psychological traumas cannot be passed down through the generations like bad genes. In the first place, the fact that the memory of such personally traumatic experiences is externalized and objectified as narrative means it is no longer a purely individual psychological matter. And in the second place, discussing the ongoing nature of the trauma in terms of such transmitted personal narratives does not capture what we really mean—that is, an unassimilable breach in the collective narrative. . . . In this way, for instance, the trauma of Auschwitz will not disappear with the death of the last survivor; nor is it carried only through those . . . who suffered its personal ripple effects: Auschwitz remains a trauma for the narratives of modernity and morality, among others. (345)

The externalization and objectification of personal memories of trauma as narrative (and we must recall here Van Alphen's warning that these memories are necessarily the construction of experience through later discursive forms and are not constitutive of the trauma event itself) transforms personal trauma into something that is no longer personal and psychological or emotional. We are talking here about collective historical trauma, a problematic concept that generalizes theories developed in the treatment of traumatized individuals to encompass communities that have been subject to historical trauma. Olick does emphasize, however, the necessity that we think of trauma not only in personal but also in collective terms, as the disruption of collective narratives such as "progress," "civilization," "modernity," and the like. As Olick suggests, the assimilation of personal trauma accounts into explanatory paradigms that remove the horror of inexplicable pre-experience or raw sensation disrupts those collective narratives and the collective values of "modernity and morality" that underlie and support them.

In Allen's narrative this disruption of collective narratives by Ephanie's personal trauma serves to underline the distinction between the destructive white narratives that have destroyed Ephanie's self-esteem to the point of destroying her subjectivity and the tribal narratives that offer the possibility of self-reconciliation and healing. This is an uneasy distinction to sustain, however, as Ephanie reveals the ostracism of her family through three generations by a tribal community that will not tolerate intermarriage with whites and the mixed-blood offspring that result from these marriages. Ephanie's alienation is equally from tribal and white communities. The opening section, "Her Name Was a Stranger," explains this double estrangement: "like her it was a split name, a name half of this and half of that: Ephiphany. Effie. An almost name. An almost event. Proper at that for her, a halfblood. A halfbreed. Which was the source of her derangement. Ranging despair. Disarrangement" (3). Her trauma is located partially in the negative narratives of Native Americans that surround her: the Vanishing American, the Indian as Victim, the romanticized view of Native peoples by certain liberal whites. After spending time with Teresa's New Age friends in Colorado, for example, Ephanie is consumed with rage because these people insist upon a view of Native Americans as the passive victims of the colonial history of the United States who continue in a passive role as victims of modernity. Ephanie is aware that her self-destructive rage confirms the negative stereotype to which she is subjected, even as her anger exposes this traumatizing collective narrative.

Dominick LaCapra offers a useful term to describe such collective trauma: a "founding trauma" is a historical event that plays a formative role in the creation of a community's collective identity and becomes a basis for the individual identity of members of the community (724). Traumatic historical events include the Holocaust, American slavery, and Native American genocide. Paula Gunn Allen's protagonist is shaped in negative ways by the legacy of genocide: she is haunted by voices that chant to her the historical message that "a good Indian is a dead Indian," and she knows that she cannot be "good" because she is alive (147); she and her community have somehow survived that which they were not intended to survive.

Personal trauma is reconciled in the narrative by the pattern of tribal symbols and the tribal mythology, the stories, which enable Ephanie to situate her trauma, to transform it into experience. The collective and historical, or "founding," trauma she suffers is, however, reconciled only through the thematics of death and the exposure of the negative collective narratives to which Ephanie, as a mixed-blood person, has been subjected.

Ephanie comes to understand the tribal account of the bringing of death to the world, and in this way she is able to situate her own experience of vision, her understanding of the symbolic parallel between the Woman Who Fell from the Sky and her own fall into falsehood and self-loathing. The collective narrative of death describes not only the disruption of tribal narratives by the invasion of Anglos, with their contrary narratives of life and death; the disruption of collective tribal narratives such as these is in itself the trauma suffered by tribal peoples. At the same time that Ephanie situates her own personal trauma in a logical paradigm offered by the tribal mythology, so she also locates her own trauma within the larger historical trauma, the founding trauma, of her people. This is a trauma that she is best placed to appreciate, in all her suffering but also in the wisdom of her knowledge, as a person of mixed-blood ancestry who has been alienated from her white and tribal affiliations but who finally comes to see a way forward for herself and, potentially, for all her people.

Conclusion

The movement from lack of appropriate symbolic forms and "failed" experience to a condition of knowledge and communicable experience is achieved in this novel not by any of the conventional strategies of linear novelistic narrative. Indeed, the narrative resists that which is linear, including the linear construction of trauma posited by influential theorists such as Cathy Caruth and Ruth Leys. It is, rather, by a process of circling, recording sensation and fragmented thought in such a way as to permit the gradual accumulation of meaning by key symbols, that the narrative is able finally to bring Ephanie's trauma into a condition of meaning. The image of circles and circling, closely associated with the activity of weaving, runs throughout the text: from the early image of Elena, the friend who will betray Ephanie, running in circles to the late image of thinking in circles: "She talked, her thoughts ran in circles. Which couldn't be helped. Indians lived in circles, did not care for lines that broken went nowhere. For her the sun was a clock, a calendar, like her body, like her eyes that were the meeting place of light and flesh, were circular. Like the winds. Like the sky. Like the entire galaxy that wheeled, holding the earth in her outflung arm. She thought in accretions, concretions. Like pearls grow. Like crystals. Like the earth. She gave up talking" (185). No talking cure, then, for Ephanie. This passage succinctly describes the novelistic strategy of Allen's text. It is an achronological strategy, such as she describes as typical of the tribal novel in the MELUS interview, published in 1983, the same year as *The Woman Who Owned the Shadows*: "What you're going to have, when an Indian writes a chronological tale, is a tale of colonization and death. That's what's going to happen. Nothing else *can* happen to an Indian in a chronological time frame. . . . But in this other structure ['achronicity'], what's happening is we're beginning to develop a structural mode that will enable us to affirm life and to talk about who we really are, as well as who we imagine ourselves to be" (19–20). Paula Gunn Allen's novel challenges the assumptions underlying the chronological structure of literary narrative. This text also challenges us to review our assumptions about the narrative nature of trauma and its representation. The construction of trauma as a pattern of linear repetitions, structured as chronological narrative, may well open the field of trauma in a convenient manner for embattled literary critics, as Caruth suggests. But trauma texts such as Allen's require that we assess carefully the interests served by the explanatory paradigms that bring all our knowledge into a condition of meaningful "experience."

Works Cited

Allen, Paula Gunn. *The Sacred Hoop: Recovering the Feminine in American Indian Traditions*. Boston: Beacon, 1986.

———. *The Woman Who Owned the Shadows*. San Francisco: Spinsters Ink, 1983.

Ballinger, Franchot, and Brian Swann. "A MELUS Interview: Paula Gunn Allen." MELUS 10.2 (1983): 3–25.

Benn Michaels, Walter. "You who never was there? Slavery and the New Historicism, Deconstruction and the Holocaust." *Narrative* 4 (1996): 1–16. Rpt. in *The Americanization of the Holocaust*. Ed. Hilene Flanzbaum. Baltimore: Johns Hopkins University Press, 1999. 181–97.

Caruth, Cathy. "Unclaimed Experience: Trauma and the Possibility of History." *Yale French Studies*, special issue, *Literature and the Ethical Question* 79 (1991): 181–92.

Felman, Shoshana. "Education and Crisis." In *Trauma: Explorations in Memory*. Ed. Cathy Caruth. Baltimore: Johns Hopkins University Press, 1995. 13–60.

Freud, Sigmund. *Dora: An Analysis of a Case of Hysteria*. 1905. New York: Macmillan, 1963.

Hanson, Elizabeth. *Paula Gunn Allen*. Western Writers Series 90. Boise: Boise State University Press, 1990.

LaCapra, Dominick. "Trauma, Absence, Loss." *Critical Inquiry* 25 (1999): 696–727.

Leys, Ruth. *Trauma: A Genealogy*. Chicago: University of Chicago Press, 2000.

Olick, Jeffrey K. "Collective Memory: The Two Cultures." *Sociological Theory* 17.3 (1999): 333–48.

Prince-Hughes, Tara. "Contemporary Two-Spirit Identity in the Fiction of Paula Gunn Allen and Beth Brant." *Studies in American Indian Literatures*, ser. 2, 10.4 (1998): 9–31.

Van Alphen, Ernst. "Symptoms of Discursivity: Experience, Memory, and Trauma." In *Acts of Memory: Cultural Recall in the Present*. Ed. Mieke Bal, Jonathan Crewe, and Leo Spitzer. Hanover NH: University Press of New England, 1999. 24–38.

7 "Keep Wide Awake in the Eyes"

Seeing Eyes in Wendy Rose's Poetry

In her most recent collection of poems, Itch Like Crazy, Wendy Rose imagines a fleeting connection over space and time with her European great-great-grandfather: "Andrew MacInnes, You Look West Just at the Moment I Look East" (43–44). This title grasps the ambiguity and ambivalence of the line of vision between Rose and MacInnes, and we are left to consider the possibility that they are, at once, looking at and beyond each other. In the three MacInnes poems, and in the other ancestral portraits included in this collection, which take the form of photographs and poems, Rose uses ambiguous eye contact, momentary glances, and lines of vision in an attempt to engage with a European lineage. Previously, Rose has used the analogy of seeing to consider the potential and limits of her American Indian heritage:

> I have not been exposed to oral traditions and this has been a big gap in my upbringing. It's like growing up with bad eyesight and being given glasses as an adult. You missed a lot and you're aware of it, and this has something to do with how you interpret the new, sharp world around you, but you can never go back and re-grow your life with good eyes. You can see, finally, but your interpretation of what you see will always be influenced by the years you didn't see clearly.[1]

Only recently, in Itch Like Crazy, has Rose employed this analogy of looking and seeing to help her engage with her European heritage, and in this essay I initially focus on the ways in which Rose constructs lines of vision with her European ancestors across geographical and historical limits. Following this, I trace alternative ways of seeing and looking in Rose's earlier work by interrogating the ways in which prevailing ideologies from anthropological and museological contexts, as well as sites of cultural performance, are met and challenged by an altogether different seeing eye/I. The central concern of this study, therefore, is to track the poetic I/eye across continents and time to reveal the strikingly consistent nature of Rose's poetry as she embraces European, Native American, and transnational experiences of violence, trauma, and recovery.

In an interview with Carol Hunter in 1983, Rose defines her mixed heritage along paternal and maternal divisions. Rose's father is Hopi, and her mother is part Miwok, part Scots, Irish, and German: "When I think of my father's people, I think of living, breathing, working, surviving, strong people in the face of whom I am weak. When I think of my mother's people, I think of confusion, tragedy, death, fragmentation, bones, and things that are gone forever. I look back at my mother's heritage, and forward at my father's" (83). Certainly, the majority of Rose's poetry to date has focused on Native American heritage and experiences, and this remains a continual source of influence. To a lesser degree, perhaps, Rose also acknowledges a Western, European heritage. In interviews and autobiographical essays she describes her Catholic upbringing, for example, and in "Neon Scars," specifically, she describes her search for the MacInnes clan tartan at the Frensco Highland Games. From this experience Rose concludes: "This is not the heritage I would have picked—to be the daughter of the invaders. It is not where my sympathies lie. Searching the grounds, I found my clan" (258). Perhaps unsurprisingly, it has taken Rose some time to fully engage with her European lineage in her poetry, but in Itch Like Crazy Rose finally does "look back" at her European heritage and begins to engage with the conflict implicit in the fact that "the colonizer and colonized meet in my blood" ("Neon Scars" 258).

The opening two poems of Itch Like Crazy characterize the experience of the colonizers and the colonized, European travelers and American

Indians; like MacInnes and Rose, one group looks west, while the other group looks east. "Imagine it like this" traces the haunting and difficult journey of early colonial travelers from Europe who "faced the cold wind" and sailed west (3); the ships are spotted on a distant horizon in a companion poem, "It happened that we were gathering shellfish," through the eyes of the Taino tribe, who welcome the "trembling," starving, and dying strangers from the east (5). On a more personal level, in an eponymous poem about her great-great-grandmother, Margaret Castor, Rose imagines another brief yet poignant moment of contact and wonders:

> Are you the astonished one
> or am I that we meet like this
> between the sailing ship
> and the silver jet
> that crosses the sky?
> (24–25)

By constructing these moments of seeing, meeting, and encountering, Rose creates a "contact zone" similar to the one Mary Louise Pratt describes: "The term 'contact zone' . . . refer[s] to the space of colonial encounters, the space in which peoples geographically and historically separated come into contact with each other and establish ongoing relations, usually involving conditions of coercion, radical inequality, and intractable conflict" (*Imperial Eyes* 6). By incorporating her Hopi and Miwok heritage (as well as the perspective of the Taino tribe) into the poetic re-creation of her European ancestors and acknowledging the "intractable conflict" in the project of colonization, Rose conceptualizes her own partial complicity and tries to resolve her personal trauma of having mixed-blood identity by asking herself: "Do I let your blood run back into my veins / or pinch them off in some desolate place / between Arizona and Ontario?" (*Itch* 48) Thankfully, Rose does not rest in this "desolate place," and her urge to look into the eyes of her European ancestors, who were slave owners, pioneers, travelers, and gold miners, demonstrates a desire to engage with what Pratt describes as the "seeing-man": the "European male subject of European landscape discourse—he whose imperial eyes passively look out and possess" (7).

Certainly, Andrew MacInnes's "imperial eyes" look west, toward and across the American continent, with the intention of possessing land, property, and people. In the MacInnes poems the reader witnesses a process of demystification as Rose rewrites her memories of a man whom she believed was a victim of the Highland Clearances, an exile, and a refugee but who was in fact "the son of cattle thieves and outlaws" and, ultimately, a slave owner:

> You were one who bought other men
> to work so you would grow rich
> beyond measure; you stole them from their land,
> their people, took their names, their languages,
> turned them into blank slates upon which you would write
> with the flick of your whip.
> ("Captain Andrew MacInnes of the Norfolk Militia" 47)

It is through this "new knowledge," and only "half-blind eyes," that Rose imagines approaching MacInnes, "in my melon-round and earth-bound form,/to find you imagining me/to be as white as you"(47). While Rose begins to draw MacInnes into a clearer line of vision and accepts a more accurate account of her personal heritage within the context of colonization, violence, and slavery, she establishes a painful but necessary contact with the seeing-man; MacInnes, however, cannot (and will not) see a granddaughter who is not as "white" or "petite" as his daughter, Henrietta.

Maintaining this focus on her European lineage, Rose follows the westward expansion of nineteenth-century North America: Joseph Bigler's "hooded home, / rolling west on wood wheels" traces another part of the seeing-man's journey ("Joseph Bigler" 27), which takes Bigler to Bear Valley, where he opens the Bon Ton Saloon. Similarly, Joseph

Barrett, an Irish ancestor, who was both a miner and a gambler, demonstrates the imperial eyes of the European immigrant who looks out across the landscape to possess the quartz and gold buried in California (51–54). In this collection Rose meets the stares of these seeing men in a contact zone where personal and political conflicts of power are exposed and examined. While the majority of poems and photographs in this collection visualize Rose's own European lineage, her personal story—which includes Scots, German, Irish, and English immigration to American as well as the journey to California—tells the larger story of colonization and the gradual process of westward expansion in the North American landscape. Resisting the temptation to construct essentialist oppositional paradigms between her white ancestors and Indian sense of self, she acknowledges the complexity of family ties and family lies:

> Much of the impetus to write this book is more personal than political. I had to come to terms not only with the obvious historical facts of conquest and genocide, but with the personal fact of being born into a family that could not keep its own secrets straight. . . . This condition [of being of her father's people and her mother's people] is a part of the "itch" that is growing in intensity as young people find themselves feeling alone because they are "multiracial." (Part 3, "Listen Here for the Voices," *Itch* n.p.)

The unraveling of cultural conflict in *Itch Like Crazy* is conceived in brutally honest and revealing autobiographical terms. Indeed, it is fair to say that a large proportion of Rose's poems are autobiographical: some are explicitly dedicated to her relationship with fellow writers, friends, and her husband, Arthur. More specifically, *Now Poof She Is Gone* (1994) is a retrospective collection of poems that Rose describes in its preface as being derived from "personal issues" and "private emotions." Similarly, *Academic Squaw Reports to the World from the Ivory Tower* (1977) was inspired by her experiences as an American Indian student, and a student of American Indian literature, at the University of California, Berkeley.

Embedded within this personal experience lies a political and cultural engagement that stretches throughout Rose's career, and this engagement can be usefully mapped through ways of looking, watching, and matching the glare of the seeing-man.

Rose's interrogation of the processes of looking, watching, and seeing, in carefully constructed contact zones are most apparent in poems that deal with both the study of cultural difference by anthropologists and the exhibition of cultural difference in museum display cases. While Rose describes herself as "that most schizophrenic of creatures, an American Indian who is both poet and anthropologist," she also claims that she is "not that kind of anthropologist" ("Great Pretenders" 403, 408). She is not the kind of anthropologist who, like her professor at Berkeley, claimed: "It's time to stop studying humanity from the worm's-eye view; anthropology has been dealing with primitives too long."[2] In addition to the ideologically and culturally constructed binary oppositions that are forged in this statement—specifically, educated and primitive or white and other—the anthropological methodology Rose objects to is conceptualized in terms that hierarchically define ways of looking. At the heart of this conceptualized way of looking is the contrast between the localized "worm's-eye view" and the view of the "classic" anthropologist, described by Christoph Irmscher as that of a "voyeur who establishes for himself a privileged position from which to view, safely, other human beings" (591).

These "voyeurs" appear in "The Anthropology Convention," one of Rose's early poems:

> From the day we are born
> there are eyes all around
> to watch our stumblings. . . .
> When we pull in the world
> about our bellies there are those eyes
> watching for exotic pots of words
> spilled from our coral and rawhide tongues.
> (*Long Division*, n.p.)

Forever in the glare of the anthropologist's gaze, objectified and exoticized, Rose's objections to this voyeuristic and ideologically constructed way of looking are enlarged by the fact that her own "anthropological study" at Berkeley was in fact a Ph.D. degree in literature by American Indians, a degree the English Literature department and Comparative Literature department refused to offer. Nonetheless, Rose engages with the prevailing academic climate and forges her own anthropological role, and in "Indian Anthropologist" she refers to that educational and cultural experience. As a starting point, Rose quotes the experience of Claude Lévi-Strauss: "There is no more thrilling aspect for the anthropologist than that of being the first *white man* to visit a particular native community."[3] Marginalized by the "white man" (the anthropologist) on the grounds of her gender, culture, and race, Rose is initially brought into the academy by professors who would have her become the "pioneer" and excavate a resistant landscape that has wakened from a "stony coma" to "throw us off her back, bucking / and hollering like stars / were whipping her." Unable to adopt a pioneer viewpoint, Rose aligns herself with "Mama Earth"; parts of her soul are "moss-covered," and she feels the "rolling and moaning" of the earth "like a shiver." "Indian Anthropologist" does not offer a final resolution; Rose can only compromise:

> I can go on like this
> only if I shut my ears but
> keep wide awake
> in the eyes.

In this unusual contact zone, where the female, Indian poetic voice becomes enmeshed with a powerful, feminized, and angry landscape, the seeing-men of this poem—Lévi-Strauss and the anonymous professors and, more generally, the "European derived institution run by the white male power structure" (Rose, quoted in Bruchac 259)—are met and challenged by resilient "wide awake eyes."

In these early poems oppositional strategies between male and female, Euro-American and Native American, enable a wider political comment on her personal circumstances and those of Native Americans in the Unites States in the late 1970s. In addition to Rose's experiences as an American Indian woman in a predominantly white, male environment at Berkeley, during the late 1960s and 1970s the momentum of the American Indian Movement led many American Indians, including Rose, to occupy Alcatraz, drawing attention to the land rights of all American Indian tribes. Rose openly discusses her role in Indian activism in her interviews with Hunter and Laura Coltelli, and in each of them she recalls sitting in front of a bulldozer and a SWAT team to protect an Indian burial ground in San Jose. Rose acknowledges that the burial ground was saved, but in the Hunter interview Rose also reveals that this kind of confrontation in California led to more personal threats on her life (Coltelli 125; Hunter 70). In this context it is perhaps unsurprising that Rose's poetry aligns American Indian identity so closely with the perceived "ownership" and use of the land; it is even less surprising that the urgency of these personal and political issues are demonstrated through oppositional strategies.[4] Rose's early work in particular demonstrates a personal experience that has defined her as other in gendered and cultural terms, and in these poems, specifically, she constructs a serious political agenda predicated on oppositional frameworks. Yet, as I have demonstrated in relation to her most recent examination of her European heritage, in her work and in her personal circumstances she acknowledges the impossibility of maintaining such arbitrary and potentially destructive essentialist oppositions. I would argue that the lines of vision and the more direct connection of eye contact that Rose constructs allows for necessary oppositional engagement but also stresses the emergence of gendered identities and cultural identities of American Indians within what Susan Castillo refers to as a "dynamic, historically constructed process" (184).

This dual process of political engagement, provoked by the "alienation and anger" that Rose has experienced and witnessed ("Neon Scars" 253), and the conscious construction of a female American Indian voice, another form of political engagement, is combined in *Lost Copper*, which N. Scott Momaday characterizes as a "literature of protest" and a "celebration of the earth" (preface, *Lost Copper* ix). Specifically, in "Mount Saint Helens: An Indian Woman's Song" Rose continues to embed gender and cultural relationships within the context of a volatile and angry earth and constructs an oppositional dynamic that does not rely on an essentialist subtext but, rather, on a reworking of "historical processes" of identity construction (100).

Initially, Rose describes her experience as an airline passenger in a flight over Mount Saint Helens, and, in a similar way as with the anthropologists and professors of the earlier poems, some passengers are described as "voyeurs" who stared

> into the bellows of her throat,
> watched the convulsions shaking her
> till she raged
> and waved her round hands
> in the sky.
> (*Lost Copper* 100)[5]

The landscape is feminized from the title of the poem, the use of pronouns throughout, and implied further from a line of vision that is established from the height of the plane down onto the objectified earth, an earth whose angry "convulsions" and "labor" signal an immanent regenerative act as her eyelids are described as "fluttering / as one slowly waking" (100). The image of opening and opened eyes establishes figurative eye contact between a feminized natural force and the curious, voyeuristic airline passengers. This dynamic of looking at the feminized earth is reminiscent of the ways in which the American continent was looked at, objectified, and represented from the literature of the early colonial period through to the twentieth century.[6] Rose's work engenders the landscape, certainly, but she revises images of passive fertility and reclaims the landscape in gendered and cultural terms by aligning the violent, powerful, and regenerative forces of nature with a female American Indian voice: "An Indian woman's song." In the final analysis, then, as the volcano awakens, we are asked to imagine that it is an

Indian woman's eyes that open to stare back at the voyeurs, or airline passengers, with a destructive and regenerative force.

In this regeneration there is an implicit political engagement linked to a prevailing ideology of possession and ownership of the land. Rose's methods are oppositional but far from essentialist: her construction of gender and cultural identity rely on an engagement with historical circumstances (a long history of the seeing-man's desire to feminize, objectify, and possess the American landscape), and she destabilizes any notion of a static sense of self by locating identity within the dynamic, regenerative features of an unpredictable and volatile landscape.

Rose's interest in staring back as a way of conceptualizing her challenge to prevailing cultural discourses is further demonstrated in her fascination with the cultural practice of turning people and cultures into curiosities by placing them in museum display cases. In "Truganinny" and "Julia" she addresses issues of gender, culture, and personal trauma by focusing on the objectification of two women who were stuffed and put on public display until some time after their deaths. Truganinny, whose story is retold in the epigraph through Paul Coe's study, was considered to be the last of the Tasmanian people; after witnessing her husband's body on display in the British Museum, she too was stuffed and mounted following her death despite her pleas to the contrary (*Half-breed Chronicles and Other Poems* 56).[7] Julia Pastrana's situation was slightly different. Julia was a Mexican Indian and a circus performer who had facial deformities and long, dark hair growing over most parts of her body. A performer and, by all accounts, a crowd puller in her own lifetime (the mid-nineteenth century), after her death and the death of her son, Julia's manager-husband preserved them and put them on display; Rose records that their preserved bodies were on display in Europe and the United States until 1975 (69). The processes of exhibiting, looking, and viewing are key to understanding these poems; as Jeanne Perreault convincingly argues:

The reader is figured, in part, as a viewer, the white reader as intended audience for the original degradation and exploitation of the trophy. But the reader is also addressed by both "Truganinny" and "Julia" as the trusted survivor. . . . The trust that informs the speakers in both poems provokes recognition of the shameful role we play as museum audience, entertained as the living are turned into the dead for commodification and trophies of power. ("New Dreaming" 129)

The exhibition of the two women should be situated within a tradition of collecting, exhibiting, and classifying cultures, which has been part of Euro-American tradition from the very earliest accounts of travel and exploration.[8] In this context, and in these two poems, the Euro-American tradition of looking and marveling at "real-life" examples of racial, cultural, and physical otherness is unapologetically apparent. James Clifford, in *Routes: Travel and Translation in the Late Twentieth Century*, has argued that the "extensive and continuous history of exhibitionary contacts . . . reveals the racism, or at best the paternalist condescension, of spectacles which offered up mute, exoticized specimens for curious and titillated crowds" (198). Within this context of visual spectacle, Rose allows the exoticized, disempowered, and "othered" woman to look back and talk back to her audience, drawing them into a cultural contact zone that forces an uneasy recognition of the reader's complicity in "conditions of coercion, radical inequality, and intractable conflict" (Pratt 6).

From their trapped and vulnerable position both Truganinny and Julia create a connection with the gaze trained upon them, establishing a contact zone that transcends time and place, literally, as both were displayed in different continents up to eighty years after their death. Truganinny challenges her viewer to "come closer" that she might tell us of her dead daughters with "eyes gone gray" (56), and she pleads to be taken out of the glare of public view: "put me where / they will not / find me" (57). In contrast to Truganinny's knowingness, Julia's gradual realization that she is with her child in a glass display cabinet creeps slowly through the poem:

Oh such a small room!
No bigger than my elbows outstretched
and just as tall as my head. . . .

in my arms
or standing near me
on a tall table
by my right side:
a tiny doll
that looked
like me . . .

It scares me so
to be with child,
lioness
with cub.
(70–71)

Unlike Truganinny, whose general plea is directed to an anonymous
though culturally defined viewer, Julia speaks directly to her manager-
husband and asks that he remember her eyes "so dark / you would lose
yourself swimming" and then begs him to repeat to her: "how you love
me / for my self one more time" (69, 71). Looks of apparent "love" from
her husband are replaced with looks or stares from curious, paying audiences whose coins "glitter" in her husband's pink fist. In this case
the stare of the seeing-man is not challenged by angry, regenerative,
or destructive forces; rather, Rose challenges a history of museological
practice, challenges a history of exhibiting and displaying indigenous
cultures through the use of "living fossils" (Perrault 130), by implicat-
ing the reader/viewer in a society that condones the creation of human
visual spectacles.

   In both poems Rose chooses to situate her museological critique
within a transnational perspective, which is in harmony with several
other poems included in *The Halfbreed Chronicles*. In this collection Rose
consciously frames her work in a context that is "larger than Hopi or even

Indian" (Hunter 86). To this end Rose tells the story of Yuriko, a Japanese child born severely retarded due to the effects of radiation from the
atom bomb that was dropped on Hiroshima in 1945. In another poem
she captures the effects of political and military conflict in El Salvador,
and in "Robert" Rose imagines the psychological and physical effects of
scientific endeavor on Robert Oppenheimer, a nuclear physicist and a
"destroyer of worlds."[9] In this collection, specifically, Rose's seeing eye
travels across continental, political, and "genetic" borders and locates
the experience of trauma and suffering in the lives of individuals from
other cultures, countries, and hemispheres.[10] Rose's traveling eye/I also
crosses cultural limits; as a Native American poet, she imaginatively re-
creates the experience of different indigenous and mixed-blood women.
Through this border crossing Rose establishes a type of contact zone
where cultural difference coexists through shared historical experiences; in these poems Rose imagines a collective opposition to glass
walls and cultural barriers that have literally and figuratively imprisoned
indigenous peoples and cultures in museum display cases.

It is within this transnational perspective, then, this traveling eye/I,
that Rose's engagement with the collection and exhibition of Native
American skeletons and artifacts should be situated. In recent years a
substantial amount of work has been done to address issues of displaying human skeletons and cultural artifacts in museum exhibitions. One
of the most comprehensive and significant contributions to this field is
Moira Simpson's *Making Representations*, which outlines the moral and
ethical pressures facing scientific and museological communities to
engage in a process of repatriating human remains and cultural "artifacts" to lineal descendants. Simpson considers scientific and museological practice in a global context, and within these wide parameters
she traces the implications of the Native American Graves Protection
and Repatriation Act (NAGPRA) of 1990, suggesting that the repatriation of remains to lineal descendants has created "a climate of sympathy
and willingness for change amongst many museum anthropologists"
(228). The battle between museological and scientific communities and
indigenous communities continues, however, and Simpson estimates

that the number of Native American skeletal remains held in private and public museums across the United States ranges from 200,000 to 2.5 million (174–75).

In this context of conflicting worldviews but some years before the implementation of NAGPRA, museum invoices and auction catalogues describing the condition and price of the clothes and skeletons of American Indians provide the inspiration for several of Rose's poems, including "Three Thousand Dollar Death Song" and "I expected my skin and my blood to ripen" (Lost Copper 26, 14–15). Engaging directly with issues of exhibiting human remains, as well as other artifacts stolen from graves or taken from bodies after the Wounded Knee massacre, for example, Rose refers to the museum as a "fleshless prison" and a "universe / of stolen things" (26–27). As a way of resisting and countering the cultural practice of collecting, classifying, and exhibiting people and cultures in museum display cases, Rose creates a collective voice for the unnamed skeletons:

From this distant point we watch our bones
auctioned with our careful beadwork. . . .
You: who have
priced us, you who have removed us: at what cost?
What price the pits where our bones share
a single bit of memory, how one century
turns our dead into specimens, our history
into dust, our survivors into clowns.
(26)

Those who look to buy, or look in scientific or voyeuristic fascination, are challenged to consider the human suffering and sacrifice through the connection between the human spirit and the human body: "Our memory might be catching . . . watch our bones rise . . . and mount the horses once again!" The static visual spectacle of the display case is, ultimately, transformed into a powerful, regenerative, ghostly uprising as the bones "march out the museum door!" (27). The implied reader, therefore, who has collected, priced, and "ground to dust" generations of cultural memory can watch, but this time with only impotent amazement; he or she can no longer control the cultural spectacle on "display."

In each of the museum poems—"Truganniny," "Julia," "Three Thousand Dollar Death Song," and "I expected my skin and my blood to ripen"—Rose reawakens and revitalizes the person and/or culture on display; read collectively, these poems signal a transnational perspective on the practice of preserving and exhibiting indigenous cultures, extending from Australia to Mexico and the United States.

This cultural crossing in Rose's poetry situates North American calls for repatriation within an international context, a context all the more appropriate as repatriation debates often occur across political and continental borders. In recent years Exeter Museum, England, returned a necklace and bracelet that belonged to the Tasmanian aboriginal Truganini (Rose's Truganniny), and in 1998 a Lakota Ghost Dance shirt, which had been taken from the Wounded Knee massacre and had been on display in Glasgow's Kelvingrove Art Gallery and Museum, Scotland (Rose's "universe of stolen things" perhaps), was returned to the Wounded Knee Survivors' Association (Simpson 276–79). Rose's museum poems are not dedicated to these events—indeed, her poems precede the repatriation of these items by some years. Nonetheless, Rose reflects a similar desire to that of the Lakota and Tasmanians to control cultural memory through the control of cultural artifacts and their place in museum exhibitions. Yet control of visual spectacles and the performance of culture is not limited to museological practices; indeed, meditations on the enactment of contemporary American Indian culture becomes more apparent in Rose's poetry and critical work when she considers the visual and literary performances of "whiteshamanism."

Instead of representing American Indian culture, Rose explains that the "whiteshaman," who is usually a white, middle-class Euro-American, adopts the persona of a shaman and speaks, writes, or performs as though drawing directly from tribal sources:

You think of us now
when you kneel
on the earth,
turn holy
in a temporary tourism
of our souls.

("For the White poets who would be Indian," Lost Copper 23)

Rose's main concern is not that individuals should be denied access or excluded from engaging with other cultures, and she is quick to acknowledge that "many non-Indian people have written beautifully and sensitively about Indian people" (Bruchac 267). Yet, as she aggressively argues: "the whiteshaman reader/performer aspires to 'embody the Indian,' in effect 'becoming' the 'real' Indian even when actual native people are present. Native reality is thereby subsumed and negated by the imposition of a 'greater' or 'more universal' contrivance." Looking "like" a shaman by wearing "buckskins, beadwork, headbands, moccasins, and sometimes paper masks intended to portray native spiritual beings such as Coyote or Raven" becomes evidence, in some circles, of "being" a shaman ("Great Pretenders" 405). Rose's objection to this kind of appropriation, or "temporary tourism," is apparent from interviews, essays, and poetry, and her objections are driven by the performance of their "becoming primitive" until the work is complete, when "you finish your poem / and go back" (Lost Copper 23). The implication of this cultural performance by the whiteshaman is that he constructs a "mythic 'Indian being'" that usurps the lived experience of the "real, live, breathing, up-to-date Indian person," making them invisible ("Great Pretenders" 413).

From the performance of the whiteshaman to the spiritless urban environment of "Vanishing Point: Urban Indian," in Lost Copper (12), and the established hierarchies and exclusions manifest in the literary and academic elite, the apparent erasure of contemporary American Indian identities is certainly a significant feature of Rose's own experience:

The great ones gather
at the university buffet
like cattle around
their alfalfa and barley.
I maintain
without willing it
an Indian invisibility.
("Literary Luncheon," *What Happened* 16)

In these poems—"For the White poets who would be Indian," "Vanishing Point: Urban Indian," and "Literary Luncheon: Iowa City"—Rose conceptualizes two aspects of invisibility, one that is imposed on Indian identity, as white shamans usurp the lived experience of Indians, and one that is self-imposed. Even in this self-imposed invisibility, Rose sees a kind of strength: "It's protective coloration, like camouflage. It's a survival trait" (quoted in Coltelli 124).

While conceptualizing and challenging Indian invisibility, throughout her career Wendy Rose has demonstrated an unquenchable desire to see and be seen by establishing a contact zone where she meets the glare of the seeing-man and challenges the coercion, inequality, and conflict manifest across political and continental boundaries—from Europe, Australia, and Mexico to the rural and urban landscapes of the United States. Remaining constant in Rose's negotiations of conflict and survival is a personal eye/I, consciously looking across borders and back through time. From her early experience as a young Catholic girl, Rose remembers looking

downward
eyes cornered so the Sisters couldn't see
how we copied the almost-women
with color on our lips.
("Remembering a Catholic Girlhood," *Lost Copper* 103)

In later years Rose remembers withstanding the gaze of the midwesterner whose "translucent eyes" "roll" over her ("Sunday Morning,"

What Happened 18). Finally, in her most recent work, *Itch Like Crazy*, she demonstrates the strength of her new "wide awake eyes" in a contact zone that allows her to face the most painful aspects of her European heritage. In an act of both destructive and regenerative power Rose draws strength from the personal and political challenges that she has encountered throughout her life and career and defiantly stares back:

> Some scars, Andrew,
> are those we keep.
> Others rise by themselves,
> ripen like berries
> on the backs of the beaten.
> And there are those that howl
> from the strangled throats of poets
> freezing in the subway steam.
> And some will take a spirit rifle
> and shoot back, Andrew, shoot back.
> (42)

Notes

1. Carol Hunter, "A MELUS Interview: Wendy Rose," 67–87, 77.

2. According to Rose, this quote was "heard at a university seminar from an anthropology professor, 1977" and is the epigraph to "Dancing with the New Katcina: Worm Song," *Academic Squaw* n.p.

3. Epigraph, by Claude Lévi-Strauss, *Tristes Tropiques* (1955), to Rose, "Indian Anthropologist: Overhanging Sand Dune Story," *Academic Squaw*; emphasis mine.

4. The use of oppositional strategies that pit men against women, and white against Native, are often criticized for endorsing an essentialist ideology that presupposes an origin or essence that defines gender, cultural, or racial identity. For more general analysis of this issue in relation to contemporary Native American literature, see Krupat; and Turner Strong and Van Winkle.

5. Rose dates her poem March 30, 1980, at which time Mount Saint Helens was emitting steam and ash, in preparation for a final eruption on May 18.

6. For further analysis of this perception of the North American continent, see Kolodny.

7. In this context I am using Rose's spelling, *Truganniny*. It should be noted that other commentators, specifically Moira Simpson, use the spelling *Truginini*.

8. For excellent commentaries on the history and traditions of collecting and exhibiting cultural "artifacts," see Feest; Ritterbush; Clifford, *Predicament of Culture* and *Routes*; and Murray.

9. In the epigraph for "Robert" Rose paraphrases Oppenheimer: "I am death, the destroyer of worlds . . . the physicists have known sin and this is a knowledge they cannot lose" (*Halfbreed Chronicles*, 63).

10. The term *genetic* is from Rose: "By 'Halfbreed,' I'm meaning something that transcends genetics. It's a collection of history, of society, of something larger than any individual" (Hunter, "MELUS Interview" 86).

Works Cited

Bruchac, Joseph. "The Bones Are Alive: An Interview with Wendy Rose." *Survival This Way: Interviews with American Indian Poets*. Tucson: University of Arizona Press, 1987. 249–69.

Castillo, Susan. "Postmodernism, Native American Literature and the Real: The Silko-Erdrich Controversy." *Notes from the Periphery: Marginality in North American Literature and Culture*. New York: Peter Lang, 1995. 177–90.

Clifford, James. *The Predicament of Culture*. Cambridge: Harvard University Press, 1987.

———. *Routes: Travel and Translation in the Late Twentieth Century*. Cambridge: Harvard University Press, 1997.

Coltelli, Laura. "Wendy Rose." *Winged Words: American Indian Writers Speak*. Lincoln: University of Nebraska Press, 1990. 121-33.

Feest, Christian F. "The Collecting of American Indian Artifacts in Europe, 1493–1750." In *America in European Consciousness, 1493–1750*. Ed. Karen Ordahl Kupperman. Chapel Hill: University of North Carolina Press, 1995. 324–60.

Hunter, Carol. "A MELUS Interview: Wendy Rose." *MELUS* 10.3 (1983): 67–87.

Irmscher, Christoph. "Anthropological Roles: The Self and Its Others in T. S. Eliot, William Carlos Williams and Wendy Rose." *Soundings* 75.4 (1992): 587–603.

Kolodny, Annette. *The Lay of the Land: Metaphor as Experience and History in American Life and Letters*. 1975. Chapel Hill: University of North Carolina Press, 1984.

Krupat, Arnold. *The Voice in the Margin: Native American Literature and the Canon*. Berkeley: University of Californian Press, 1989.

Murray, David. *Museums, Their History and Their Use*. Glasgow: MacLehose, 1904.

Perreault, Jeanne. "New Dreaming: Joy Harjo, Wendy Rose, Leslie Marmon Silko." In *Deferring a Dream: Literary Sub-Versions of the American Columbiad*. Ed. Gert Buelens and Ernst Rudin. Basel: Birkhäuser, 1994. 120–36.

Pratt, Mary Louise. *Imperial Eyes: Travel Writing and Transculturation*. London: Routledge, 1992.

Ritterbush, Philip. "Art and Science as Influences on the Early Development of Natural History Collections." In *Papers Presented at a Symposium on Natural History Collections Past—Present—Future*. Ed. Daniel M. Cohen. *Proceedings of the Biological Society* 82 (1969): 561–78.

Rose, Wendy. *Academic Squaw Reports to the World from the Ivory Tower*. Marvin SD: Blue Cloud Quarterly, 1977.

———. *Lost Copper*. Banning CA: Malki Museum Press, 1980.

———. *Long Division: A Tribal History*. 1976. New York: Strawberry Press, 1981.

———. *What Happened When the Hopi Hit New York*. New York: Contact II Publications, 1982.

———. "Neon Scars." In *I Tell You Now: Autobiographical Essays by Native American Writers*. Ed. Brian Swann and Arnold Krupat. Lincoln: University of Nebraska Press, 1987. 252–61.

———. "The Great Pretenders: Further Reflections on Whiteshamanism." In *The State of Native America: Genocide, Colonization and Resistance*. Ed. M. Annette Jaimes. Boston: South End Press, 1992. 403–21.

———. *The Halfbreed Chronicles and Other Poems*. 1985. Albuquerque: West End Press, 1992.

———. *Bone Dance: New and Selected Poems, 1965–1993*. Tucson: University of Arizona Press, 1994.

———. *Now Poof She Is Gone*. Ithaca NY: Firebrand Books, 1994.

———. *Itch Like Crazy*. Tucson: University of Arizona Press, 2002.

Simpson, Moira. *Making Representations: Museums in the Post-Colonial Era.* Rev. ed. London: Routledge, 2001.

Turner Strong, Pauline, and Barrick Van Winkle. "'Indian Blood': Reflections on the Reckoning and Refiguring of Native North American Identity." *Cultural Anthropology* 11.4 (1996): 547–76.

8 Anamnesiac Mappings

National Histories and Transnational Healing in Leslie Marmon Silko's *Almanac of the Dead*

Generating some notable critical hostility upon its publication in 1991,[1] Leslie Marmon Silko's contentious novel *Almanac of the Dead* has since been hailed as "a radical, stunning manifesto" that offers a graphic, brutal, and highly political analysis of America and the Americas at the turn of the twenty-first century.[2] Confronting the willful amnesia that pervades contemporary U.S. society regarding the history of settlement and of subsequent Anglo-Indian relations, Silko offers an anamnesiac consideration of the trauma of contact and a celebration of the significance of memory in the face of cultural assimilation and of the power of remembrance to heal individuals, communities, and nations.

Published to coincide with the quincentennial celebrations of Columbus's "discovery," *Almanac* is an abrasive indictment of five hundred years of colonialism, inhumanity, and genocide in the Americas, where Silko provocatively claims that "the Indian wars have never ended."[3] Alluding to Karl Marx's image of Europe haunted by the specter of the oppressed, Silko populates the Americas with the ever-present, inescapable souls of millions of slaughtered indigenous peoples and African slaves, "spirits that never rested and would never stop until justice had been done" (424). By tracing the unavoidable presence of the dead, *Almanac* exposes the carefully elided history of American settlement, illustrating the direct links between the multiple legacies of that history and U.S. society and social policies at the close of the twentieth century.

Yet Silko's "America" is truly transnational, refusing accepted "national" geographies and histories in order to illustrate the complex cultural and colonial relationships within the Americas as a whole and between the "New" World and the Old. To this end *Almanac* erases all borders: between time and space; between history and geography; between living and dead; between forms of oppression; between nation-states; between continents. As a result, Silko's characters are firmly hybrid: transcultural and transnational, they inhabit an inter-national space of possibility. Yet this approach has drawn criticism: while celebrating Silko's "fearless[s] assert[ion]" within *Almanac* of "a collective indigenous retrieval of lands stolen through colonization" (89), the Dakota critic Elizabeth Cook-Lynn has nonetheless been highly critical of Silko's focus upon multiculturalism and pan-tribalism — that is, the incorporation and inclusion of all, regardless of ethnicity, who would adhere to a worldview that recognizes, celebrates, and respects their fellow humans and the natural world. In this sense Cook-Lynn suggests that Silko's approach mirrors that of Gerald Vizenor, "the feeling that 'whoever wants to be tribal can join the tribe'" (85). She maintains that such an approach effectively works against tribal sovereignty; in Cook-Lynn's terms, Silko's focus upon "cosmopolitanism" erases a much needed (and hard fought for) focus upon tribal "nationalism" (78). In many ways her point is highly valid: the battle against persistent and highly prevalent popular understandings of Native Americans as apolitical and ahistorical is ongoing and far from resolved, and concepts of tribal nationalism, indeed perceptions of national tribal consciousness, have been hard-won.

I would argue, however, that Cook-Lynn's is nonetheless too swift and simplistic a dismissal of Silko's analysis of the transcultural, and of her consideration of the complex ways in which oppressed peoples are interconnected, which ultimately runs the risk of shortsightedness. The call for a more engaged tribal nationalism among Native American fiction writers is an increasingly problematic position to take, given that some of the most tribally oriented, or tribally engaged, writers — for instance, Gerald Vizenor and Wendy Rose, to name but two — are also those who are adopting increasingly transcultural and transnational approaches. Ultimately, Cook-Lynn's dismissal of Silko's emphasis upon the effects and impact of transcultural oppression fails to recognize the key premise of *Almanac*: the role and power of the imagination within both story and history. In her assertion of the prophesied "disappearance of all things European" (*Almanac* map legend), Silko addresses a particularly insidious form of colonialism: unhealthy and ultimately hostile Euro-American worldviews. Thus, in her essay "Fifth World" she states that "the prophecies do not say that European people themselves will disappear, only their customs" (125). In this sense Silko clearly engages with Ngugi wa Thiong'o's assertion that the decolonization process is not only political or land-based but, crucially, also the process by which we can "decoloniz[e] the mind."[4] In direct contrast to Cook-Lynn's assertions, *Almanac*'s extended celebration of the holistic — Silko's exploration of a specifically Native epistemology that recognizes the ramifications of individual and communal actions and values balance and cooperation of all kinds — indicates that it is, perhaps ironically, one of the most "indigenous," or "tribally conscious," of contemporary Native American novels.

It is, for example, within the transcultural as a hybrid space of possibility that lies *beyond* the nation, *beyond* the national, and *beyond* nationalism that the potential strength of Silko's characters lies — and from which they can, potentially, derive the capacity to heal wounded individuals and communities. It is no accident that, at the close of the text, multiple characters converge at the appropriately named "International Holistic Healers Convention" (709). As a hybrid space of possibility, the Convention clearly symbolizes the need for, and the significance of, some kind of therapeutic cultural process to deal with the colonial experience. The very term *holistic* represents a clear warning not only that the social "ills" in the Americas are transcultural and interrelated but also that any therapeutic process needs to address social problems as part of a larger inter-national cultural healing process. In this sense Silko's emphasis upon the transcultural also calls attention to the psychological and spiritual damage caused by colonization, both to the colonized and to the colonizer: within the text the colonizers become "infected with [the] bloody compulsions they had indulged in the colonies" (425–26). As Albert Memmi argued in his analysis of the psychology of empire, "The colonial situation manufactures colonialists, just as it manufactures the colonized" (56).

It is in this context that the value of postcolonial theory in the analysis of Native literature can be located, in spite of its sometimes hostile dismissal by many Native American Studies academics, including Cook-Lynn. The problem lies largely in the name — "postcolonial" — which itself belies the complex types of academic analyses that are being undertaken by "postcolonial" theorists and encourages one-dimensional interpretations by those unfamiliar with or unwilling to investigate the field. Indeed, because there has long been an emphasis within Postcolonial Studies upon former colonies such as India and Africa, Cook-Lynn's assumption is that postcolonial theorists are in effect "decolonization theorists" (78), or theorists of the postcolonial.[5] Given that the United States is not, nor ever has been, a postcolonial nation because it includes indigenous peoples who continue to be colonized, the general tendency within Native American Studies has been to dismiss postcolonial theory as inapplicable: to cite Louis Owens, we need to "keep carefully in mind that America does not participate in what is sometimes termed the 'colonial aftermath' or postcolonial condition" ("As If an Indian" 214).

Yet this is again too swift and simplistic a denial of a highly complex field, which deliberately reads against the grain of cultural hegemony to ground analyses carefully within historical and cultural specificities. Postcolonial theory is not necessarily applicable only to former colonies or to peoples who have been decolonized, and many theorists are engaged both with "colonial texts" and with texts produced by colonized peoples under colonialism. More important, postcolonial theory has drawn attention to texts that resist and challenge the colonizing power and assert cultural difference in the face of assimilation. In this sense postcolonial theory is wholly applicable to Native American literature, especially in the wider context of global anticolonial critiques, such as those involving other indigenous peoples in regions as geographically (and culturally) diverse as Australia, New Zealand, and Central and South America.[6] Thus, Owens, for one, identifies his own position — albeit with some highly justified reservations regarding the further marginalization of Native literature by postcolonial theorists — in postcolonial terms: he is not only "migrant" or "diasporic" due to "many generations of displacement and orchestrated ethnocide" but, significantly, situates himself within a "transcultural location" (208).[7] This transcultural location is illustrated by Silko's International Holistic Healers Convention as a hybrid space of possibility that is specifically *active*, a place where action and even activism can take place. Here the textual convergence of the oppressed of many nations and cultures undoubtedly marks the point at which the ostensibly passive concept of healing can be equated with the active: with political action and with militant social activism. Thus, Silko's "manifesto" — itself an implicitly violent political term deriving from the Latin *manifestus*, literally translating as to "strike with the hand" (*Collins English Dictionary* [CED]) — concurs with Frantz Fanon's (in)famous assertion that to achieve absolute sociocultural and political change requires "absolute violence" (*Wretched of the Earth* 37).

The desperate need for political action and social activism (or postcolonial resistance) is highlighted throughout the text: *Almanac* is in effect an elaboration and an extension of the types of oppressive and destructive attitudes and worldviews that Silko outlined in her celebrated 1977 novel, *Ceremony*. The text is, therefore, a detailed illustration of the "witchery" that operates wherever tyranny triumphs and the poor, politically weak, and socially expendable are exploited and oppressed. In *Almanac* Silko moves beyond the local focus of *Ceremony* (the social forces operating within/upon the Laguna Pueblo community) to address the global: the powerful and persistent sociocultural values, or lack of values, that continue to produce the acquisitive and destructive imperial impulse. Here Silko traces the interests, actions, and repercussions of those who lack sociocultural ethics, morals, and values: the "Destroyers." *Almanac* unflinchingly depicts a wide range of moral and ethical corruption: from the human sacrifices of Montezuma and the atrocities committed by Cortés and the Catholic Church to the "new work of the

Destroyers" evident in the vast profits of the international trade in arms and weapons, in the financial rewards reaped from the misery of illegal immigrants and refugees, and in the "destruction and poison" of the uranium industry in New Mexico, among other things (760). As Adam Sol comments, the contemporary Destroyers that Silko portrays are those "who hold political, financial, and military power in the Americas" and who "have in common a taste for violence [and] a disregard for humanity and the earth" (35). The concerns of the text are therefore centered upon the five hundred–year legacy of American settlement, describing a wide range of American societies that are, as a direct consequence of their links to (and perpetuation of) a history devoted to destruction and oppression, inherently both corrupt and depraved.

Thus, Silko's Tucson houses "an assortment of speculators, confidence men, embezzlers, lawyers, judges, police and other criminals" (map legend). *Almanac* produces an exhaustive and appalling list of social ills: suicide; homicide; infanticide; genocide; racism; prostitution; drug trafficking; gun running; hit men; gangsters; outlaws; political assassinations; blood and organ trafficking; pornography; snuff photography and movies; videos of torture, of violent sexual assault, of sex change operations, of female circumcisions, of abortions, of fetal dissections; bestiality; pedophilia; rape; cannibalism; the trafficking of illegal immigrants; environmental destruction; and the racist heritage of genetic research. As this highly comprehensive list suggests, one legacy of colonialism in the Americas is an ongoing inter-national social disrespect and disease. And it is a disease that, for Silko, demands a radical cultural and spiritual "cure."

The International Holistic Healers Convention: "Cures of All Kinds"

The International Holistic Healers Convention is a significant narrative moment within the text: the meeting place of "medicine makers" offering "cures of all kinds" (716). It is a demarcated textual space through which the dangers of the cultural and spiritual attitudes identified with the Destroyers can be demonstrated but through which, simultaneously, the potential benefits of adopting more respectful, moral, ethical, and spiritual attitudes can be emphasized. In this sense the convention represents an opportunity to promote a more holistic — indeed tribal — worldview that recognizes the interrelatedness of human and non-human societies and the potentially irreparable damage that is caused by selfish and disrespectful attitudes to the poor, to the oppressed, and to the Earth itself. Silko's use of the term *convention* is highly significant, as its primary definition, according to the CED, is specifically both holistic and political: it is a "contract" or "agreement between states for [the] regulation of matters *affecting all of them*" (emphasis mine). To employ Mary Louise Pratt's terminology, the conference is a transcultural "contact zone" that illustrates both the often "radically asymmetrical relations of power" ordinarily evident within "colonial encounters" and their simultaneously subversive potential: their "interactive [and] improvisational dimensions" (7).[8] Thus, the individual dispossessed members of the inter-national meeting in Room 1212 can be interpreted as representatives of specific local, national, and even global interests, who have a clear agenda to discuss and a plan of action to decide on and implement. In this context an analysis of the convention as a "space" of opportunity becomes highly significant: as a discrete textual *space*, the convention can be interpreted specifically, in CED terms, as a "continuous [that is, indefinite] expanse" that bestows the "freedom or scope to live and/or develop as one wishes."

The freedom, indeed the very opportunity, to live or develop as one wishes is constantly under threat from what Silko herself acknowledges are the dangerously "toxic" and diseased cultural and spiritual values that pervade the pages of the text (quoted in Arnold 7). The extensive nature of these values, and, more significantly, their contagious/communicable nature, is evident in the initial descriptions of the convention itself. Here an absence of the truly spiritual within Euro-American societies — the "urgency and desperation" of many of the Euro-Americans attending (719) — is interpreted by the Yaqui psychic Lecha as a result of the historical excesses of Christianity. Critiquing the second traditional foundation, or cornerstone, of Euro-American society — state-organized

religion in the form of Christianity—Almanac states quite bluntly that
the "tortures and executions performed in the name of Jesus" indicate
not only that "Europeans had arrived in the New World in precarious
spiritual health" but also that "a church that tortures and kills is a church
that can no longer heal" (717, 718).⁹ This Euro-American spiritual hunger is depicted as one cause of an ongoing appropriation of indigenous
cultural and spiritual traditions: "Most of the new-age spiritualists were
whites from the United States, many of whom claimed to have been
trained by 110-year-old Huichol Indians" (716). The convention is full
of "white men from California in expensive new buckskins, beads, and
feathers who had called themselves 'Thunder-roll' and 'Buffalo Horn'"
(719), addressing the types of cultural appropriation highlighted by the
Hopi-Miwok poet Wendy Rose as the "temporary tourism of our [In-
dian] souls." Like Silko, Rose argues that this exploitation and usurpa-
tion of tribal traditions is the sole point at which Native Americans, as
an oppressed minority, become visible to mainstream American society:
"You think of us only / when your voice / wants for roots" before "You
finish your poem / and go back" ("For the White Poets Who Would Be
Indian" 22).

Significantly, the types of exploitative Euro-American attitudes
that Silko critiques are equally and dangerously apparent within the
dispossessed and marginalized groups themselves, suggestive not
only of the infectious and assimilative nature of those attitudes but
also of their attraction. The Yaqui Lecha states that her grandmother,
Yoeme, "used to brag that she could make white people believe in
anything and do anything she told them because whites were so desperate" (719). Lecha herself is a "TV talk show psychic" (42), who
uses her spiritual powers almost solely in relation to violent death,
helping police locate the bodies of murder victims robbed of life and
potential; while her twin, Zeta, smuggles drugs and guns across the
U.S.–Mexico border. Likewise, the Cuban-trained Mayan revolutionary Angelita, who works alongside the prophet twins, Wacah and El
Feo, leading the unarmed indigenous People's Army north from Mexico to invade U.S. national space peacefully, has also taken the "war

name" La Escapía and makes secret arrangements for weapons with which to "defend the people from attack" by the Mexican and American governments (712). And there are many other examples that can be drawn from the dispossessed group who meet at the convention, including the disgraced Korean academic Awa Gee, the extremist ecoterrorist group Green Vengeance, the armed homeless Vietnam veterans, the "Army of Justice" (423), and the Bare Foot Hopi, all of whom are ready to participate in a supportive and diversionary "multinational . . . uprising" (727).

These plans of action are ostensibly dangerously close to the attitudes of the Destroyers, and Silko indicates that they are often the result of a deep-seated cynicism and suspicion, ingrained through years of oppression: "The Hopi and the twin brothers might sincerely believe their recovery of the Americas could take place without bloodshed, but Lecha had her doubts . . . violence begat violence" (739). Yet the reasoning behind all of these potentially destructive plans is strikingly at odds with the selfish and self-centered attitudes of the Destroyers that *Almanac* critiques. As Leslie Wootten comments, these actions are identified as "political work" that, far more significantly, is specifically designed and undertaken "for the common good" (63). Holistic rather than individualistic, with the bigger picture kept at all times firmly in view, the majority of *Almanac*'s dispossessed characters are interested in acting for their community as a whole. In this sense the subversive and revolutionary plans of action are made for the benefit of large numbers of multiethnic and multinational poor and oppressed, rather than to protect the power of a minority social elite whose very privilege is maintained at the expense of the many. The "common good" here is quite clearly the political struggle of the dispossessed of all nations to reclaim their place in society. The meeting in Room 1212 is the point at which highly diverse characters are brought together and cultural, ethnic, geographical, political, and national differences become insignificant in the face of a common and potentially overwhelming bond: a shared history of oppression and dispossession.

The Convention as a Critique of Global, Economic Forces

Silko's analysis of oppression and dispossession considers a whole range of ongoing ramifications: of American settlement; of African slavery; of poverty within the United States; of the Vietnam War; of the legacies of medical epidemics such as HIV/AIDS; and of the environmental abuses of science and technology.[10]

While the textual characters have clear "individual" agendas—the reclamation of lands stolen from indigenous peoples; the reclamation of elided African-American histories; and the social reintegration of the homeless, to name but a few—nonetheless, the radical forces that converge at the International Holistic Healers Conference have equally clear communal goals: to eradicate poverty and racism, to provide homes for the homeless, and to ensure enfranchisement for all. Moreover, enfranchisement is here interpreted as both liberation and political power. In this context a key feature of the convention is economic: the text is an exploration of the forces of economic globalization, and in particular of the ramifications of the concept of "free trade" in the Americas. Thus, *Almanac* anticipates both the introduction of the 1994 North American Free Trade Agreement (NAFTA) to align the economic markets of the United States, Canada, and Mexico and the simultaneous Zapatista response: the indigenous uprising in Chiapas. Thus, in Silko's text the Mayan People's Army emerges from the same Chiapas region to march for justice upon the United States. More significantly, Silko also predicts the economic outcome of NAFTA. In 2001, in response to plans to extend the treaty to produce a continent-wide Free Trade Area of the Americas (FTAA), the Economic Policy Institute (EPI) argued that "the current imbalanced structure of NAFTA is clearly inadequate for the creation of an economically sustainable and socially balanced continental economy. . . . Rather than attempting to spread a deeply flawed agreement to all of the Americas, the leaders of the nations of North America need to return to the drawing board and design a model of economic integration that works for the continent's working people."[11] The EPI's conclusions, that NAFTA is "deeply flawed" due to its emphasis upon investors and financiers (the privileged minority) at the expense of labor and social development (the oppressed majority, "the continent's working people," for whom the economy is far from "socially balanced"), concurs with *Almanac's* assertion that trade is "free" only for the select few. While Marxist thought, a variety of twentieth-century theoretical evolutions and practical applications of Marxism, and even Marx the man are all analyzed in detail by the Cuban (Marxist)–trained Angelita La Escapía, such ideas are eventually dismissed because Marx, as a European, "understood the possibilities of communal consciousness only imperfectly" (291). Significantly, in the context of the concerns of the convention, it is, as Edward Huffstetler suggests, "Marxism's lack of spirituality and lack of connection to the land [that] means ultimately that it will fail in the Americas" (12).

The convention thus highlights the role played by economics and exchange—in this case the lack of exchange—in the dispossession of large sections of society. As a result, the dispossessed healers at the convention take part in a subversive redistribution of wealth, to fund the types of radical political action that are required to force fundamental social change and to promote cultural and spiritual healing. Significantly, the redistribution subverts what Dorothea Fischer-Hornung has identified as the powerful and almost overwhelming "global economic parasitism" operating within the text (199).

The redistribution of wealth signifies, although only partially and momentarily, that the hybrid convention is also the site of a redistribution of power, both spiritual and political. Silko's use of the hybrid, however, is itself not without problems: hybridity has become a contentious theoretical position, in part due to the horticultural meanings, which suggest some form of inherent cultural elision. As Bill Ashcroft and others comment, despite having been used by critics such as Homi K. Bhabha to signify an empowering space in which "cultural difference may operate" and cultural exchange occur, the term has subsequently been greatly criticized for "negating and neglecting the imbalance and inequality of the power relations it references."[12] Indeed, they argue that the primary criticism of theories of hybridity derives from the suggestion that the term "replicat[es] assimilationist policies by masking . . . cultural differences" (*Reader* 118–19). Such a position concurs with Pratt's analysis of the "radically asymmetrical relations of power" within the colonial relationship (7). Yet Silko's engagement with the textual space represented by the convention is primarily *about* relationships and power relations: between individuals and communities, between peoples and nations, between cultures and ethnicities.[13] In this sense the convention is a space much like the "Third Space" advocated by Bhabha (*Location of Culture* 36), in which transcultural exchange of all kinds can take place; in which the hierarchies of colonialism can be subverted, inverted, diverted. As Bhabha argues, the significance of this Third Space is its very fluidity and lack of closure: it is a site in which an "international culture" can be "conceptualized" and the "politics of polarity" can be "elude[d]" (38–39).

Alter/native Memories and Histories

The emphasis within Silko's convention is upon the potential of the transcultural and of inter-national fluidity, demonstrating the social possibilities that can be drawn from the numerous "Medicine Makers" offering "cures of all kinds" (716). These "cures" (or "solutions") are implicitly spiritual and holistic: the Latin *cura* translates, according to the CED definition, as "cure of souls." In part the social and spiritual cures that are offered are dependent upon historical and political awareness: it becomes ever more noticeable throughout Silko's text that historical amnesia — the denial of the less than savory aspects of national history — is a key part of international sociocultural disease. Consequently, both memory and the power of remembrance are celebrated as a form of cultural cure for individuals, communities, and nations; as a means by which local communities and national or international societies can be healed and "made whole." As Susan Scarberry has noted, in this sense memory is "medicine" and therefore represents a "powerful" and potentially curative "life force" (22).

Within the text memory becomes, to cite Fischer-Hornung, very appropriately an "econom[y]" in its own right (199). Memory is therefore a potent political textual force and embodies Silko's commitment to anamnesis, or the refusal to forget, as a direct response to America's historical amnesia. *Almanac* therefore provides an anamnesiac mapping of elided cultural memories and histories, demonstrating a form of "remembrance" that demands that we be "mindful" (from the Latin *memor*) of alter/native memories. In this context Silko includes a variety of alter/native memories, stories and histories that Virginia Bell identifies as forms of "counter-chronicling" (5). These alternative "chronicles" are politically powerful not only because they mimic and subvert the authority of established European forms of historiography, but also because they are "records" by which to "re-call" the elided memories and knowledges that remain at the very "heart" (both physically and emotionally) of oppressed cultures.[14] The political significance of memory lies in its ability to empower individuals and communities, in its power to provoke action and activism. As Joanne Rappaport argues in her analysis of the uses of history and historical analyses among Native groups in the Colombian Andes, the political significance of memory is its ability to "move people into action" (189).

By taking control of their pasts and thus acquiring political agency, the dispossessed groups of Silko's text also acquire the ability to take control of the future and work actively to change it. Angelita's collection of Mesoamerican tribal histories/memories provides, for example, a vast and highly comprehensive catalogue of "Native American resistance and revolution," from the "first Native American revolt against European slave hunters" in Cuba in 1510 to the formation of the "National Federation of Peasants" in Bolivia in 1945, fighting to "restore Indians' rights" (527, 528). Angelita's timeline spans the histories of the Americas from the moment of "contact" to the present day, illustrating the ongoing colonization and oppression of Native American peoples continent-wide. Indeed, it is through the political power of this chronicle that Angelita successfully challenges, tries, and executes the Cuban revolutionary Bartolomeo for "crimes against tribal histories": his persistent denial of tribal memory. Bartolomeo's contention that the Mayan Indians are "jungle monkeys and savages" who "have no history" is an illustration of the types of destructive and contagious international sociocultural disease for which Silko demands a cure (525). As Angelita succinctly comments, "More than five hundred years of white men in Indian jurisdiction were in trial with Bartolomeo" (526). A further example is Clinton's compilation of African-American histories, which he plans to disseminate through "liberation radio broadcasts" (426). For Clinton entire peoples can become oppressed and dispossessed when they are erased from 'national' histories, and denied their own cultural memories. Significantly, it is his contention that "slavery is any continuing relationship between people and systems that results in human degradation and human suffering" (427). In this context Clinton is convinced that memory — the dissemination of knowledge and thus power — is the most effective cultural cure, that it is designed to provoke political action/activism because "the most complete history is the most powerful force" (316). Both examples are, as Bell notes, effective forms of "historiographic practice" (22), and in her inclusion of these "unauthorized marginal storytellers" Silko demonstrates a "narrative commitment" to the "inclusion of everyone's testimony" within a transcultural perspective (Donnelly 248–49).

From this transcultural perspective the public address by the poet-lawyer Wilson Weasel Tail is the most arresting example of memory at the convention. Opening with a paraphrase of Pontiac's address detailing the dangers of forgetfulness, Weasel Tail warns, "You forg[e]t everything you were ever told" only at the danger of cultivating destructive attitudes of "envy . . . and poisoning" (721). Significantly, Weasel Tail includes a re-vision of the Ghost Dance, emphasizing that its power lay (and, for Weasel Tail, still lies) not in its *physical* ability to offer protection against bullets but in its *spiritual* ability to promote the curative power of remembrance. The Ghost Dance is therefore presented as a demonstration not only of holism but of the necessary incorporation of the spiritual within the political. For Weasel Tail the political act of remembrance focuses upon the "sixty million dead souls who howl for justice in the Americas" (723). Weasel Tail's proclamation is a direct assertion of alter/native histories: "We dance to remember . . . . the Ghost Dance has never ended" (722, 724).

Yet perhaps the most significant example of alter/native memories and histories is the ancient almanac of Silko's title, kept (and transcribed) by Lecha and Zeta. Basing her almanac upon pre-contact Mayan texts and cultural concepts of time and history, Silko uses the textual form to illustrate the holistic nature of indigenous concepts of memory and change. This provides a powerful political and cultural challenge, in which "nothing is lost, left behind, or destroyed" ("Notes on *Almanac of the Dead*" 137). By incorporating a constantly moving and fluid Mayan textual form at the heart of her own text, Silko further erodes the borders of the nation and of national consciousness in the Americas, to promote the potential power of the transcultural. As a result, the almanac's significance is immense: it is a vivid and vital assertion of Native presence in the Americas, "somehow includ[ing]" within it the story of the Yaqui children (247), the "last of their tribe" (246), who flee north with the text in order to preserve it. Charged with the preservation of the almanac, these children are culturally but also physically *sustained* by the text, consuming the pages and savoring the "wonderful flavor" of the stories after they have been memorized (250).

The living organic nature of the text, whose pages hold "many forces within them" (252), is illustrated by Silko's description of the words that detach themselves from the page like a flock of birds as each sheet is consumed (249). In this sense the almanac is a "living power" that acts as a vessel of identity for the community, or communities, to whom it belongs (569). For the people the almanac provides spiritual sustenance, carrying vital information on "who they were and where they had come from"; thus, "if even part of their almanac survived, they as a people would return someday" (246). Within the transcultural focus of the text Silko's assertion applies equally to the survival (and dissemination) of holistic worldviews that promote healthy cultural, ethical, and moral values. Appropriately, it is this organic nature of the almanac that allows it to function, as Daria Donnelly comments, as a site of remembrance where "unauthorized marginal storytellers" can find both place and voice (248). The almanac is also therefore an account of its marginal keepers and their lives, through which various characters "succeed in speaking themselves into the texture of the story," or history (Taylor 52). In this context Lecha notes that "some sections had been splashed with wine, and others with water or blood" (*Almanac* 569). Moreover, included in the "margins," there are "scribbles and scratches" that trace the "scribbled arguments" through which Yoeme has engaged in direct dialogue with the text, with its multiple voices, and with its memories and histories (570).

The constant addition of stories to the margins—Yoeme's tale of her miraculous escape from American "justice" and execution and the Euro-American Seese's insertion of her own dream about her lost son (580, 595)—emphasizes the almanac's role as a receptacle for a communal history and identity that is truly transnational. In this sense the almanac is a storehouse of the marginalized testimonies of all of the dispossessed. The power of the almanac is especially visible in the naming of the fragments and notes of which it is composed: they are "mouths" and "tongues" that give a voice to those who are otherwise actively silenced and erased by oppression and dispossession (142). Consequently, it is a communal identity based on shared worldviews and values that moves beyond the ethnic confines of individual societies to embrace all politically, socially, and economically oppressed peoples. As Donnelly comments, in her discussion of the transnational Silko provides a "shift toward Pueblo storytelling" — and so toward a holistic and curative worldview — "as the most essential and enduring guarantor of community and a just future." *Almanac* is, therefore, "more intensely Laguna in its prophecy and capricious style" (Donnelly 254). Kept in a "wooden ammunition box" (245), Silko's almanac is thus a powerful and effective cultural and political weapon, the embodiment of a transcultural curative remembrance.

Conclusions

It is within the context of transcultural curative remembrance that Clinton reviews the sociocultural/political situation after the convention at the close of the text. Considering the Mexican Calabazas's fears that, in the face of social unrest, "the battle lines would fall along skin color" (738), Clinton addresses his own concerns that the "black war vets" within his own Army of Justice might be "misled by fanatics or extremists screaming 'Black only! Africa only!'" (742). Clinton's concomitant fear is that the sociopolitical power of the vast and diverse army of the dispossessed might therefore be curtailed, even derailed. Ultimately, however, he agrees with the Bare Foot Hopi's contention that the dispossessed have far more in common than they have dividing them. Moreover, it is a common ground that is undeniably related to a whole variety of economies: cultural, financial, political, social. The battle is, as the Bare Foot Hopi argues, one of possession and dispossession, between "the haves, whatever their colors were," and "the have-nots" (738).

It is, therefore, within the economies of memory, transculturalism, and healing that Clinton offers his concluding analysis of transcultural opportunity — a succinct summary both of the role of the convention within the text and of Silko's detailed analysis of transcultural potential. Clinton offers a direct challenge to current popular ways of thinking and seeing, reiterating Silko's ongoing textual message of the necessity of incorporating the spiritual within the political. Moreover, Clinton offers a stark warning of the very real dangers of failing to reject the corrupt and pervasive worldview of the Destroyers and of failing to surmount the national by embracing the inter-national: "Nothing could be black only or brown only or white anymore. The ancient prophecies had foretold a time when the destruction by man had left the earth desolate, and the human race itself endangered. This was the last chance the people had against the Destroyers, and they would never prevail if they did not work together as a common force" (747).

Notes

1. For two examples, see Alan Ryan, "An Inept 'Almanac of the Dead,'" *USA Today*, January 21, 1992, D6; and Sven Birkerts, "Apocalypse Now: A Review of Leslie Marmon Silko's *Almanac of the Dead*," *New Republic*, November 4, 1991, 41.

2. Linda Niemann, "New World Disorder," *Women's Review of Books* 9.6 (March 1992): 1.

3. Leslie Marmon Silko, *Almanac of the Dead* (New York: Penguin, 1991), map legend.

4. Emphasis mine. While Ngugi's concern is clearly with the role of education and the use of the English language within the process of African colonization, his principles nonetheless can be applied in this context because he deals with the power of colonial worldviews and the significance of imaginative decolonization to successful cultural and political resistance.

5. It is these "decolonization theoreticians" whom Cook-Lynn accuses of promoting "cosmopolitanism" at the expense of "nationalism" (78). Homi Bhabha and Timothy Brennan are mentioned specifically.

6. In this context Wendy Rose clearly bridges nations and cultures to consider the fate and treatment of the Tasmanian Truganinny and the Mexican Indian Julia Pastrana alongside of her explorations of Native American histories. In this sense Rose engages with the same type of transnational recognition of oppression as Silko. See Kathryn Napier Gray's essay, in this collection, for a full discussion of Rose's transculturalism.

7. Owens quite rightly notes that the majority of the "big names" in postcolonial scholarship have ignored and, as a result, have elided the Native American experience. See his essay "As If an Indian," 212–14.

8. For a development of Pratt's "contact zone" in the context of *Almanac*, see Dorothea Fischer-Hornung's consideration of Michael Taussig's more complex "second contact" theory, which she considers to be "better suited . . . to the complexities and ironies of Silko's project" ("Economies of Memory" 200).

9. Silko's critique is specifically directed toward organized forms of religion (especially those sponsored by the nation-state) that have been historically employed to oppress, and to justify the oppression of, a range of social groups.

10. Within *Almanac* Silko addresses a wide range of popular fears. For example, HIV is shown to be a scientifically engineered "designer virus" that has been created "specifically for targeted groups" primarily in Africa, where the designers hope that "malnutrition would enhance the virus's power" to ensure that "the [racially] filthy would die" (*Almanac* 547–48).

11. See Jeff Faux, "NAFTA at Seven: Its Impact on Workers in All Three

Nations," *Economic Policy Institute Briefing Paper*, April 2001, www.epinet.org/briefingpapers/naftao1.

12. See Homi K. Bhabha, *Location of Culture*.

13. Silko's analysis also extends to explore the relationships between humankind and the land, a highly complex topic that is, unfortunately, beyond the scope of this essay.

14. One example is the *Anglo-Saxon Chronicle*, whose authority and value as a historical and cultural document is firmly established.

Works Cited

Arnold, Ellen. "Listening to the Spirits: An Interview with Leslie Marmon Silko." *Studies in American Indian Literatures* 10.3 (1998): 1–33.

Ashcroft, Bill, Gareth Griffiths, and Helen Tiffin, eds. *The Post-Colonial Studies Reader*. London: Routledge, 1995.

Bell, Virginia E. "Counter-Chronicling and Alternative Mapping in *Memoria del Fuego* and *Almanac of the Dead*." MELUS 25.3–4 (2000): 5–30.

Bhabha, Homi K. *The Location of Culture*. London: Routledge, 1994.

Cook-Lynn, Elizabeth. "The American Indian Fiction Writers: Cosmopolitanism, Nationalism, the Third World, and First Nation Sovereignty." 1993. *Why I Can't Read Wallace Stegner and Other Essays: A Tribal Voice*. Madison: University of Wisconsin Press, 1996. 78–96.

Donnelly, Daria. "Old and New Notebooks: *Almanac of the Dead* as Revolutionary Entertainment." In *Leslie Marmon Silko: A Collection of Critical Essays*. Ed. Louise K. Barnett and James L. Thorson. Albuquerque: University of New Mexico Press, 1999. 245–59.

Fanon, Frantz. *The Wretched of the Earth*. 1961. Reprint. New York: Grove Press, 1965.

Faux, Jeff. "NAFTA at Seven: Its Impact on Workers in All Three Nations." *Economic Policy Institute Briefing Paper*, April 2001, www.epinet.org/briefing-Papers/naftao1.

Fischer-Hornung, Dorothea. "Economies of Memory: Trafficking in Blood, Body Parts, and Crossblood Ancestors." *Amerikastudien / American Studies* 47.2 (2002): 199–221.

Huffstetler, Edward. "Spirit Armies and Ghost Dancers: The Dialogic Nature of American Indian Resistance." *Studies in American Indian Literatures* 14.4 (2002): 1–17.

Memmi, Albert. *The Colonizer and the Colonized*. Boston: Beacon Press, 1965.

Ngugi wa Thiong'o. *Decolonizing the Mind: The Politics of Language in African Literature*. London: Heinemann, 1986.Niemann, Linda. "New World Disorder." *Women's Review of Books* 9.6 (1992): 1, 3–4.

Owens, Louis. "As If an Indian Were Really an Indian: Native American Voices and Postcolonial Theory." *I Hear the Train: Reflections, Inventions, Refractions*. Norman: University of Oklahoma Press, 2001. 207–26.

Pratt, Mary Louise. *Imperial Eyes: Travel Writing and Transculturation*. London: Routledge, 1992.

Rappaport, Joanne. *The Politics Of Memory: Native Historical Interpretation in the Colombian Andes*. Cambridge: Cambridge University Press, 1990.

Scarberry, Susan J. "Memory as Medicine: The Power of Recollection in *Ceremony*." *American Indian Quarterly* 5 (1989): 19–26.

Silko, Leslie Marmon. *Almanac of the Dead*. New York: Penguin, 1991.

———."The Fifth World: The Return of Ma ah shra true ee, the Giant Serpent." *Yellow Woman and a Beauty of the Spirit: Essays on Native American Life Today*. New York: Simon and Schuster, 1996. 124–34.

———. "Notes on *Almanac of the Dead*." *Yellow Woman and a Beauty of the Spirit: Essays on Native American Life Today*. New York: Simon and Schuster, 1996. 135–45.

Sol, Adam. "The Story as It's Told: Prodigious Revisions in Leslie Marmon Silko's *Almanac of the Dead*." *American Indian Quarterly* 23.3–4 (1999): 24–48.

Taylor, Paul Beekman. "Silko's Reappropriation of Secrecy." In *Leslie Marmon Silko: A Collection of Critical Essays*. Ed. Louise K. Barnett and James L. Thorson. Albuquerque: University of New Mexico Press, 1999. 23–62.

Wilson, Norma C. "Beyond False Boundaries." *Studies in American Indian Literatures* 6.1 (1994): 71–82.

Wootten, Leslie A. "'We Want Our Mother the Land': Female Power in Leslie Marmon Silko's *Almanac of the Dead*." *North Dakota Quarterly* 64.4 (1997): 57–69.

4. COMPARATIVE MYTHOLOGIES, TRANSATLANTIC JOURNEYS

9 Vizenor's Trickster Theft

Pretexts and Paratexts of *Darkness*
in *Saint Louis Bearheart*

We Indians are great storytellers and
liars and mythmakers.
SHERMAN ALEXIE, *Ten Little Indians*

"When I was seeking some meaning in literature for myself," Vizenor recalls, "some identity for myself as a writer, I found it easily in the mythic connections" (quoted in Owens, *Other Destinies* 239). His earlier autobiographical essays, collected in *Interior Landscapes: Autobiographical Myths and Metaphors*, equate fact with myth and myth with truth in accordance with the etymology of *myth*: "word, truth, speech" (Greek *muthos* < *Indo-European *mudh*, "to think, imagine"). In early Greek usage myth designates an oral pronouncement made to an audience, and Vizenor follows this mold as a maker of myth, neither in the Tolkien political or C. S. Lewis religious veins of mythological fantasy but as a sacred history of truth.

Vizenor's *Darkness in Saint Louis Bearheart* sounds new myth over the stale European story sowed on native North American ground.[1] Although popular imagination relegates myth-making to the distant past, in *Darkness* "myth bec[o]me[s] the center of meaning again" (158). With its mythic allusions, scope, and import, the novel conjoins fundamental European founding myths and many of their romance derivatives.[2] The myth of Zeus, who in the guise of a bull ravages Europa, the bearer of the founder of Minoan culture, is archetypal, and his rape of Leda in swan shape sires a Greek-Trojan civilization. In later legend comparable shape-shifting and sexual violence characterize the founding of Roman civilization by Aeneas after he wins Lavinia in battle. In Celtic legend Uther Pendragon shifts shape to couple with Igrayne and sire the Arthur, who founds a British court of courtesy and honor. Shape-shifting sexuality is common in Native American story as well. In Anishinaabe (Ojibwe, Chippewa) myth the sun Giisis uses winds to engender Manidou sons with civilizing spirits. Appropriately in *Darkness*, Vizenor's ursonymic narrator explains that his hidden book is about "sex and violence" (xiii), principal components of the Anishinaabe creation story. Tricksters all are these makers, and the bloodstream of the lives made is mixed. Mixed-blood violence and sexuality are central to *Darkness*, and to that mix Vizenor adds language violence and generation. In effect he conjoins native with imported story to produce something radically new while bringing the old up to date.[3]

Similar to its classical precedents, *Darkness* is a chronicle of the end of one world and the birth of another but also provides a mixed vulnerary for the diseased language of a moribund culture. In short *Darkness* is about shape-shifting of both life and language forms. Its language participates in a *Logomachy*, a word war between political, social, and spiritual forces of language, which is a feature of trickster discourse on all terrains. Although sacred myth has through time lost its prominence to secular and banal "facts" of religion, rule, and social and commercial intercourse, myth survives in modes of dynamic flexible orality that contrast with dry written secular fact. The style of *Darkness* draws the reader to assume a trickster mythographic stance and participate imaginatively in the war of words that Vizenor wages to dis-member the current secular word and re-member the English language with the mystery of myth. In this respect *Darkness* is an emetic that purges both diseased sounds and graphic shapes of words. Appropriately, Bearheart's story is called a "word war," and its introduction is both prelude to and ludic heart of its warring issues.

The book's wordplay opens with confusion symptomatic of and suitable to the entire story performance. Bearheart tells his American Indian Movement (AIM) interrogator that his book lies among "heirship documents" (vii). Whether the book contains them or is one of them is purposefully vague, as is the range of meaning in heirship, though in the context of the Bureau of Indian Affairs it designates inherited land rights of American Indians. Etymologically, heir can be traced back through French hoir and Latin heres to Sanskrit jahati, "he leaves"; and –ship, like German –shaft, is cognate with the English shape, create. Thus, etymologically, heirship can be read as "abandonment of creation." Further punning possibilities are legion once the AIM woman hears "hairship" (ix). Bearheart uses hairship for a register of "the names of the tribal people who would own land if the tribal people who have died had owned the land" (xii). Hairship also designates Bearheart's bear pelt. The aspirate h sounds hare as well. Unaspirated, the term produces an heir/air pun that reflects the Greek ær, "mist, haze," and Attic aura, "fresh/cool breeze." An airship is a vehicle of transportation over a long distance, which is what Darkness is about and what it performs for its readers. Among these homophonies is the unpronounced rhyme Bearship that would allude to the story's bear-led migration, which culminates in Proude Cedarfair's ursotropic assumption.

Such implicit and explicit wordplay collide senses everywhere. Bearheart's "Grave Reports from the Cultural Word Wars" distorts Mercutio's grave pun in Shakespeare's Romeo and Juliet (3.1.99); and word wars echoes world wars, in which the first two Proude Cedarfairs fought. Puns, of course, are the trickster's tools of the trade, but Vizenor's revised title term heirship is enough to qualify the plot chronicle broadly as mankind's unwelcome inheritance of a waste world that will come to an end sometime in the near future, perhaps on December 23, 2012, the date posited by Mayan calendars. Once engaged in the text, the reader-critic finds himself drawn into the vortex of Vizenor's mixed ludic style.

Bearheart's mythopoeia is in the form of a sinuous quest of "Cedarfair Circus and the bears traveling to the fourth world" (Darkness xiii), led by the old shaman and mouth warrior Fourth Proude across an energy-wasted terrain. On the sacred geography they inscribe between the cedar woods of Minnesota and Chaco Canyon's Pueblo Bonito in a New Mexican desert, Proude and his mixed animal-human troupe engage in a number of battles with word arms against the white occupier of his land and Indian collaborators, who aim Euro-American logos arrows at the "white Indian," or mixed-blood. Bearheart's word warfare is a combat to manumit the Indian and his discourse from "static artifact[s] within the discourse of the American myth" (Owens, *Mixedblood Messages* 84). Nonetheless, *mixed-blood* alludes historically not only to North American Indians but to virtually all Europeans and Euro-Americans alike. We are all essentially genetically and culturally mixed. Vizenor's concern with "static utterances that exist on their own authority" addresses racial and social groups of all ages and places (Owens, *Mixedblood Messages* 156). Static qualifiers of Indian and white are, like written land deeds, fixed, while traditional Indian discourse, with its shifting vectors, is oral. It takes the trickster voice to revitalize a linguistic static worldview, and Vizenor, Bearheart, and Fourth Proude are three-in-one trickster myth-makers.

The stylistically mixed manner in *Darkness* of chronicling a passage from a wasted third world to a fourth world, Rigal-Cellard says, is a "brilliant firework of borrowings . . . from western apocalyptic art and literature" ("Doubling" 93). It is, however, much more than an exposé of apocalypse or even, as Owens observes, a "postapocalyptic rejection of modernist despair" (*Mixedblood Messages* 83). It is a narrative mosaic collage exposing malefic monstrosities of Western civilization. Owens remarks in his afterword to the reprint edition of *Bearheart* that the story of passage "takes on ironic overtones in a parody not merely of the familiar allegorical pilgrimage found in *Canterbury Tales*" but in "the westernizing pattern of American 'discovery' and settlement" (248–49). Actually, *Darkness* both mirrors and deconstructs a broad range of European and American secular stories both prior to and following Chaucer.

The core sense of *Darkness* emanates from and constitutes three overlapping mythic and post-mythic genre paradigms: exodus, pilgrimage, and quest. An exodus is a voyage of escape from a hostile ethnic, national, or cultural locus, a pilgrimage is a commemorative voyage to a shrine, and a quest is a search for an article of great value. "Motion is genetically encoded in American Indian being," notes Owens (*Mixedblood Messages* 164), and in *Darkness* Bearman leads his pilgrims in a *movida* across a wasted and depleted land full of accumulated shards of Western civilization.

Such pathways are common in Western myth and secular story "imported" and traced by the immigrant European over the indigenous myths of the New World. The biblical tale of Moses, Asian in origin but European by adoption, is a prototext for escape to a sanctuary. The trail of Moses with his exiles toward a "promised land" is a distant image of Proude's anabasis with exiled Indians, mixed-bloods and whites from pristine and fertile Anishinaabe cedar forests and lakes to the lifeless barren Anasazi desert. Typically, European myths of forced or voluntary exodus carry civilizations across cultural borders. Daedalus, in his flight from Crete across the Mediterranean, carries Minoan culture to the Peloponnesus. Aeneas ships Trojan culture to Rome, and Nicodemus sails with Christian story freight from Jerusalem to Massalia and on to Britain. Each of these moves, like Proude's exodus, is from a familiar locus to an imagined one. Nation-founding migrations such as these reflect the ur-myth of the settlement of Western Europe from the Eden of the Near East northwestward to the Danai of Greece and northwestward to the Danu of Celtic Ireland. Darcy McNickle's *Runner in the Sun* and Leslie Marmon Silko's *Almanac of the Dead*, albeit distinct in form, purpose, and effect, reflect traditional North American autochthonous myths of forced purgative migrations to renovate cultural identities. The by-product of migration in all these instances is a new and stronger mixed bloodline, what Virgil identifies in his Daedalus story as *mixtum genus*, "mixed-blood strain" (*Aeneid* 6.4–26), and Ovid as *biformis*, "double-formed" (*Metamorphoses* 8.156; see Latin *mixtus*, Modern English *metis* and *mestizo*).

Proude and his fellows, along with being on a forced exodus, are on a pilgrimage to a sacred site that reflects the Prudentian *Psychomachia*, a battle between virtues and vices. The morality play *Everyman* and John Bunyan's *Pilgrim's Progress* are examples of the *pélérinage de la vie humaine* from a fallen *hic et nunc* to a salvific residence *in aeternum*. The mythic process of Bearheart's world, however, is not the linear spiritual vector of Christian Providence but Nature's cyclical procession. In Toltec myth mankind is now in the age of the fifth sun (*tonatiuh*), while Vizenor's Bearheart moves between third and fourth worlds (vii).

As pilgrimage, *Darkness* resembles Chaucer's fourteenth-century human comedy of man's fallen state in *Canterbury Tales*. Besides being a forced exodus from an endangered geographical location to a place of revitalization that occasions a succession of narrative diversions, *Darkness* chronicles a move toward a renewed state of being. Both pilgrimages end at a shrine of conversion, both feature pilgrim tale telling during a long trek, and both have outstanding women like Chaucer's Wife of Bath and Bearheart's Belladonna, whose person and story define female sexuality and "Indianness," respectively. Chaucer's domineering and childless Wife and Vizenor's Pio Wissakodewinni (Eternal Sister / Parawoman) merge gender characteristics. Vizenor's Inawa, like Chaucer's Pardoner, tells a story about death (128). Like Chaucer's Harry Bailly, Vizenor's Proude is a gambler, and, like the three rioters of the Pardoner's Tale, he gambles with Death (124). Vizenor's Word Hospital in Bioavaricious, Kansas, involves the same nominalist inquiry into language that Chaucer offers.

Of course, there are minor differences in the two pilgrimages. Of twenty-nine pilgrims that leave Chaucer's London and two more that join them en route, thirty arrive before the gates of Canterbury, whereas, of thirteen pilgrims who leave Red Cedar Reservation, only a handful arrive before the vision window in Pueblo Bonito. While Chaucer impugns static Christian social and religious creeds, Vizenor's comic hallucinatory satire impugns American Indian quests to define and preserve a viable sense of self. Chaucer's pilgrims move through the tertium quid between sin and grace, while Proude and his fellow "cedarclown pilgrims" move from a vanishing paradise to a desert shrine limen between an evil third world and an animal-regenerated fourth world.

Besides exodus and pilgrimage, Bearheart chronicles a quest that reflects European mythic searches for tokens of eternal life. The classical literary prototext is the quest of the Sumerian Gilgamesh who travels from Mesopotamian sands to Lebanon cedars. Proude goes the other way, from cedars to desert, on his way to retrieve the essential life force.

In Greek myth Theseus and Demeter descend to the Underworld to rescue Persephone, and Orpheus to retrieve Eurydice. Ulysses voyages from Troy to Ithaca to recover both realm and wife. The obvious fertility issues in these stories and in Bearheart's chronicle recall the Egyptian myth of Isis to re-member Osiris. The descents of the Nordic god Odin, Aeneas, and Dante to underworlds have eschatological implications. Like Proude, they are on quests for transcendental rebirth.

Comparable to Vizenor's story is the Irish epic *Táin Bó Cuailnge* (The Cattle Raid at Cooley), whose hero, Cuchulain (Hound of Culann), is a shape-shifting "outsider" who battles the magical force of Morrigan, the queen of demons.[4] A more romanticized Celtic analogue is the quest of the Holy Grail. In Thomas Malory's fifteenth-century version, of the scores of knights who leave Arthur's Round Table, Perceval, Bors, and Galahad achieve the Grail and then disappear from the landscape, while only Proude and Inawa of Bearheart's thirteen pilgrims pass into the fourth world through the vision window. The terrain traversed in search of escape in both stories is blighted physically, morally, and spiritually, and the movement of the questers in both reshapes the landscape both topologically and nominally.

Fertility is central to Vizenor's mythopoeia as much as it is in the non-mythic fiction of Chaucer and Malory. The Wife of Bath and Arthur's Guinevere are childless, and Vizenor's Parawoman, like the Toltec Om-téotl, is dual-sexed but sterile due to botched Euro-American punitive medicine. The sexual quest for (re-)generation is common to indigenous American myth. Locke Setman's rehabilitation in Momaday's novel *The Ancient Child* is marked by his impregnation of Grey, who had dreamed of mating with a bear and will bear a mixed-blood heir for a Kiowa/Navajo world (74). Both *Ancient Child* and *Darkness* play with names. *Setman* signifies "Bearman" in Kiowa/English, and, as a young boy, Set is told about bee-wolves (74). *Bee-wolf* duplicates the name of the Anglo-Saxon quest hero Beowulf (both North American and European oral traditions are replete with Bear Child myths).[5] Names have disposable logo-kinetic power that shifts from one adventure to another, and Vizenor's and Malory's characters adapt nominal laminations to punctual exigencies.

There are many other significant correspondences between *Darkness* and Malory's Grail legend. One is the curious match of the name Bearheart with the Celtic name Arthur, glossed by Latin *ursus horribilis*, "horrible bear." The honor and plunder pursued by Malory's knights incite the same sex and violence that fill Bearheart's chronicle. The rules of the Round Table that define knighthood anticipate Belladonna's reply to the question "What is an Indian?" The magic and shape-shifting exercised by Merlin and the knights of the Round Table (Lancelot, Tristram, and Kay) are matched by all four Proude Cedarfairs and his meta-masked pilgrims. Guinevere and Belladonna are both undone by poison, the one by an apple and the other by a cookie. Both groups of seekers move across blighted landscapes through zones of magic and engage in battles of words and physical weapons. The majority of Bearheart's pilgrims and Arthur's knights fail in their quest, and few understand what it is. Quest and migration alike are often waste displacements without purpose or effect. Malory himself is a distant mirror of Vizenor's terminal believers, who, like Plato's troglodyte viewers, can see only a shadow of reality.

A focal issue in both Malory's romance of nostalgia and Vizenor's barbed critique of Euro-American cultural territorialism is "terminal creeds," Vizenor's neologism for "terminal definitions of 'Indianness' imposed upon indigenous Americans for five hundred years" (*Mixedblood Messages* 85). For Elvira Pulitano the creeds are "destructive stereotypes of Native Americans created by the Euroamerican imagination" (*Critical Theory* 146), but she recognizes the appropriateness of the term to any set of beliefs that impose static definitions upon a group. Whereas Arthur's knights are bound by the terminal creeds of the rules of the Round Table, Proude and his fellow Indians are "terminal believers . . . believing in only one vision of the world" (Blaeser, *Gerald Vizenor* 49). Like Malory's Arthur and his knights, who hold desperately to a terminal belief and faith in a courtly and chivalric creed of behavior that is rendered meaningless in the dust of senseless destruction, they are entrapped in cultural and spiritual terminal creeds. Proude's word warriors are also victims of racial creeds.

A century and a half after Malory, Miguel de Cervantes (1547–1616) questioned the high ideals, the terminal creeds, of knight errantry in a low mimetic parody of heroic legend. His Don Quixote believed in the true possibilities of what he had read in romance literature and tilted at imagined giants and evildoers futilely until, on his deathbed, "with many forceful arguments . . . expressed his abomination of books of chivalry." Like Vizenor long after him, Cervantes invites scrutiny of the creeds to be combated.

In effect, in its conjoining with and "irreverent doubling of the great works of European literature" ("Doubling" 94), *Darkness* takes off where Cervantes ended. While Vizenor could look to other European models of European literary attacks on static hegemonic political, racial, and moral ideologies, his immediate literary paratexts are American. In *Leaves of Grass* Walt Whitman calls for an American liberation from European "creeds and schools" ("Song of Myself" [1891], 1), and celebrates the generative mix of Euro-American immigrant and Red Indian (10). In the preface to his 1855 edition he invites a "new order" and predicts that "the poems distilled from other poems will probably pass away." In his reply to Ralph Waldo Emerson's praise Whitman wrote: "what is to be done is withdraw from precedents (*Poetry and Prose* 1330). As Vizenor was to do, Whitman reconciled opposites in search of a homogeneity of being among all living creatures. Another nineteenth-century work that informs *Darkness* is *Moby-Dick; or, The Whale* (1851), Herman Melville's mythic quest story that brings into question Euro-American religious, racial, and sexual terminal creeds. Among Ahab's mixed-race crew only one survives to tell the story of a failed quest to destroy the monster whale that incarnates a principle of evil. In a Lima café Melville's narrator speaks from the persona of "Ishmael," while Vizenor's speaks from the bear in him.

The major "myth" behind Vizenor's *Darkness*, it seems to me, is Mark Twain's *The Adventures of Huckleberry Finn*, a story that Europeans tend to view as the quintessential exposition of American civilization and exemplum of a distinct American literary canon. *Darkness* conjoins *Huck* in a comic "compassionate trickster" indictment of Euro-American terminal creeds (*Darkness* 16). Comparable plot and thematic elements abound. First and foremost, both author-to-narrator textual relationships are confused. Vizenor has Bearheart tell Proude Cedarfair's (Bearman's) chronicle story locked away from his place of confinement. Twain tells a story that Huckleberry—whose name is synonymous with hurtleberry, whortleberry, and blueberry—relates to an unidentified audience somewhere as a complement, corrective, and counter to Twain's novel *The Adventures of Tom Sawyer*. Both Vizenor and Twain, in effect, construct mises en abîme, stories within stories in which the "authors" wear meta-masks of a fictive trickster teller.

The tales run parallel. Huck flees with black Jim from Missouri southward from terminal creeds of frontier life that include domineering social, moral, and racial attitudes; Proude flees southward with a band of different blood strains from similar static creeds. The water route Huck takes down the Mississippi River with the renegade slave Jim is Proude's route southward from the Red Cedar Reservation on the Misisibi. The biblical Exodus is the archetypal prototext behind both migrations, and Huck disdains the stereotypical reading of that myth when he recalls that the Widow Douglas "learned me about Moses and the Bulrushers . . . but by and by she let out that Moses had been dead a considerable long time . . . I don't take stock in dead people" (626; a pun on bul[l] is evident). In *Darkness* the Canadian River recedes like the Red Sea (209), allowing Proude and his disenfranchised peoples to cross and reach a new homeland.

The plot and style correspondences between *Darkness* and *Huck Finn* are too numerous to explore here, but consider the following. Both feature fake nobility: Sir Cecil Staples (etymologically, "blind market / commodity") and Benito Saint Plumero (the feathered) recall the Duke and King, who impose themselves on Huck's wigwam raft. "Meta-mask" disguises abound in both texts. Huck, apparently dead, parades as Sarah Williams to avoid detection and later passes himself off as Tom Sawyer (679, 841). Huck's Jim is dressed as King Lear and then identified as a sick Arab (779). In *Darkness* both Proude and his flock change sex, names, and shapes frequently. The ontological conundrum "What is a man?" that Huck and Jim fail to solve anticipates Vizenor's challenges to Indian self-definition. On their escape routes Huck and Proude meet riverboat and land vehicle wrecks (689–90), respectively, while "wrecks" of language, the vital mediation between author and his characters, clutter the landscapes of both. Huck sets his narrative somewhere between "the truth, mainly" and "one time or another lie" (625). Both *Huck Finn* and *Darkness* are about heirship, fraudulent claims of parentage, and rights of inheritance (815–23).

Bearheart chronicles "travels through terminal creeds and social deeds escaping from evil into the fourth world where bears speak the sacred language of saints" (*Darkness* xii). Pristine worlds in which the language of all living things is mutually understood are topoi in creation myths, and, as Proude and Inawa soar through the vision window into the fourth world as bears (241), we can assume that they achieve primal speech. The wasted world of words they fly from is comparable to frontier civilization, where Huck overhears boatmen prepare for fisticuffs in a stereotypical logomachy that obviates physical contact.[6] In his argument over language with Jim he defends linguistic forms in foreign fictional texts that the uneducated Jim neither fathoms nor respects (701–3). A comparable linguistic inquisition attends Proude Cedarclown and his troupe when they tour the Avaricious Kansas Word Hospital and are instructed on degenerate grammar and the nursing of terminal creed vocabulary (162–67).

Imprisonment is ubiquitous in both novels. Jim is enslaved in Missouri, imprisoned on a raft, and, finally, incarcerated on the Phelp's farm. Proude and his comrades are jailed in the Santa Fe Plaza Palace of Governors (222), but, more drastically, they are fettered to a stereotypical ethnic design of the white world in which they are "terminal prisoners." Impulse for exodus incites escape, and both Huck and Proude flee civilization. Proude and Inawa fly from a wasted world through the vision window at Pueblo Bonito—ironically, a pueblo that was abandoned in the thirteenth century. Huck will set out for Indian Territory already in the process of being wasted by white invaders incited by terminal beliefs of manifest destiny. It is cruel irony that Huck drifts past Cairo, Illinois

("Little Egypt"), where a turn northeastward would have led him and Jim to freedom up the Ohio. The biblical Moses brought his people to freedom out of "Cairo." At the end of his journey Huck decides to escape the terminal impediments of civilization: "But I reckon I got to light out for the Territory ahead of the rest, because Aunt Sally she's going to adopt me and sivilize me and I can't stand it. I been there before" (912).

To obviate the "there," Twain and Vizenor trace, retract, and erase collective vestiges of European creeds imposed on the North American landscape. Where *Darkness* goes significantly further is in its assault on terminal language. Vizenor's neologisms, freed from terminal connotative limits, are as radical as James Joyce's. His characters communicate in ad hoc languages of animals, cripples, and with soundless gestures. Vizenor also dis-figures trite metaphor, for example, when the pilgrims are challenged to "eat your fucking hearts out" as they dine on innards and when Belladonna's poisoned cookies become her "just desserts" (170, 193).

The most startling examples of stylistic conjoining of this sort are words and phrases wrenched loose from their contexts in the "terminal canon" of Western arts. Like Ezra Pound and T. S. Eliot before him, Vizenor makes collages of literary tropes. Besides echoes of scriptural names and phrases as well as classical myth (esp. 124, 187), he twists familiar literary phrases into "firewords overture" (120; George Frideric Handel), "the mind is the perfect hunter (188; Carson McCullers), "nothing to fear but silence" (205; Franklin Delano Roosevelt), and "across the river but not into the hills" (207; Ernest Hemingway). Most remarkable is a cleverly camouflaged haiku that echoes Pound's poem "In a Station of the Metro": "Crows retreated and waited in the trees. Black blotches in the cedar" (15). Although one might claim that by repetition and allusion, Vizenor condones the terminal creeds he would abrogate; his retracing is an erasing.

Collectively, *Darkness* conjoins the heritage, or "heirage," of these and other texts in the Western canon as a distinct dismembering and re-membering of cultural inheritance.[7] At first sight it may seem that Vizenor's Proude, like Twain's Huck, abandons the world he would redeem.

Huck flies from a world of innocence in the throes of ruination, leaving behind, however, the one he has led toward freedom, while Bearheart's Fourth Proude Cedarfair leaves behind him the remains of the female contingent he had led toward the fourth world. Both flights seem to mark the end of a world in imagination, but, because Huck is alive to tell his story, we can suspect that his innocence is still intact; and, as Sister Eternal Flame and Rosina hear the signifying roar of bears, they sense that Proude, like Quetzalcóatl, will return to mark the Ce Acatl, or Year One, of a new world.

For the reader of Bearheart's chronicle who cannot traverse an evil world to reach the Pueblo Bonito of the human spirit, Proude is a model for those left behind. To escape a prison one must realize that he is in prison then have the means of escaping and finally the instruction of one who has already done so. Bearheart's chronicle is a manual of escape: "Return with our book and we will tell how to read and understand the hairship documents" (xvi); that is, how to emigrate from the wasted third world of lost innocence, terminal beliefs, and blinded visions to a non-mixed-blood universality of being.

In *Bearheart* Vizenor offers his reader a model for conjoining Native American with European and Euro-American myth with a style that produces a radically new mixed myth. His text deconstructs and recontextualizes the literary tradition it draws upon, informing it with meaning pertinent to the mix of language and culture that is, after all, the hallmark of American arts.

Notes

1. Gerald Vizenor, *Darkness in Saint Louis Bearheart* (Saint Paul MN: Trucks Books, 1978). Because the opening chapter is drastically abridged in the reprint *Bearheart: The Heirship Chronicles* (Minneapolis: University of Minnesota Press, 1990), I refer to the first edition unless otherwise noted.

2. Bernadette Rigal-Cellard cites Vizenor's "irreverent doubling of the great works of European literature" ("Doubling" 94).

3. *Conjoining* translates to *conjointure*, a term used in French criticism to describe the addition to a literary form of something new, therefore modifying it.

4. In *Postindian Conversations* Vizenor revealed his totem as the dog (102).

5. "Name is fame," said Dante, and Vizenor's informs his authorial posture. *Gerald* (Germanic *ger* + [w]ald) signifies "wielder of sword," and *Viz en or* echoes a number of Latinate terms that are "in gold"; the abbreviation *viz.*, for *videlicet*, has its roots in the Latin words for "to see" and "to be permitted."

6. The flyting of riverboat men in an early manuscript of *Huck Finn* appears in chapter 3 of *Life on the Mississippi* (242–43).

7. The literary influence of *Darkness* is evident in David Seals's novel *Sweet Medicine* (New York: Orion, 1992), a pilgrimage story of flight from white imprisonment that features a violent reappropriation of Native rights. It concludes with a Cheyenne quest to commemorate Indian victims of American massacres. Seals's creation myths and a horse raid recall James Welch's *Fools Crow*, and, in his retracing of cultural forces stolen from the Indian, he catalogues Indian clown tricksters.

Works Cited

Blaeser, Kimberly. *Gerald Vizenor: Writing in the Oral Tradition*. Norman: University of Oklahoma Press, 1996.

Bowers, Neil, and Charles L. P. Silet. "An Interview with Gerald Vizenor." MELUS 8 (1981): 41–49.

Momaday, N. Scott. *The Ancient Child*. New York: HarperCollins, 1990.

Owens, Louis. *Other Destinies: Understanding the American Indian Novel*. Norman: University of Oklahoma Press, 1992.

———. *Mixedblood Messages*. Norman: University of Oklahoma Press, 1998.

Pulitano, Elvira. *Toward a Native American Critical Theory*. Lincoln: University of Nebraska Press, 2003.

Rigal-Cellard, Bernadette. "Doubling in Gerald Vizenor's *Bearheart*: The Pilgrimage Strategy or Bunyan Revisited." SAIL 9.1 (1997): 93–114.

Seals, David. *Sweet Medicine*. New York: Orion, 1992.

Swann, Brian, and Arnold Krupat, eds. *I Tell You Now: Autobiographical Essays by Native American Writers*. Lincoln: University of Nebraska Press, 1987.

Twain, Mark. *Mississippi Writings: The Adventures of Huckleberry Finn*. New York: Library of America, 1982.

Vizenor, Gerald. *Darkness in Saint Louis Bearheart*. St. Paul MN: Trucks Books, 1978.

————. "Crows Written on the Poplars." In *I Tell You Now: Autobiographical Essays by Native American Writers*. Ed. Brian Swann and Arnold Krupat. Lincoln: University of Nebraska Press, 1987. 99–110.

————. *Manifest Manners: Postindian Warriors of Survivance*. Hanover NH: Wesleyan University Press, 1991.

Vizenor, Gerald, and A. Robert Lee. *Postindian Conversations*. Lincoln: University of Nebraska Press, 1999.

Whitman, Walt. *Poetry and Prose*. New York: Library of America, 1982.

10 *"June Walked over It like Water and Came Home"*

Cross-Cultural Symbolism in Louise Erdrich's *Love Medicine* and *Tracks*

The opening section of *Love Medicine* (1984, rev. 1993) closes with the death of June Kashpaw, "a long-legged Chippewa woman," on the eve of Easter Sunday: "The snow fell deeper that Easter than it had in forty years, but June walked over it like water and came home" (1, 7). Such overt Christian symbolism has prompted the Native American poet and critic Elizabeth Cook-Lynn (Crow Creek Sioux) to criticize Erdrich for her supposed adulteration of aboriginal writing and "the myths and metaphors of sovereign nationalism" with "Christian-oriented" prose (84, 85). The majority of critics, however, read Erdrich's use of Christian symbolism as highly qualified and often ironic,[1] seeing her fusion of Western and Native mythologies as an instance of cross-cultural fertilization,[2] or, as Simon J. Ortiz (Acoma Pueblo) has put it, "they [Western cultural materials] are now Indian because of the creative development that the native people applied to them" (8).

This essay will focus on the symbolic importance of water in two of Erdrich's early works, an importance that the writer herself has stressed. In a 1986 interview with Hertha D. Wong, Erdrich agreed that the main image in *Love Medicine* was the recurring image of water as "transformation" and "a sort of transcendence" and that water/river imagery is "elaborated on in [her] other books" (44). Louis Owens, in his essay on Erdrich in *Other Destinies*, also mentions the importance of water in Erdrich's fiction and in Chippewa storytelling, "a people whose traditional homeland was once the region of the Great Lakes" (197). Owens stresses Erdrich's mixed-blood identity, which allows insights into both American mainstream and Native American worlds, frequently setting up in her fiction a dialogic hybridized discourse that can be read in (at least) two ways. Thus, Owens reads June's "homecoming" at the opening of *Love Medicine* as "the feminine Christ-figure resurrected as trickster" (196). Taking up the notion of ironic cultural interchange, I shall explore the fusion of Christian symbolism and Anishinabe legends related to water, showing how the two cultures contrast, interpenetrate, and at times ironize each other.

Erdrich's work relies on a fusion of Christian and Native symbolism, but overt Christian symbolism is often placed within a Native context that interrogates and ironizes it. In *Love Medicine*, for example, any overdetermined Christian reading that would equate June's walking over the water as a Christ-like miracle is undermined by the allusions that precede it in which water is more associated with desperation and obliteration than with miracles. June, seeking against all the odds for human contact, looks through the "watery glass" of the Rigger Bar window for her savior (1). He, however, turns out to be a "mud engineer," who later on passes out into a drunken coma while attempting to have sex with June in his pickup (3). Inside the bar she struggles toward the "beacon" of a blue [Easter] egg, held in the engineer's hand (2). Temporarily blinded by the bright reflected light of the snow outside, the "murky air" of the bar makes her feel as if she is "going underwater" (2). This is a portrait of a woman who is drowning and is clutching at straws, suggesting that a purely transcendent reading of the ending would be simplistic.

The opening of *Love Medicine* links death and water, associating death more with emptiness and annihilation than with a Christian heaven. Obliteration is evoked by June's memory of an oil engineer killed by a hose of pressurized water that with one blast had "taken out his insides." The realization of being "totally empty," annihilated, is something June can empathize with: "she thought she knew what it might be like" (3). The water hose, "snaking up suddenly from its unseen nest . . . striking like a live thing," evokes the world of avenging Native gods, like the Anishinabe water monster Misshepeshu, not the world of Christian spirituality. Thus, June's walking over water toward "home" alludes to both Christian and Native symbolism. The image at one level suggests transcendence, but water in this opening section is also associated with its reverse—emptiness and destruction. Water, ultimately, is an ambivalent element that can deceive, like the supposedly "mild and wet" Chinook that June chooses to deceive herself with (6), which in fact is a freezing wind that kills her.

My reading has stressed the subversion of an affirmative Christian reading in the first chapter of *Love Medicine* and has focused on the association of water with annihilation of the self. Returning to Owens's essay on Erdrich is to be reminded that June's cracking into "many pieces" should set the Euro-American reading in dialogue with the Native American perspective: "In a Euramerican context it underscores June's alienation, approaching schizophrenia, her loss of a centered identity. Fragmentation in Native American mythology is not necessarily a bad thing, however. For the traditional culture hero, the necessary annihilation of the self that prefigures healing and wholeness and a return to the tribal community often takes the form of physical fragmentation, bodily, as well as psychic deconstruction" (195). We should note here that both readings are possible. June's psychic breakdown is real, but its significance in the Native context links the individual with the community and ultimately the cosmos. June's walking over water and coming home may sound like a Christian affirmation, but the cyclical structure of the novel, the repeated motif of "coming home," shows that the event needs to be placed within a tribal context. It needs to be placed in that epistemological framework that Western readers need to consider if they want to engage in rewarding "crossreading" experiences. Elaborating further on these issues, Owens, in *Mixedblood Messages*, writes: "Just as the oppressively literate modernists felt justified in demanding that readers know a little Greek and Roman mythology as well as the entire literary history of the Western world, Native American writers have begun to expect, even demand, that readers learn something about the mythology and oral histories of Indian America." And, quoting Dell

Hymes, he concludes by saying that cross-cultural reading, whether it involves *Beowulf, The Tale of Genji,* or Vizenor's *Bearheart,* ultimately requires "some understanding of a way of life" (10).

Owens's notion of Erdrich's dialogic, hybridized utterances, which juxtapose both Euro-American and Native perspectives, is apparent even in the chapter headings of *Love Medicine.* Headings such as "The World's Greatest Fishermen," "Saint Marie," "Crown of Thorns," "Resurrection," and "Crossing the Water" would appear to allude directly to Christian symbols, but closer investigation shows that Erdrich has indigenized these allusions. Given that the book's opening narrative begins with June's death at Easter, the book's first chapter, "The World's Greatest Fishermen," might appear to play upon the notion of Christ calling his disciples to be "fishers of men" or the miracle of the five loaves and two fishes. The title refers, however, to a patch on June's son's (King's) hat and ironically refers to King's belief that he maintains the backwoods hunting skills of the "old-time Indian" (32). King's hunting skills are highly questionable, the only verified kill being a skunk he got when he was ten. King, in fact, is a deeply unhappy man. He has been raised by a father and mother who were frequently absent and is cut off from an older generation of hunting/fishing Indians such as Uncle Eli, so that his hat is a symbol of what he would wish to be. According to his abused white wife, Lynette: "They think the world of him down in the Cities. Everybody knows him. They know him by that hat" (36), but the fame of this urbanized Chippewa would appear to be imaginary or at best token, symbolic, and stereotypical in the white community of Minneapolis–St. Paul. King's drunken aggression on his brief return to the reservation also shows he is equally homeless there. This opening chapter undermines a potentially Christian reading by linking fishing not to saving souls or miracles but to the empty bravado of a displaced and confused Indian.

The following chapter, "Saint Marie," continues Erdrich's ironic exploitation of Christian symbolism associated with water and fishing. "Saint Marie" alludes directly to the Virgin Mary, and on her way to the Sacred Heart Convent Marie Lazarre imagines herself becoming an iconized saint: "I'd be carved in pure gold. With ruby lips. And my toenails would be little pink ocean shells" (43). The reference to maritime shells is picked up later when she is called "Marie. Star of the Sea" by one of the sisters. Marie, however is a fraud, passing as white and entering an institution for "nuns that don't get along elsewhere" (45), with inmates like Sister Leopolda, who herself disguises her real identity as Marie's mother. The opening sentence, "So, when I went there, I knew the dark fish must rise" (43), links back to the fishing motif found in "The World's Greatest Fishermen" and extends it to include the notion of "fishing for souls." Marie offers herself as bait, and the sisters swallow her whole: "You ever see a walleye strike so bad the lure is practically out its back end before you reel it in? That is what they done with me" (44). Sister Leopolda is the most voracious of hunters, and the metaphor shifts as Marie becomes a fish rather than the bait, Leopolda plunging a hook pole into the Satan in Marie's heart like spearing a fish: "I was afraid of Leopolda's pole for the first time . . . I felt the cold hook in my heart. How it could crack through the door at any minute and drag me out, like a dead fish on a gaff" (47). The "black hook" that spears and links them together is a love-hatred that takes the form of a battle for dominance over the other's soul (48). Leopolda later boils the Devil from Marie's mind by scalding her with boiling water, as the battle escalates in violence. "Saint Marie" transforms Christian symbolism by rewriting the trope of "fisher of men," depicting it as a deadly battle between two Native women relying on traditional hunting skills to gain spiritual victory.[3]

Adding to the complex cross-cultural layering, this chapter is shot through with European folktale motifs, producing a tragic-comic Grand Guignol effect. Marie is the Cinderella to Leopolda's wicked stepmother, "You'll be sleeping behind the stove, child," she says (49). Then the lethal mother-daughter battle takes on shades of "Hansel and Gretel," as Marie attempts to send Leopolda flying into the jaws of the hot oven.[4] The Witch, however, is not consumed; bouncing back, she spears her daughter's hand with a fork and, as though stunning a struggling fish, lays her out with a poker. Ironically, Marie's speared hand

becomes the saintly sign of stigmata, raising her perpetually spiritually
ascendant over her mother. But Marie's victory is Pyrrhic; momentary
elation is replaced by pity for her mother.

Images associated with water—fishing for souls, scalding the
devil, Leopolda's "desperate eyes drowning in the deep wells of her
wrongness"—are replaced at the chapter's end by dryness, the handful
of dust associated with spiritual despair:

> "Receive the dispensation of my sacred blood," I whispered.
>
> But there was no heart in it. No joy when she bent to touch the
> floor. No dark leaping. . . . Blank dust was whirling through the
> light shafts. My skin was dust. Dust my lips. . . .
>
> Rise up! I thought. Rise up and walk! There is no limit to this
> dust! (60)[5]

Significantly, the following chapter sees Marie escaping from the convent, rejecting the burden of sainthood, and embracing the world beyond Leopolda's deathly convent. She ceases to be Saint Marie, a Virgin
Mary, by willingly engaging in sex with Nector Kashpaw. Afterward,
Nector holds her hand and thinks of a wounded animal that "hasn't
died well, or, worse, it's still living" (66). The bodies of such animals,
he feels, are like "killed saints" (67). Marie has willingly killed her sainthood, she has "died into life," but the rebirth is not without a sense of
loss at breaking from her spiritual mother and her imagined vocation.

A later chapter, "Crown of Thorns," again directly alludes to Christian symbolism associated with spiritual thirst and spiritual cleansing.
The symbols, however, are ironically transformed—spiritual thirst is
rewritten as an alcoholic Native man's search for a bottle, and spiritual
cleansing takes the form of a cool bath an insomniac nun only dreams
about. This short narrative, like so many of the episodes in *Love Medicine*, focuses on the effects of June's death on the Chippewa community,
in this case the effect on her husband, Gordie. The chapter begins, "A
month after June died Gordie took the first drink" (212). Driving to get
to town to buy a bottle, he hits a deer, which he places on the backseat,

but realizes that the deer is only stunned, their eyes meeting in the rear-view mirror: "Her look was black and endless and melting pure. She looked through him. She saw into the troubled thrashing woods of him, a rattling thicket of bones. She saw how he'd woven his own crown of thorns. She saw how although he was not worthy he'd jammed this re-lief on his brow" (221). But Gordie, unwilling to accept that his troubles are of his own making and that he has brought pain upon himself as a "relief," destroys the moment of revelation by killing the deer. In his alcoholic delirium, however, the deer becomes June, forcing him to rec-ognize his role in her disconnected life and ultimate death.

Erdrich draws from a well of Christian imagery but transforms con-ventional symbolic decodings by placing them within a Native American framework. Gordie, a token Catholic who has not been to confession for ten years, stumbles toward the Sacred Heart convent for absolution. Erdrich ironically equates the life of one of the sisters, Sister Mary Mar-tin de Porres, with Gordie's. Both are troubled, are having yet another sleepless night, and both are partly responsible for their own malaise: "Her nights were enjoyable while she was having them, which was part of the problem" (222–23). The spiritual desiccation of Gordie's "rat-tling thicket of bones" seems momentarily contrasted with the "cool bath" that Sister Mary is drawing for herself: "She thought that once she stripped herself and crawled into the tub, she would change, she would be able to breathe under water" (222). But this vision of absolu-tion and cleansing comes to her in a dream, and we realize that their lives are parallel and intersect. Gordie comes to her "through the wet grass" (224), "weeping" (226), confessing to his wife's murder, a story that finally becomes real for Sister Mary too, and her tears fall along with his. Mary's discovery that it is a deer and not a woman's body in the car strangely causes not relief but breakdown, as though she sees her despair in his: "Suddenly and without warning, like her chest were cracking, the weeping broke her . . . a wild burst of sounds that emptied her" (228).

In *Love Medicine* chapters that have overtly Christian headings and marked Christian symbolism alternate with chapters with a more Native focus. Thus, "Crown of Thorns," with its traditional (albeit ironized) Christian imagery of spiritual desiccation and spiritual cleansing is followed by "Love Medicine," a section that centers on traditional Chippewa love medicines and the healing power of touch. This section in turn is followed by "Resurrection," with its overt allusion to Christ. "Resurrection" concerns the return of the alcoholic Gordie, an ironic Christ figure, who returns to his mother Marie as though risen from the dead. He sprawls on the "spent grass that Marie cultivated with the leavings of her kitchen water . . . focused on the bitter green as some minor salvation" and then sleeps "like he was dead" (261). Any hope of salvation or resurrection into a new life is soon dashed, however, as Gordie erratically moves between wheedling charm, his face taking on the fake innocence of "altar boy slyness" (265), to self-destructive violence in his desperate need for a drink.

In "Crown of Thorns" water imagery again abounds. The chapter opens with Marie putting together her husband's (Nector's) ceremonial pipe, which at one end depicts "a horned man radiating wavering lines of power" (259), the water monster Misshepeshu. Putting the pipe together connects "earth and heaven" (260), brings back the old Native ways, but that resurrection is still to come; the pipe is put away for Lipsha, the hope of a future generation. The opening sentence of the chapter connects Marie with cleaning, with boiling, sterilizing, and canning--as though attempting to maintain a pure space in which traditional customs and ways, such as stocking up for winter, can be preserved. Gordie's presence erupts into this cleansed space, vomiting, scattering food, destroying. As in chapters such as "The Red Convertible," a brief idyll from the past is presented, which serves in effect to highlight the hopelessness of the present. Gordie remembers his honeymoon with June, swimming in a green lake, catching their own fish. The prelapsarian overtones, however, are countered by June's near drowning of Gordie and their failed lovemaking, foreshadowing the eventual breakdown of their relationship. The chapter ends brutally with Gordie's fatal drinking of Lysol, described as a "harsh rapture" (273), as though it were a form of transcendental religious experience. To stop him from killing himself, Marie sits at the door of her son's bedroom with an ax, like the Roman guard at Christ's sepulchre. Gordie's subsequent death,[6] the passing of his spirit, is depicted as an apocalyptic resurrection, the walls of the bedroom opening like the boulder rolled away from Christ's tomb: "She felt the walls open. He connected, his heart quit, he went through with a blast like heat. Still, she sat firm in her chair and did not let go of the ax handle" (275). Unlike the Bible, which focuses on the transcendent miracle of Christ rising from the dead, Erdrich closes with the stoicism needed for the living to carry on.

A number of critics have noted that "Crossing the Water," the final section of *Love Medicine*, brings the novel full circle.[7] As Susan Farrell puts it, "Lipsha's 'coming home' is an explicit rewriting of his mother June's suicidal 'homecoming'" (112). Lipsha's return to the reservation at the close suggests that the ghost of June's "failed 'homecoming,'" which haunts the whole novel, is finally laid to rest. Karla Sanders questions the usual interpretation of *home* as the reservation in the closing line ("there was nothing to do but cross the water, and bring her home"), persuasively arguing that *her* refers to June: "the car no longer represents June, it *is* June" (152).

The close of *Love Medicine* brings together many motifs and points to the complexity of Erdrich's water imagery. Erdrich, interviewed by Wong, has said that "the river is always this boundary" (45), and at the end of the novel Lipsha comes to a bridge over the "boundary river" (*Love* 366), *boundary* here being the borders of the reservation. Stopping in the middle of the bridge suggests his newfound ability to balance the Native and non-Native aspects. Looking in the water, he thinks of June and imagines the water playing over sunken cars, a clear reference to Lyman driving Henry's car into the river after his suicide by drowning. His imagination widens to envisage the ancient ocean that once covered the Dakotas "and solved all our problems" (367), water here suggesting death and the peaceful resolution of earthly pains. The vision of oblivion is appealing but ultimately rejected, as Lipsha acknowledges that "we live on dry land," and a clear morning is ahead. Lipsha crosses the waters and carries on. Lipsha's crossing has a specific Native American context, but the Western (or Westernized) reader may also bring to the text a whole series of images (Moses crossing the Red Sea and leading his people home; Caesar crossing the Rubicon; Washington crossing the Delaware) that reinforce the perception of river crossing as a symbol of significant change.

Water links the opening and closing narratives, but critics have interpreted this imagery in different ways. Sanders argues that "throughout the novel, dust is associated with death . . . while water represents life and love" (135). Farrell, by contrast, writes that "in the novel, water is associated with suicide, with death and oblivion, and with giving up rather than surviving" (110), giving as examples Henry Junior's suicide by drowning and the painting depicting Nector Kapshaw as a doomed Indian brave plunging from a high cliff to certain death in the water below. The most sophisticated reading is given by Catherine Rainwater, who demonstrates how Erdrich deliberately raises conflicting possibilities, "an hermeneutical impasse," so that no single cultural code (Christian or Native) is privileged, and false syntheses of antithetical possibilities are resisted (410–12). I would add to Rainwater's argument that literary and cultural context influence how the imagery is decoded.

Greg Sarris, in his essay "Reading Louise Erdrich," has raised the question of ethnocentric readings of Native American literature, urging critics in particular to question their literary criteria and assumptions with a view to keeping intercultural channels of communication open. The question "How am I reading?" is a vital one that requires the critic to acknowledge and make transparent cultural biases and at the same time does justice to the Indian writer's specific cultural experiences, which the text mediates for the reader. In my reading (a Eurocentric one) I have suggested that positive Christian imagery (such as baptism, spiritual cleansing, the miracle of walking on water, the water of life, and being led by clear waters) is a cultural backdrop against which Erdrich plays variations out of which ironies spring. An example of this would be Lipsha's blessing a turkey heart with holy water to ensure a powerful love medicine, an act that results in the death of his adoptive grandfather, Nector Kashpaw, by choking. In this context Lipsha's addition of a Christian blessing to an Anishinabe custom can be read as an ironic comment on simplistic attempts to syncretize cultures. Another example of the effect of cultural context in determining meaning would be the passages in which Erdrich introduces negative associations with water derived from Anishinabe culture, particularly the horror of death by drowning. In Lulu Lamartine's life, for example, nothing hurts her more than the memory of Henry Junior's death by drowning: "Moses told me . . . how drowning was the worst death for a Chippewa to experience. By all accounts, the drowned weren't allowed into the next life but forced to wander forever. . . . There was no place for the drowned in heaven or anywhere on earth. That is what I never found it easy to forget" (*Love* 295). Such passages take on an extra force for Western readers precisely because they come from a culture in which water and spirituality have predominantly positive associations. A Chinese reader would no doubt be equally affected but more by the shock of recognition, the surprise of cultural similarities.[8]

As Erdrich herself has pointed out in her 1986 interview with Wong, each of her first four novels were tied to one of the four elements—*Love Medicine* to water, *The Beet Queen* (1986) to air, *Tracks* (1988) to earth, and *American Horse* (later retitled *The Bingo Palace* [1994]) to fire—but these patterns of imagery are more intuitive than programmatic, and water symbolism is a feature of all her works (45). Earth is important in *Tracks* as a major theme of the novel is the dispossession of Native land around Matchimanito Lake by lumbering companies, but the lake contains Misshepeshu, the Anishinabe water monster, whom Erdrich calls in *Tracks* a "real plot device" (Wong 45), representing Native resistance to white encroachments.[9] *Love Medicine* and *Tracks* are complementary and interrelated texts.

Love Medicine is set primarily in the 1980s (with chapters dipping back into the 1930s, 1950s, and 1970s), whereas Erdrich's third novel, *Tracks*, takes the reader back to the same Chippewa community between 1912 and 1924. *Love Medicine* begins with the death of a Native woman in the snow; *Tracks* starts in winter 1912 with the death of most of the community through consumption, brought by white settlers. In both novels the theme of cultural annihilation as well as resistance to cultural annihilation is foregrounded: in *Love Medicine* June dies, but her spirit lives on in the community; in *Tracks* the tribe is decimated, but Nanapush and Fleur survive.

In *Tracks* the character who provides the strongest resistance to settler invasions of Native land and culture is Fleur, who is identified by all as the consort of Misshepeshu, the water monster of Matchimanito Lake. In traditional Anishinabe stories Misshepeshu is an ambivalent figure, a malevolent water god who drowns the unwary but also a powerful deity who helped create the world. In *Tracks* he is associated with resistance and, according to Victoria Brehm, "represents the power of American Indian spirituality and tradition, which are being drowned in American culture" (682). *Tracks* presents more starkly the battle between Christianity and Native spirituality than *Love Medicine*, shown in the climactic scene in chapter 8, in which Pauline Puyat, a mixed-blood Chippewa and a fanatical Catholic, sets out to do battle with Misshepeshu. In *Love Medicine*, by contrast, Lipsha has only heard of Misshepeshu, the implication being that the old gods no longer play an active resistant role, the majority of the community being either practicing or at least token Catholics, but in *Tracks* Misshepeshu is still a force to be reckoned with.

I have argued that in *Love Medicine* Christian symbolism is ironized and appropriated, a form of counter-discourse in which Western materials lose their power to represent dominant (white) cultural values and become indigenized. In *Tracks*, although the Catholic presence is strong, the balance between Christian and Native spirituality is more evenly balanced, and this is reflected in the cultural references in the text, for there is much more reference to Anishinabe myth in *Tracks* than there is in *Love Medicine*. This changes the nature of the ironic allusions in the texts. In *Love Medicine* Erdrich appropriates Christian symbolism; in *Tracks*, in the character of Pauline Puyat (later known as Sister Leopolda in *Love Medicine*), we have a converse irony—a Catholic convert appropriating Anishinabe spiritual lore to pursue her evangelical mission to kill the Native Devil. To Pauline, Christ has succumbed to the water monster, "overcome by the glitter of copper scales" (*Tracks* 195), and she takes on the armor of the water monster, *becomes* the water monster, in order to win her battle.[10] She takes on "the cunning of serpents" (Misshepeshu has scales like a snake), and the hands she has scalded in an excess of religious devotion shed skin and become webbed and clawed. Reprising the narrative of women's confrontations with Misshepeshu in Anishinabe tales or, alternatively, the eternal battle of the Anishinabe sky gods, the Thunderers, with the water god, Pauline pushes her boat out onto the lake. The battle, depicted in terms of sexual congress, ends when Pauline strangles the monster with her rosary beads, though as light breaks she realizes she has killed Napoleon Morrissey, the man who had towed her boat to land and the father of her child. The chapter ends with her water monster identity curiously combined with her new Christian role as a nun. The "now sanctified" Pauline, in *Tracks* (204), becomes Sister Leopolda (the name Leo-polda evoking the water monster, which can take "the body of a lion" [11]). The "unfamiliar syllables" of her new name crack in her ears "like a fist through ice" (205); this refers directly to Pauline's mortifications in the nunnery, where she breaks the water bucket ice with her bare hands (164), but also (possibly) to Misshepeshu rising to the surface of the lake in winter. Magdelena Delicka has argued that this composite mythology reflects Pauline's inability to identify fully with either Catholic or tribal beliefs. I would counter this by saying that Pauline thoroughly identifies with Catholicism and that her appropriation of tribal legend is purely a means of accessing power to pursue her missionizing ends: "New devils require new gods" (195).

Tracks is constructed dialogically, the events around Matchimanito Lake between 1912 and 1924 being told from the perspective of alternating narrators: Nanapush and Pauline. In the novel Pauline's grotesque battle with the water monster, leading to the death of Napoleon, needs to be placed beside another "water battle," Nanapush's trickster tale in chapter 6, which causes Pauline to wet herself. Pauline has devised a number of medieval tortures for herself to mortify the flesh, restricting herself to only two visits to the outhouse each day. Deliberately punning on the word *call* (spiritual calling and the call of nature), Nanapush observes to Pauline, "You never have to answer the call" (147). He proceeds to tell the tale of a girl caught in a flood and the phallic "sticking-out thing" that rescues her (149), a story, aided by strong sassafras tea, that will teach Pauline to respect the demands of the flesh. The communal function of Trickster tales, besides providing laughter, is to educate, to laugh fools out of their folly, and the tale ends with Nanapush's gleeful words "I'm only telling this for your benefit!" (151). Nanapush's tale relates to Pauline on many levels — it critiques her absurd denial of the body, her perversion of sexuality into power (the ending of Pauline's passionate relationship with Napoleon coincides with her increased religious extremism), and her lack of love for her daughter (Pauline abandons her daughter, and in Nanapush's tale the offspring of the girl and the phallus is "nothing but water" [151], held in a condom that bursts). Comparing Pauline's battle with Misshepeshu in chapter 8 and what might be called the Battle of the Outhouse in chapter 6, we see a series of dichotomies set up: denial of the body versus acceptance of the flesh; death and negation versus life and fertility; the will to power versus the power of story; tragedy versus comedy; and so on. Placed before Pauline's battle of Matchimanito Lake, the Battle of the Outhouse casts an ironic light on later events, both humanizing and critiquing Pauline's religious fanaticism.

I have focused on the ironic cultural interchanges playing under and on the surface of two of Erdrich's early works. Irony depends on an intimate knowledge of systems of signification, and inevitably readers from different cultures will access different cultural information. My analysis of Erdrich's work reflects my Eurocentrism, my greater knowledge of the Bible than of Anishinabe myths and legends, though cultural ignorance can at least be partly overcome by secondary reading and also by the information provided by the writer herself. In the second chapter of *Tracks*, for example, the narrator, Pauline, provides us with this vital cultural information about Misshepeshu: "Our mothers warn us that we'll think he's handsome, for he appears with green eyes, copper skin, a mouth tender as a child's. But if you fall into his arms, he sprouts horns, fangs, claws, fins. . . . He's a thing of dry foam, a thing of death by drowning, the death a Chippewa cannot survive" (11). A European reader would not be wrong to link Misshepeshu with worldwide water monster legends or to European cautionary animal groom/demon lover tales such as "Little Red Riding Hood" or "Beauty and the Beast."[11] Such a reading, however, although not wrong, would be inadequate as it would exclude the cultural specificity of the myth—water taboos and the fear of drowning, women's power in the Anishinabe community, warnings against the abuse of shared food resources (Misshepeshu floods the world after Nanapush with the aid of wolves greedily decimates the available game), and so on. Erdrich's novels too, of course, provide their own specific frames of reference, her transformation of both Christian and Native mythologies making large but rewarding demands on her readers.

In interviews Erdrich herself has frequently stressed her bicultural mixed-blood identity, a "dual citizenship" (Bruchac 96) allowing her to "flourish on the edge" (Chavkin and Chavkin 230). Talking with Bill Moyers in 1989, she said, "Once one is a citizen of both nations, it gives you a look at the world that's different. There is an edge of irony" (144). Erdrich's irony involves juggling with cultural codes in which we as readers need to consider both the Native and the Euro-American context. As this essay has shown, no single cultural code is privileged in Erdrich's work; indeed, the literary and cultural hybridization of her fiction seeks to deconstruct binary categories such as European versus Native. It is important to take the Native context into account, but Erdrich's novels are bicultural works that encourage bi- (or multi-) cultural readings at the same time as they challenge epistemological assumptions for both Native and Western readers.

Notes

1. See, for example, Catherine Rainwater, Susan Farrell, and Karen Janet McKinney.

2. See, for example, Roberta Rosenburg.

3. I am reading retroactively here. The reader is only aware that Sister Leopolda is a mixed-blood Native woman after having read *Tracks*.

4. Susan Castillo (18) and Patricia Riley (20) have also noted the allusion to "Hansel and Gretel" but not the reference to Cinderella.

5. Here Marie's thoughts are a collage of biblical allusions—Isaiah urging redemption: "Shake yourself from the dust; arise, and sit down, O Jerusalem" (Isaiah 52:2); Christ exhorting the sick, "Arise, and take up thy bed and walk" (Mark 2:9); and Christ raising Lazarus from the dead (John 11:43–44). Erdrich's irony here is that Marie's decision to leave the convent is couched in biblical terms.

6. Rainwater writes that Gordie "perhaps goes insane or dies" (408). In addition to the reasons given in my analysis, I interpret the closing of "Resurrection" as Gordie's death not least because the word death occurs in the final paragraph but also because Gordie subsequently disappears from the novel and is next referred to in the closing chapter (set three years later) by Lulu Lamartine as having died: "June's dead. Gordie too" (Love 336).

7. The significance of circular form in Native American fiction is explored by Hartmut Lutz.

8. For a fictional representation of the Chinese belief that the drowned become malevolent ghosts, see "No Name Woman" in Maxine Hong Kingston's novel The Woman Warrior.

9. Misshepeshu is of great importance in Erdrich's Tracks as a symbol of Native resistance to white encroachments. For the cultural significance of Misshepeshu, see Victoria Brehm and Theresa S. Smith. The pre- and post-contact significance of Micipijiu (Misshepeshu) is presented particularly well by Brehm, who writes that texts incorporating Micipijiu have been influenced and changed by contact with other cultures (678–79). Brehm's point that Erdrich's fiction creates a new set of variants that refigure the traditional Anishinabe oral narratives on Micipijiu complements my own argument that Erdrich invites a bicultural reading that deconstructs the essentialist assumptions of both Native and Western readers.

10. The medieval overtones of this passage are unmistakable. Pauline sees herself as "armored and armed," redeeming a lost Christendom as "his champion" (Tracks 195). The most obvious parallel is Saint George and the Dragon, but there may also be allusions to the Grail legend, which contains marked water imagery. The hero's spiritual duty is to restore water and fertility to the wasteland, and it is a further instance of Erdrich's irony that Pauline throughout Tracks is associated with dryness, ice, and death rather than life-giving fer-

tility. Space limitations prevent me from developing such parallels any further here.

11. See Michel Meurger and Claude Gagnon.

Works Cited

Brehm, Victoria. "The Metamorphoses of an Ojibwa Manido." *American Literature* 68.4 (1996): 677–706.

Bruchac, Joseph. "Whatever Is Really Yours: An Interview with Louise Erdrich." 1987. In *Conversations with Louise Erdrich and Michael Dorris*. Ed. Allan Chavkin and Nancy Feyl Chavkin. Jackson: University Press of Mississippi, 1994. 94–104.

Castillo, Susan. "Women Aging into Power: Fictional Representations of Power and Authority in Louise Erdrich's Female Characters." *Studies in American Indian Literatures* 8.4 (1996): 13–20.

Chavkin, Nancy Feyl, and Allan Chavkin. "An Interview with Louise Erdrich." 1993. In *Conversations with Louise Erdrich and Michael Dorris*. Ed. Allan Chavkin and Nancy Feyl Chavkin. Jackson: University Press of Mississippi, 1994. 220–53.

Cook-Lynn, Elizabeth. "The American Indian Fiction Writers: Cosmopolitanism, Nationalism, the Third World, and First Nation Sovereignty." *Why I Can't Read Wallace Stegner and Other Essays. A Tribal Voice.* Madison: University of Wisconsin Press, 1996. 78–96.

Delicka, Magdelena. "American Magic Realism: Crossing the Borders in Literatures of the Margin." *Journal of American Studies of Turkey* 6 (1997): 25–33.

Erdrich, Louise. *Love Medicine.* 1984, 1993. Reprint. Rev. and exp. ed. New York: Perennial, 2001.

———. *Tracks.* 1988. Reprint. New York: Perennial, 2004.

Farrell, Susan. "Erdrich's *Love Medicine.*" *Explicator* 56.2 (1998): 109–12.

Lutz, Hartmut. "The Circle as a Philosophical and Structural Concept in Native American Fiction." *Approaches: Essays in Native North American Studies and Literatures.* Augsburg: Wissner-Verlag, 2002. 195–208.

McKinney, Karen Janet. "False Miracles and Failed Vision in Louise Erdrich's *Love Medicine.*" *Critique: Studies in Contemporary Fiction* 40.2 (1999): 152–60.

Meurger, Michel, and Claude Gagnon. *Lake Monster Traditions: A Cross-Cultural Analysis.* London: Fortean Tomes, 1988.

Moyers, Bill. "Louise Erdrich and Michael Dorris." 1989. In *Conversations with Louise Erdrich and Michael Dorris*. Ed. Allan Chavkin and Nancy Feyl Chavkin. Jackson: University Press of Mississippi, 1994. 138–50.

Ortiz, Simon. J. "Toward a National Indian Literature: Cultural Authenticity in Nationalism." MELUS 8.2 (1981): 7–12.

Owens, Louis. "Erdrich and Dorris's Mixedbloods and Multiple Narratives." *Other Destinies: Understanding the American Indian Novel*. Norman: University of Oklahoma Press, 1992. 192–224.

———. *Mixedblood Messages: Literature, Film, Family, Place*. Norman: University of Oklahoma Press, 1998.

Rainwater, Catherine. "Reading between Worlds: Narrativity in the Fiction of Louise Erdrich." *American Literature* 62.3 (1990): 405–22.

Riley, Patricia. "There Is No Limit to This Dust: The Refusal of Sacrifice in Louise Erdrich's *Love Medicine*." *Studies in American Indian Literatures* 12.2 (2000): 13–23.

Rosenberg, Roberta. "Ceremonial Healing and the Multiple Narrative Tradition in Louise Erdrich's *Tales of Burning Love*." MELUS 27.3 (2002): 113–32.

Sanders, Karla. "A Healthy Balance: Religion, Identity, and Community in Louise Erdrich's *Love Medicine*." MELUS 23.2 (1998): 129–55.

Sarris, Greg. "Reading Louise Erdrich: *Love Medicine* as Home Medicine." *Keeping Slug Woman Alive: A Holistic Approach to American Indian Texts*. Berkeley: University of California Press, 1993. 115–45.

Smith, Theresa S. *The Island of the Anishnaabeg: Thunderers and Water Monsters in the Traditional Ojibwe Life-World*. Moscow: University of Idaho Press, 1995.

Wong, Hertha D. "An Interview with Louise Erdrich and Michael Dorris." 1986. In *Conversations with Louise Erdrich and Michael Dorris*. Ed. Allan Chavkin and Nancy Feyl Chavkin. Jackson: University Press of Mississippi, 1994. 30–53.

11 Encounters across Time and Space

The Sacred, the Profane, and the Political in Linda Hogan's *Power*

> I think of my work as part of the history of our tribe and as part of the history of colonization everywhere. LINDA HOGAN, in Wilson, *Nature of Native American Poetry*

> The one faith is expressed in different ways. . . . Not only is Christianity relevant to the Indian peoples, but Christ, in the members of his Body, is himself . . . Indian. POPE JOHN PAUL II

In 1994, when I was completing a research grant at the University of Arizona, I attended N. Scott Momaday's classes. I was surprised to learn that he had visited Bulgaria twice during Communism, on invitations from the Bulgarian Union of Writers. We talked about the similarities between Bulgarian and Native peoples' folk songs and stories, especially about stories featuring bears, Momaday's favorite animal. In the course of our discussions, and as my knowledge of Native American traditions grew, I began to perceive a mode of reciprocity between Bulgarian traditional literature and that of Native peoples and the way the two talk to each other, encounter, and enrich each other, without for a moment losing their unique linguistic mastery and poetic beauty. Ironically, during Communism works by Native American writers were used only to illustrate the imperialist policies of the United States and to affirm, by implication, the internationalist policies of equality of Communism. Yet people saw the subtext in the sacred stories, and its political message was not lost; age-tested folk wisdom and national memory survive the harshest oppressive system. In those days the works of Native American writers inspired a stronger awareness in their Bulgarian audience about the inexhaustible resources and mysterious power of their own traditions. The "ecological thinking" in the works of Native American writers now stimulates a new awareness for the pressing need for interaction with and care for the Earth that we all share (Katharine Chandler, quoted in Cook 17).[1]

In her 2002 interview with Barbara Cook, when asked about the unity of the spiritual and the political in her works, Linda Hogan answers that "for Native Peoples there is no difference. Decisions are made, and they may be political decisions" (11). The legal conflicts in her novels—*Mean Spirit, Solar Storms,* and *Power*—are based on actual events, yet the fictionalized form in which she renders them reveals deeper mysteries than the intricate procedures of the courts in each work are able to resolve. The political and spiritual aspects of Hogan's narratives are inextricably connected with the process of individuation and self-perception of the main characters. *Power* has been defined as a "bildungsroman" by *Bloomsbury Review*, a critique of apocalyptic narrative" (Hardin 135), and "auto-history in the face of Amer-European hetero-history" (Weaver 163). I will argue that the book is a borderland text and an example of ceremonial literature that "contains an entire ecosystem, what is now called a textbook of knowledge" (Hogan, quoted in Cook 12). The rediscovery of the mystery of being, the restoration of the severed ties between the self and a larger and more encompassing concept of the "other," is the basic policy that the author advocates to stop the collision course modern history has taken toward the Earth and its marginalized peoples.

Nevertheless, despite Hogan's message of cosmic healing, *Power* ultimately perpetuates the binary thinking of Western epistemology by using a rhetoric of good versus evil, Native versus Christian. The validation of the ancient stories in the modern time of historical progress leads inevitably to a juxtaposition of cultural values in which Christianity is perceived as the ideology of colonization, which justifies racism and exploitation both of land and people. The "extensive critique of Christianity" in *Power* has been noted by many scholars (Hardin 148), and more particularly by Michael Hardin, who discusses Hogan's criticism of apocalyptic narrative and ultimately concludes that, although she uses Christlike characteristics for her main characters, Hogan does not validate the Christian myth. In my reading of those seemingly competing theological systems, I will suggest that, in spite of Hogan's criticism of Christianity in an attempt to attribute a sense of "exclusiveness" and romantic aura to Native American spirituality, ultimately she cannot escape the dynamic symbiosis between cultural epistemologies and symbolism in the constructions of the sacred and produces a highly hybridized borderland text.

The ceremonial is often the realm of the sacred, and every initiated human being becomes part of the cosmic cycle of life. The everyday life of such a person is a reenactment of different aspects of the sacred that imply a participation in a larger and timeless mystery of being, as opposed to modern perception of the individual as a distinct, autonomous self, defined by linear time and collapsed space. In the novel the incursion of fragmentary, historical time is experienced as a desecration of cyclic ritual time, a rupture that also distorts the perspective of the old stories. They need to be "updated" to meet the challenges of a traditional community living in a modern world. When Ama, the protagonist's mentor figure in *Power*, says, "the old ways are not enough to get us through this time" (23), she expresses her belief that an ancient story has to be rewritten in such a way as to reassert its validity in relation to the new historical context. As I will show later, with her ritualistic killing of the Florida panther, Ama writes the modern counterpart of an ancient myth, an act that is a leap both of faith and of imagination.

I will address the issue of rewriting ancient myths also by discussing the functions of Christian spirituality in another marginalized, non-Western culture, in this case Bulgarian culture. There are striking similarities between the history and the fate of the Bulgarian people and that of Native peoples. The Bulgarians were under Ottoman domination for nearly five hundred years, as long as Native American people have been resisting the encroachments of a dominant, aggressive culture. The expansion of the Ottoman Empire and the conquest of the Balkans at the end of the fourteenth century were motivated and legitimized by the calling of Islam in the same way that the conquering of the New World was legitimized by the Pilgrims' claim for covenant with Christ. In both cases the profane, the undiscerning and self-serving interpretation of the religious message, masquerades as the sacred, thus discrediting the very nature of spirituality and justifying the politics of dominance and control. The first centuries of the conquest of the Balkans saw assimilation policies enforced by conversions and massacres in which conversion was resisted. The Bulgarians have been repeatedly imaged and imagined as semi-barbarous Christians of the East or exotic primitive people and are at present "being discovered" by the West. They have survived and preserved their national identity by resorting to the same strategies as the Taiga people in Hogan's novel have done—sustaining and reliving the memory of their sacred beginnings as the first Christian Slav people in Europe, with an alphabet and culture of their own, in the face of a formidable and relentless Muslim colonizer. In both cultures spirituality has been the most effective tool for preserving national and individual identity. Yet, with the lifting of the ban on religion after 1989, many Bulgarians have chosen to define themselves not as Orthodox but as Pentecostal, Methodist, Lutheran, Buddhist, among other, in the same way in which some American Indians have chosen to identify themselves as Native Christians. Is this good or bad? Does it make them less Bulgarian or less native Indian? Hardly so. In a complex world of increasingly intersecting destinies, cross-cultural communities and interreligious dialogue, the paradigm good/bad, or inferior/superior, is deeply simplistic and misleading.

The Bulgarian sense of national identity and history is as closely connected to the land as it is for the Native people. In the preface to their anthology of Bulgarian oral and literary tradition, The Balkan Range, John Colombo and Nikola Rousanoff explain their choice of title in this way: "The Balkan Range has been the cradle, the hearth, and the fortress of the Bulgarian people. . . . Take away the Balkan Range from the history of these people and there will be nothing left—no folk, no lore, no literature" (11). The Balkan Mountains for Bulgarian people, then, are what the Black Hills, for example, are for the Sioux people or the Florida semi-wilderness is for the Taiga community in *Power*.

Significantly, the first line of the Bulgarian national hymn evokes the Balkan Range and goes on to catalogue the beauties of the land and to claim the indissoluble link between its majesty and graciousness and Bulgarian national destiny:

> Proudly rise the Balkan peaks
> At their feet Blue Danube flows;
> Over Thrace the sun is shining,
> Pirin looms in purple glow.

These examples clearly show that not all Christian nations look at the environment as a commodity, a major point Hogan makes in her novel. As the first epigraph at the beginning of my discussion suggests, the author is aware of the existence of parallels between Native American traditions and those of other cultures in terms of the common strategies they use to resist dominant cultures. Norma Wilson argues that in the poem "Folksong" Hogan "parallels the experience of the Latvians, whose nation was controlled by the Soviet Union, to that of the Chickasaw, controlled by the U.S. government since the early 19th c." (93). Yet the dominant ideology that former socialistic countries such as Latvia had to resist was atheistic Communism in which there was no connection between institutionalized Christianity and power, as was the case with the conquest of the Americas. My argument is that the biblical texts do not necessarily preach subjugation and exploitation of nature, as Hogan seems to imply in *Power*, given that there are clear examples in them of man's obligation to nature as a caretaker and the perception of nature as God's sacred creation.[2] Neither do they preach colonization but state clearly, "Thou shall not oppress a stranger / for strangers you were in Egypt" (Exodus 23:9). The specific practices of an imperialist, money-oriented, and acquisitive society, in which politics and morality have parted company, should not be confused with the deeply spiritual and inclusive messages of the Bible.

In *Power* Hogan connects in a most explicit way the idea of historic landscape that goes beyond the boundaries of a specific locale to the protagonist's fashioning of identity in the borderland spaces between two cultures. By evoking the landscape as a "storied land" (Fisher-Worth, quoted in Cook 53), imbued with sacred wisdom, the sixteen-year-old protagonist, Omishto, enters into a dialogue with the pragmatic discourse of the dominant culture that has formed her as a young person. This is the starting point of her journey of self-discovery and search for a community in which narrativity, identity, and politics become one. As the novel opens, Omishto is in her boat, near Alma's cabin, on the reservation of the Taiga people, and feels that "the earth was bleeding. . . . It's as if I am curled inside the opening leaf in this boat covered with algae, as if I am just beginning to live" (1). In this fetus-like position the girl seems to be experiencing the beginning of life in the womb. The violent rainstorm that uproots trees and kills animals represents symbolically the painful process of being (re)born, for it is during the storm that Omishto's initiatory journey with Ama takes place. After the rainstorm subsides, the protagonist sees her dress hanging from a tree and realizes that she is naked, as if she has just been baptized by nature. The motif of rebirth is reinforced by the pervasive water symbolism, the primary element in which all life begins. This makes the narrator kin to all creation.

On another level the devastating hurricane evokes on a smaller scale the drama of the Old Testament flood. In "Standing Naked before the Storm" Hardin contrasts the protagonist's interpretation of the storm as a "regenerative force" with her Christianized mother's view of it as "a destructive, punishing force" (145). It seems to me somewhat glib to claim that "within an apocalyptic structure there is no renewal, only devastation and removal" (150). The biblical flood is a regenerative force that restores a harmonious and moral world in the place of a fallen and dissolute one, in the same way in which the hurricane in the novel blows the Taiga people into existence. As Omishto speculates, in Taiga mythology: "We were blown together by a storm in the first place. It was all created out of storms" (43). Similarly, in the Book of Revelations John sees "a new heaven and a new Earth" (21:1), in which "there shall be no more death, neither sorrow, nor crying, neither shall there be any more pain" (21:4, 5). In both Hogan's novel and the biblical account a new earth must be created because the first one has been destroyed by wars and calamities that humans inflicted upon themselves and upon the earth. It is human beings' failure to comply with the moral and practical laws that God has laid out that brings total devastation, not a wrathful God who visits destruction upon his people. There is clearly an ecological consciousness in the biblical texts. Such archetypal examples, as the flood in *Power*, highlight the pervasive syncretism in the construction of the sacred rather than distinctly discernible and conflicting traditions for its conceptualization.

Although Hogan sets up a binary between Native and Christian spirituality and privileges the first as exceptional and the "more spiritual," ultimately the logic of her narrative defies such a separatist ethos, for both beliefs converge linguistically and conceptually in Omishto's consciousness and speech. Hardin recognizes the fact that, despite the critique of Christianity in *Power*, Ama and Omishto find themselves "within events evocative of those Christ supposedly experienced," yet he still sees the two systems only as competing and conflicting. "I am not suggesting," the author goes on, "that Hogan is validating the Christian myth, merely that she is appropriating some of Christ's more mythic, archetypal qualities" (148). I perceive two problems with this kind of reasoning because of Hardin's "selective appropriation" and his discrimination between "more" and "less" mythic and archetypal aspects of Christ. Christ is the absolute value, both the myth and the archetype. In all cultures the sacred, conceptualized as perfection itself, does not allow for any relativism, binarism, for more or less of the sacred. If we accept Hardin's principle of selective appropriation, then we must dismiss Hogan/Omishto's criticism of mainstream environmentalists' appropriation of native beliefs when she complains that "they are taking up our beliefs and judging us" (177). My second point is that the Christlike characteristics in Omishto's narrative cannot be avoided, for they are deeply ingrained in her consciousness. This is a symbolic language she has known, and, although she is acquiring new knowledge and a new symbolical order for making sense of things, this first language still functions as a valid code for interpretation. In trying to decipher the meaning of present and past events, of symbolic and ritualistic acts, Omishto is code switching all the time, borrowing freely both from Christian and Native American traditions.[3]

From the very beginning of her narrative Omishto sees her life story as an identity story and clearly defines the conflicting forces that try to claim her. "I am my sister's project," the girl confides, "but I do not want to look pretty in the house with my mother and stepfather looking at me, his eyes always looking too much in places they do not belong." The open spaces are perceived as dangerous by the civilized mind: "My mom says it's not good to sleep in my boat . . . but it is the safest place there is, surrounded all around by water. It's like I am a continent, a whole continent," the protagonist reasons (7). Home and civilization imply confinement and stunted development, while Ama's house, which is perceived as a natural extension of the semi-wilderness, affords growth and opening up of the self to include the outside world. The wild, with its contiguity to the woods and the unseen, allows Omishto to perceive it as boundless and felicitous.

The protagonist's soulful experience of the wild affords an immersion into the mystical and the visionary, yet there is a price to pay for the return to the sacred totality. She has to go through the painful drama of liminality, the transitional stage from which the individual emerges with a new identity and, depending on this identity, is either reintegrated into society with a new status, is trapped by it, or leaves it entirely. During this initiation rite the adolescents have to make hard choices, and, as I suggest on another occasion, they "have to be placed in isolation, in order to perceive themselves as subjects, and engage actively in self-fashioning" (Krasteva 160). Liminality enables the drama of change in the experience of individuation, the transition from innocence to maturity, and is bracketed, as in *Power*, by both time and space.[4] Omishto becomes an unwitting accomplice to Ama's cunning tracking of a Florida panther, a sacred animal for the Taiga people and an endangered species for the white people. As soon as she realizes that Ama is hunting the sacred cat, everything changes; the whole landscape comes to life, "as if space has eyes and ears. . . . What will happen has been in the air all along, and in Ama's face. . . . She hears something speaking to her, calling, and I hear nothing, but I go with her, as if I have no choice." As she is entering the realm of the sacred, Omishto is terrified by the unknown: "I want to split in two," she confesses, "so part of me can turn back, can go home to where there are radios and schoolbooks, full of knowledge, that will begin my life, but there is no turning back" (58). These reflections illustrate the heroine's continuous awareness of having two lives, of living in two worlds—the one in which all the choices about who she is and how she is supposed to live have already been made for her and a whole new, unfathomable, mysterious world that exists only in the stories and where, if she enters it, she will acquire the kind of knowledge that will help her take possession of her life, for, ultimately, we are who we are on the basis of the choices we make or fail to make.

The network of relationships between the human and the natural world, between the past, present, and future, in *Power* confirms the possibility of the self's being defined not by boundaries and divisions but by a quest for community and wholeness. For Native people nature and the animal world are not only essential to survival but are characterized in kinship terms and through the ritual of caretaking. More than simply a sense of place, this view of "creation as kin" implies the idea of permeable borders and dissolution of borders. Seeing landscape as another self, rather than as other, allows it to function as a participant in the dialogue by which meanings are constructed. This ideal of interdependence is embodied also by Christ, for he blurs all dualities that man has set up, between man and woman, white and colored, Jew and gentile, rich and poor. Significantly, the New Testament establishes a radical shift from the paradigm of conquest in the Old Testament to the paradigm of home, in which home is infinity and oneness with the universe, a community of all creation. Every Christian contains in himself the macrocosm by becoming the temple of the living Christ on earth. This temple is a miniature model of the cosmic home. "There are many dwelling places in my Father's house," Christ assures his disciples, "otherwise, should I have said to you I was going away to prepare a home for you" (John 14:2). If some Christians choose to privilege the Old Testament paradigm of conquest and domination to the New Testament paradigm of home and the ritual of caretaking, then they have not made the transition to true Christianity. A radically new quest for the cosmic Christ, on the other hand, has become the hallmark of a Native Christian discourse that, in James Treat's words, "brings a fresh new perspective to the global liberation theology movement" (1). Rather than seeing "Native" and "Christian" identities as competing and mutually exclusive, most native Christian writers share Charles Eastman's conviction "that there is no such thing as 'Christian civilization.'" "I believe," Eastman posits, "that Christianity and modern civilization are opposed and irreconcilable, and that the spirit of Christianity and of our ancient religion is essentially the same" (quoted in Treat 6).[5] Cross-cultural mediation and translation, then, is the paradigm that defines this new theology.

Significantly, in the paradigm of home as the world, whether it is in the Christian tradition or in Native American stories, the blurring of boundaries is complete. As Omishto watches the drama between Ama and the cat unfold, she realizes that it is "as if the panther is a place and it holds her, as if they've always known and lived inside one another. "You've killed yourself Ama," the girl cries out. "I know it. Don't I just know it" (67), Ama retorts, for she believes "skin was never a boundary to be kept or held to; there are no limits between one thing and another, one time and another" (188). In healing ceremonies the scratch from a panther's paws works miraculous recoveries. When Omishto's mother is left in the wilderness by her new husband to die, it is a wolf that shows her the way home and to safety. This anthropomorphism of nature, miraculous recoveries, and mystic exchanges with the supernatural can be encountered also in the Bulgarian literary tradition.

Stories about animals saving and taking care of people abound in Bulgarian folklore. There are different variants of the paradigmatic story of a wolf transmitting to people the supernatural powers of the wild, which they use to protect their people from the enemy. The most striking variant of this story appears in an epic poem written by Bulgaria's best-known poet of all time, Christo Botev. The eulogy he wrote in 1876 for a leader of an insurgent band (*haiduks*) is the eulogy that Bulgaria sings for all who have sacrificed their lives for their motherland, including the poet himself. The dying hero is drenched in blood," yet he does not die, for he "is mourned / by earth and sky, by beast and land," and the Balkan Range echoes with the songs that minstrels sing about him:

> An eagle makes his shade by day,
> A wolf, it meekly licks his wound;
> Above a falcon, hero's bird
> The hero like a brother treats.
> (Colombo 77)

The poet translates the hidden responses from the natural world to his knowing audience through visual evocation of the silent language of nature and of the mysterious but familiar agents of the unseen. The sacred narrative is evoked by the totemic presence of the wolf, the falcon, and the eagle. As the day draws to a close, the whole world stands at attention, and the universe opens its portals to receive the spirit of the dying hero:

> The evening comes, the moon appears,
> The stars light up the heaven's vault;
> The forest rustles, breeze blows,
> The Balkan Range sings haiduks' song.
> (Colombo 77)

In this intimate, interactive setting, the forest sprites, which are always female, perform the ceremony of the last rites. Their white bridal attire implies also the rite of celestial marriage, elevating the young hero into mythic proportions, welcoming him into an eternal cosmic embrace. The poet uses ritualized language that raises the physical and the profane into the sacred and the immortal and restores forgotten relationships from when people were lower only than angels. At this moment the dying hero is identified with Christian sacrifice, the absolute value, the sun in the Bulgarian cosmos, for every fighter for Bulgaria's freedom takes his vow of loyalty on a pistol and a dagger, placed upon a Bible. As the hero dies and his blood soaks into the earth, he returns to his people in the form of yet another wondrous myth, restoring and renewing their belief in the validity and power of the ancient stories and sustaining the vision of their national destiny. In the poem the natural and the ceremonial become the main venues to spirituality. The mysterious is transmitted to us by what Hogan calls "a form of sacred reason . . . linked to the forces of nature" (Dwelling 19) and made available to us through the spiritual power of the storyteller.

Like the dying hero in Botev's poem, Ama is immortalized in the myth that Omishto invents about her when she tries to imagine where Ama might have gone after being exiled for four years by the Taiga people for failing to give them the hide of the animal: "Maybe she laid herself down on the ground and reached into clay," the girl reasons, "until she sank into the mud and earth and closed her eyes in the shining clay and stopped her own breath until there would be another time four years from now, when once again she could surface" (227). This new story transforms Ama into a cyclic mysterious force of renewal in the complex order of nature. Omishto's reading of the killing of the panther, on the other hand, tells of a higher truth than the partial truths that the two courts establish—the truth that all visionaries, while seemingly breaking tradition with their acts of renewal and redemption, are actually working within the tradition by extending the range of the sacred to include the present moment. Ama sees what others fail to see, that the degeneration of the godlike Sisa, the paradigmatic Panther Woman, into the worn-away, sick, and nearly destroyed cat, parallels the fate of the Taiga people. She wants to break the vicious cycle before they realize the truth and lose hope. The redeemer figures in all sacred stories are almost always misunderstood, exiled, or killed by their own people. Yet, through their sacred sacrifice, the visionaries restore the lost connection with the spiritual realm and make possible the next cycle of renewal.

After Ama's banishment, Omishto casts her fate with that of the Taiga community and begins to dream Ama's dreams about the golden cat. At Ama's place the girl is surprised by a beautiful panther: "Standing still looking back at me, the golden cat, large and with a tawny fur loose and healthy, lean-muscled. I do not move . . . then I say 'I mean no harm, Aunt, Grandmother'" (222). The girl welcomes the cat as the one Ama killed, "returned fully grown and beautiful, or the one that was born alongside me at my beginning" (233). The completion of her search for self and community could be read as the fulfillment of the old story that Ama enacted but also as another story in which "Panther Woman went back into the black trees and returned finally, with magic words which she withheld until the time the world teetered on the brink of death and then she spoke them" (231). By claiming Sisa, the godlike cat, as her relative, Omishto is transformed into the Panther Woman, who speaks the magic words of renewal. This story and the one the girl invents about Ama's exile become different stages of the modern counterpart of the myth of the Panther Woman in which Ama and Omishto merge into one personality in a sacred kinship. They are both Panther Woman come back to life.

The protagonist exults in her new freedom, in the final breaking up of boundaries. "Me, I am a dissolved person, like salt in water," she declares, "at the end of the road is a different story. On the little patch of land behind the swamp, they are still human. The world they live in is still alive" (231). Although Omishto repeatedly sees Christian beliefs and symbols as misleading and tries to distance herself from them, even when she strives to define a new identity, she uses Christian metaphors. "The salt in water" simile, evoking Lot's wife, is an example of Freud's theory of the return of the repressed. Omishto's struggle to articulate a sense of self illustrates the extent to which European heritage has become part of her hybrid identity through the symbiosis between Judeo-Christian and Native American traditions.

On the other hand, to set up Christian and Native mythologies as members in a binary relationship, and not see them as invariants in a larger and more encompassing symbolic order, would mean to treat them as closed and complete systems, as exotic museum pieces, rather than as living, "open-ended series of connections" (Holquist 10), in what Bakhtin defines as an "open unity" (quoted in Holquist x). It is this romantic response to Native American cultures that seems to make Hogan attractive to "new age" environmental spiritualists. My interpretation of the ways in which Christian and Native traditions encounter and reciprocate with each other confirms Bakhtin's theory that "a meaning only reveals its depth once it has encountered or come into a contact with another, foreign meaning" (*Speech Genres* 7). As links in an infinite chain of meanings, these cultures are "renewed again, and again, as though [they] were being reborn. . . . Each retains its own meaning and *open* totality, but they are mutually enriched" (quoted in Holquist ix). Any local system, then, is part of a larger whole and, like the individual human being, is alive and capable of renewal and rebirth once it comes into a contact with another open-ended and unfinished entity.

At the end of Omishto's initiation journey through the "storied earth and the storied lives" of her ancestors, the heroine emerges from her marginality and uncertainty to a self-defining position as a Taiga person and produces an auto-translation and an alternative history in the face of Euro-American history. In the same way the Bulgarian ceremonial literature and literary works that borrow from it evoke the memories of a dismembered colonial past in order to put together a broken world of trauma and loss and move beyond the sense of victimhood. Not surprisingly, after centuries of slavery Bulgaria's longing for freedom was awakened by a highly spiritual person, Vassil Levski, a humble monk, reverently called "the Deacon" and "the Apostle of Freedom," who, in the words of the colossus of modern Bulgarian literature Ivan Vasov, "had been sent by providence, leading a host of apostles and martyrs for freedom, to wake up the people, to challenge history, to create the future" (quoted in Colombo 82). Levski symbolizes everything that Bulgarians hold sacred and dear; he is the Golgotha of Bulgaria's suffering and resurrection. And, again, it was Christo Botev who wrote an elegy for his death on the gallows, "The Hanging of Vassil Levski," which to all purposes has become another sacred story.[6]

In the years of Communism, when socialist realism was the norm for artistic expression, anything smacking of abstractionism, modernism, avant-gardism, postmodernism, and the like was denounced as decadent Western art. Instead of following in the steps of Western traditions and risking being denounced on similar grounds, many writers resorted to the magic realism of Bulgarian folklore, thus resisting both Communist dogma in art and keeping the people's national identity alive. Most typical examples of such resistance are the works of the world-famous storyteller Yordan Radichkov. His plays and novels explore the clash between peasant cultures and modernity. They are populated by eccentric characters to whom extraordinary things happen in a drama of mystery and suspense, as, for example, in the play *January*. The inhabitants of the inn argue about the meanings of boggart, vampire, goblin, ghostie, woodpecker, and yuckle. They bemoan the disappearance of the supernatural beings, for, as one of them laments, "where would you find boggarts in the age of technology?" (Radichkov 92). Eventually, the mystery of the disappearing wolf hunters is resolved in a letter, sent by a person who died a year ago, but, because a cat jumped over his coffin, he became a boggart and is running all kinds of earthly chores. It is not difficult to recognize Gerald Vizenor's strategy of "tricksterish deconstruction" in such dramatic situations (quoted in Pulitano 151). The presence of the supernatural, legitimized by its existence in the national imaginary, is a thinly veiled subversion of the constraining ideological norms of socialist realism at the same time that it posits alternatives to socialist reality.

As I read *Power*, I cannot help searching for those yet not fully recognized systems of spiritual wisdom in my own culture that have kept me always on the alert, always questioning and looking for hidden meanings. It is the pervasive syncretism of Native and Christian worldviews in borderland texts, such as *Power*, that makes discovering unexpected semantic depths in both cultures legitimate for a reader like me. I am not a Western reader, although, as an American Studies person, I am steeped in Western theory; I am not an "East European" reader either, for there is hardly any such category. The position from which I speak and interpret texts is the position of a crossroads at which each perspective is highly destabilized as it enters into a dialogue with the others it encounters. The inhabitants of such hybrid cultural locations are both outsiders and insiders; they exist in a typical condition of frontier liminality in which new meanings are constructed through the mode of reciprocity, as we "explore new ways of opening up rather than closing down ideas in language" (Pulitano 101). I hope that in my interpretations of different epistemological traditions from this highly dynamic position, I am learning to apply what Louis Owens calls "crosscultural reading" (112), a creative understanding that builds bridges between cultures and allows us all to participate in healing ceremonies, working together for transformative changes of renewal.

Notes

1. Mainstream American writers who engage with environmental issues, such as John Cheever, Don DeLillo, and John Updike, reflect a "toxic consciousness" that sees America as a wasteland, while writers such as Linda Hogan, Leslie Marmon Silko, Alice Walker, Ofelia Zepeda, and Gary Snyder form the more politically oriented discourse of "environmental justice," which establishes a connection between race, the location of hazardous waste, and environmental racism (Adamson 56).

2. For example: "And six years thou shall sow thy land, / and shall gather in the fruit thereof: / But the seventh year thou shall let it rest and lie still; that the poor of thy people may eat: and what they leave the beasts of the field shall eat. In like manner thou shall deal with the vineyard, and with thy olive yard" (Exodus 23:10–11). "Behold the fowls in the air, for they sow not, neither do they reap, no gather into barns, yet your heavenly Father feedeth them. . . . / Consider the lilies in the field, how they grow; they toil not, neither do they spin, / and yet, even Solomon in all his glory was not arrayed like one of these" (Matthew 6:26, 28–29). God's longest speech in the Bible, in the Book of Job, is another impressive example of ecological thinking.

3. Omishto's mother, for example, is a typical marginal figure of the bor-

der. Although the protagonist denounces her as a mentor because, as a convert to Christianity, she "has given herself to a distant God" (187), is "of a split mind," and "want[s] to pass as white," ultimately the girl concludes that "she still believes in the power and owner of breath, Oni, but by another name . . . my mother, I know, is one of us" (188). This final acceptance of the mother is also recognition of the syncretism of the sacred and, in fact, a validation of the Christian myth. In a personal, informal conversation at the Native American Literature Symposium at the Soaring Eagle Casino in Mt. Pleasant, Michigan (April 6–8, 2006), Linda Hogan said she considers Native spirituality of higher value "because it is a 'knowledge system,' whereas Christianity is a 'belief system.'" Yet there are many Christians who have acquired knowledge through a personal relationship with God. The interpretation seems to rest on the definition of knowledge.

4. I am fully aware of the current debates about whether the modalities and terminology of Western cultural theory are adequate for the interpretation of American Indian texts. My belief is that, because American Indian writers use narrative structures that are clearly recognizable not only in Western but in many other cultures (as, for instance, the initiation story) as well as all kinds of symbiosis of symbols, images, and linguistic strategies, the recourse to such terminology is justified. See Pulitano.

5. Native Christians today face a false dilemma: Native or Christian? Greeks and other gentile nations encountered the same issue when at the dawn of Christianity Paul preached the Gospel to them. Yet none of those nations seemed to have had a problem with preserving its cultural identity. There is, however, a significant difference: the Greeks and the other nations at that time made the choice freely, when Christians were persecuted and Christianity was practiced in its purest form, and not as an ideology of conquest or state policy. But the difference is one of context, not of essence. James Treat's anthology *Native and Christian* and his most recent collection of essays, *Writing the Cross Culture*, are the most impressive and comprehensive collections of texts that, in Treat's words, document "the emergence of a significant new collective voice on the North American religious landscape" (*Native and Christian* 1).

6. There are interesting similarities between Levski's life and myth and that of Crazy Horse. Both were visionaries, spiritual leaders, ideologists of national resistance, and superb strategists. Both were betrayed and died at the same age. Their graves are unknown. Both occupy the highest place in the

hierarchy of the sacred within their respective cultures. For lack of space, I cannot further explore this fascinating parallel here.

Works Cited

Adamson, Joni. *American Indian Literature, Environmental Justice, and Ecocriticism: The Middle Place.* Tucson: University of Arizona Press, 2001.

Bakhtin, M. M. *Speech Genres and Other Late Essays.* Ed. Caryl Emerson and Michael Holquist. Trans. Vern W. McGee. Austin: University of Texas Press, 1986.

Colombo, John Robert, and Nicola Roussanoff, eds. *The Balkan Range: A Bulgarian Reader.* Toronto: Hounslow Press, 1976.

Cook, Barbara, ed. *From the Center of Tradition: Critical Perspectives on Linda Hogan.* Boulder: University Press of Colorado, 2003.

Fisher-Wirth, Ann. "Storied Earth, Storied Lives." In *Ecofeminism: Women, Culture, Nature.* Ed. Karen J. Warren. Bloomington: Indiana University Press, 1997. 53–66.

Hardin, Michael. "Standing Naked before the Storm." In *From the Center of Tradition: Critical Perspectives on Linda Hogan.* Ed. Barbara J. Cook. Boulder: University Press of Colorado, 2003. 135–55.

Hogan, Linda. *Dwellings: A Spiritual History of the Living World.* New York: W. W. Norton, 1995.

———. *Power.* New York: W. W. Norton, 1998.

Holquist, Michael. Introduction to *Speech Genres and Other Essays.* Ed. Karl Emerson and Michael Holquist. Austin: University of Texas Press, 1986. Ix–xxiii.

John Paul II, Pope. "Celebration of the Word." Address at the Martyr's Shrine, Huronia, September 15, 1985, www.wyandot.org/missions/pope.htm.

Krasteva, Yonka. *The West and the American Dream: Studies in Twentieth Century American Literature.* Sofia: Paradigma, 2000.

Pulitano, Elvira. *Toward a Native American Critical Theory.* Lincoln: University of Nebraska Press, 2003.

Radichkov, Yordan. "January." In *Contemporary Bulgarian Plays.* Ed. Anna Karabinska and Josepha Jacobson. Trans. Judith Sprostanova. London: Tantalus Books, 2002. 61–126.

Treat, James, ed. *Native and Christian: Indigenous Voices on Religious Identity in the United States and Canada*. 2nd ed. 1996. Reprint. New York: Routledge, 2006.

———, ed. *Writing the Cross Culture: Native Fiction on the White Man's Religion*. Colorado: Fulcrum Publishing, 2006.

Weaver, Janice. *That the People Might Live: Native American Literatures and Native American Community*. New York: Oxford University Press, 1997.

Wilson, Norma C. *The Nature of Native American Poetry*. Albuquerque: University of New Mexico Press, 2001.

12 Double Translation

James Welch's *Heartsong of Charging Elk*

1

In a well-known essay William Bevis put forward a theory of Native American literature by juxtaposing Western and Native American plot structures. "American whites," he observed, "keep leaving home" in search of better opportunities "in a newer land" (581). These (gendered) stories typically portray an individual striving for success, trying to stand up to the test of unforeseen hardships and conflicts by keeping true to himself. The existential pathos of living in a hostile world is only slightly modified by the hero's ability to build relationships with others; as Bevis notes, romantic love typically serves as an antidote to isolation, as it provides a mode of recognition without which individual identity would be adrift in the changing contexts of a world continually in the making. In such canonical self-representations of America the implied "philosophy for a new, permanently unsettled rhythm of creation and destruction" celebrates ongoing transformation and resists the authority of the given (Fisher 3). From the point of view of American mainstream culture, loyalty to an ethnic group must therefore be regarded as a transitional phenomenon, as Philip Fisher argues:

> Mobility includes the right to go somewhere else and to be someone else, the right to start over, the option that the young above all have to make what is called "a fresh start." It also includes the right of children on their way to adulthood to select from, discard,

forget, and create their own emphasis within the many things inherited from parents as "their natal identity." . . . Mobility is spatial and temporal. It governs difference of place as well as the right to renew, discard, and invent categories of life and experience. (171)

In contrast, as Bevis showed persuasively, Native American novels construct a different plot: the hero comes home. His return typically goes hand in hand with a reevaluation of tribal spirituality and ethics. While this may include a redefinition of tradition and an invention of new modes of individual self-expression, the emphasis of the text usually lies on a representation of Native American identity as fundamentally different from hegemonic American culture. By reaffirming tribal law as a binding and guiding force for the individual, restating a collective allegiance to a tribal homeland, and appealing to the past as the foundation of individual and cultural being, Native American novels present an alternative to individualism. Based on circular structures, the pattern of return and reintegration articulates a refusal of the American Dream. As Bevis poignantly summarizes his argument, "Tribal reality is profoundly conservative; 'progress' and 'a fresh start' are not *native* to America" (587).

Read in this light, James Welch's last novel, *The Heartsong of Charging Elk* (2000), seems a marked departure from the Native American literary tradition and from the author's earlier work. The hero leaves home. He goes to Europe, choosing a life in exile over a return to the reservation. While he never stops yearning for home, he makes a decision to stay in France because he does not want to leave his French wife and his unborn child, opting for an unknown future in an alien country whose customs he shares only in a superficial fashion and to whose traditions he never develops an allegiance; in time he becomes a French citizen without ever claiming membership in French culture. This plot summary suggests an adoption of a white American pattern of individual self-fashioning and a concurrent dissolution of Native American identity. And, indeed, several Native American critics denigrated the novel as a corroboration of the theory of the "Vanishing Indian" (Cook-Lynn, quoted in Ruoff

195). But the historical setting of the novel—Charging Elk leaves the New for the Old World at the turn of the nineteenth century; that is, the story takes place at the climax of European immigration to the United States—should alert us right from the start that Welch's objectives are reversals of a very particular kind. As I will try to show, the notion of "homing in" is articulated perhaps ever more forcefully in a complex rewriting of the temporal and spatial trajectory of the American way of life. Welch translates a Native American existential condition into the structural framework of the Euro-American bildungsroman, but, in doing so, he translates the latter's abstract plot of individual freedom and self-realization into a thickly woven tapestry of embodied and unembodied voices that sustain a tribal context for him.

Cultural translation is a practice regularly performed by Native American literature. Bevis's argument rests on it: if the plot patterns of the novels he writes about invoke tribal storytelling and their politics may come close to advocating cultural separatism, it is nevertheless obvious that the texts are produced at a specific conjunction with American mainstream culture; the transformation of orality into writing and the adaptation of English as the medium of expression testify to the historical pervasiveness of colonial technologies of power. In fact, all practices of signification by Native American literature operate in the discursive field of interculturality. The resulting translational dynamics proceed in two directions simultaneously, however, and make the literary text into a site of cultural contention as far as notions of a "source" and "target" culture are concerned.[1] In The Heartsong of Charging Elk Welch makes use of a double translation and foregrounds it as a textual strategy—not only in order to highlight the novel's design of cultural dialogism but also to avoid being misread as advocating assimilation. While Welch's protagonist lives an isolated life in Europe, Charging Elk does not seek better opportunities for himself. Nor does Welch's novel give credit to the theory of the Vanishing Indian; composing Charging Elk's "heartsong," not his death song, the author clearly wishes to indicate Charging Elk's integrity and resilience in spite of his life in Europe. With decades spent in France, the most profound layers of Charging Elk's subjectivity consist of his unbroken commitment to Lakota cultural tradition and spirituality and his sense of belonging to a Lakota homeland. It is in constant reference to a Lakota cultural semantics that Charging Elk reads the European world around him.

In this way the novel affirms the continuity of Native American tradition in spite of colonial domination and dispersal and extends it beyond (Native) American space and place. But, while this extension is in and by itself a powerful gesture of cultural self-affirmation, it is also a statement of mourning and loss. The novel takes place in the aftermath of the conquest of Lakota territory. "Home" is irretrievably located in the past, for the expatriate Charging Elk just as for any Lakota; Pine Ridge reservation is a place of expulsion and oppression, from which Charging Elk tried to stay away even before he went to Europe. Like most Native American writers and scholars, Welch professes his commitment to a culture prior to conquest. But, in contrast to his celebrated earlier novel *Fools Crow*, in his final novel the recuperation of the past is not possible (cf. Owens; and Krupat). Rather, the past is a figure of memory and of profound longing.

What makes the novel unique as a Native American text is not the portrayal of intercultural encounters but the interdiscursive complexity brought about by an imaginative condensation of and response to various histories of transatlantic travel. In the dominant American cultural lexicon, moving to Europe is either linked to an immigrant's return (and hence to a failure of the project of a fresh start) or, with the expatriate writers, to a gesture of repudiation in favor of a European cultural climate more favorable to artists. For African Americans a move to Europe, and to France in particular, is typically inscribed in the complex contact zones of the black Atlantic and signifies a diasporic black culture in the West. From a European perspective *The Heartsong of Charging Elk* must be linked to relativist critiques of civilization that use the other in order to question European notions of cultural supremacy.

All these contexts help to assess the multilayered provocations of Welch's text. By shaping his novel as a bildungsroman, as an engagement with Western constructions of Indians, as an intertextual meditation on different minority cultures in the West, and as an allegory of contemporary Native American identity, Welch constructs his protagonist both as an individual and as a discursive figure of speech, forcing readers to observe the text from several vantage points. A hegemonic construction of reality is challenged by a demonstration of the incompatibility of different cultural worldviews. Just as the condensation of different plot patterns, the alternation between different representational modes, and the allusion to other minority histories require both Native and non-Native readers constantly to recontextualize the narrative construction of *The Heartsong of Charging Elk*.

2

Bevis argued that in Welch's earlier novel *The Death of Jim Loney* the tension between the white and the Indian plots makes up the conflict of the novel (616), and this is true for *Charging Elk* as well. The markedly different endings of both texts—Jim Loney dies violently and alone, while Charging Elk lives with his wife and unborn child—signal a new concept of Native American "survivance," to use Vizenor's term.

At the beginning of the novel Welch shows the eminent pressure of assimilation his protagonist has to contend with on the reservation and then presents a unique chronicle of experiences and choices that build up to a nuanced vision of Native agency in a colonial context. Charging Elk is a Lakota youth whose cultural identity is based on an identification with Crazy Horse's heroic resistance against the *wasichus*. His trip to Europe as a member of Buffalo Bill's Wild West Show turns into a nightmare once he falls sick and is left behind in Marseille, where he becomes the object of various institutions (the hospital, the prison, the American consulate, the press, Catholic charity) and is forced to submit to their respective disciplining practices.[2] But Charging Elk is not broken by these experiences. His ability to live in the present and accept it as a given and simultaneously hold on to his memories and to the tribal religious universe allows him to survive decades of obligatory assimilation without losing his dignity and sense of self.

As a boy, Charging Elk takes part in the Battle of the Little Big Horn. When the Oglalas finally surrender and move to the reservation, he is forced to attend reservation school. But he leaves his family and flees from the reservation to join a small group of Indian men who live the solitary lives of outcasts, roaming a territory that once was the Oglalas' home but is now controlled by the U.S. military, exploited by miners, and settled by farmers. While Charging Elk's life at the Stronghold allows for limited self-determination and a continued practice of tribal religion, it does not offer a chance to have a family and raise children. With the continuous encroachment of white settlers, this life is a doomed anachronism. After some years the group of refugees dissolves. Faced with the fate of his father, who had once held a respected position in the tribe but is now reduced to "sitting idly in his little shack, drinking the black medicine and sometimes telling the holy beads" (17), Charging Elk decides to join Buffalo Bill's troupe. He agrees to perform "the Indian way of life" as an entertainment for white audiences for a variety of reasons: he opts for the risk and adventure of transatlantic travel as a mode to continue a warrior's vision of self predicated on personal courage; he loves "to show off before thousands of people"; and he makes more money than he can spend (33). The most important reason, however—a wish to get away, escape from the prison-house of the reservation, avoid a fate forecast by his father—is only hinted at.

Once in Paris at the world exhibition, a routine of performance, off-duty hours, and sightseeing sets in. When the show moves on to Marseille, Charging Elk has become an item in a huge machine of illusion and entertainment. But the Indian actors enjoy their life nevertheless and try to be thought of by their audience as "men who quietly demonstrate courage, wisdom, and generosity—like the old-time leaders": "Of course he [Charging Elk] knew that it was all fake and that some of the elders back home disapproved of the young men going off to participate in the white man's sham, but he no longer felt guilty about singing scalping songs or participating in scalp dances or sneak-up dances. He was proud to display some of the old ways to these French because they appreciated the Indians and seemed genuinely sympathetic" (51,

52). Charging Elk clearly prefers the mask the colonizers impose on the Native to what he perceives as the effacement, or rather defacement, of Oglala identity by Pine Ridge reservation life, where Americans would "be only too happy to help the Indians disappear" (52). Many years later he reflects on a certain liberating effect of the show: "When he thought about it, the only time Charging Elk had been at ease among the *wasichus* was when he was performing with Buffalo Bill's show. For the only time in his whole life he had been safe from the *wasichus*" (167). Only by fulfilling the stereotype and playing up to the crowd's idea of Indianness, Charging Elk feels secure from efforts to dominate and "civilize" him. But there's more to that than irony. If the Wild West of the show produces a vision of the past that is retrospectively controlled by the whites, Charging Elk's own memories—of Crazy Horse, the battle with the soldiers, his family, his life at the Stronghold—create a different imaginary world of Indian autonomy into which he is constantly withdrawing. These memories form the core of his identity, as they provide him with concepts and moral standards to make sense of and judge the foreign European world, but they also contribute to his loneliness. The psychological dialectics of exile become even more pronounced as, in addition, and to a degree also in contrast, to such conscious withdrawals into memory, dreams and visions come to him unbidden and confront him with wishes and anxieties that he at times cannot but try to push aside in order not to be struck by pain, while at other times he welcomes them as helping him to find his way. In a Euro-American text such visions would be regarded as metaphors of alienation or indications of imminent schizophrenia; in Welch's text, however, they cannot be reduced to Western concepts of the unconscious because they belong to a Lakota spiritual heritage that is unassimilable to Western culture.

Religion thus forms an ethnic boundary—both in the text and for the readers—and the frequently cited critical notion of cross-cultural perception does not erase that fact. Nowhere is the incompatibility between Native and Euro-American cultural and psychological interpretations of the story and the protagonist's interiority more fully articulated than in the scene when Charging Elk kills a homosexual assailant, Breteuil, who uses blackmail in order to make the prostitute Marie drug her lover Charging Elk and then tries to rape him. Charging Elk is convinced that he has killed a *siyoko* and is therefore proud of his deed, while the French who rally to his defense argue a case of self-defense and psychological distress.[3] Juxtaposing these two perspectives, the text steers a complex course of maintaining a middle ground; the omniscient narrator elaborates the psychological and cultural worlds of all the characters and in so doing produces arguments for both interpretations.

The actual scene of rape and murder is foreshadowed by two earlier chance meetings of Charging Elk and Breteuil. The first incident takes place at the beginning of Charging Elk's life in France, when the authorities placed him with a fishmonger's family. Charging Elk helps the fishmonger, René Soulas, sell fish in the market, where he meets Breteuil, a customer of René's. Breteuil promptly engages in exoticist sexual scenarios of subjugation, favorably comparing "this *indien*" to tall and powerful "*nègres*" (141). Knowing about Breteuil's sexual orientation and fervently despising homosexuals, René warns Charging Elk to keep away from him: "You must stay away from that creature. He is an evil one. . . . They are the devil's own spawn, a pox sent by Satan to tempt young men of limited intelligence and morals" (144). At this point Charging Elk hardly speaks French and does not understand a word of René's "chattering," but he feels that Breteuil will play an important part in his future. The role he conceives for Breteuil, however, is that of a *heyoka*, a Lakota notion of a sacred clown, whom he imagines has been sent by Wakan Tanka to help him. René in turn knows nothing about Charging Elk's thoughts but reads Charging Elk's face as a confirmation of his own words.

The second encounter between Charging Elk and Breteuil takes place in the red-light district of Marseille four years later. It is the first time ever that Charging Elk explores the area. When he discovers Breteuil by peering through a leaded-glass window, his old hopes for a *heyoka* sent for his help are revived, but so are memories of René's warnings. This time there is no interaction between Charging Elk and Breteuil, who remains unaware of being gazed at. But suddenly Charging Elk's confusion changes to conviction: "He did not know why but he knew that this street was *sica*, a bad place, and the one he thought was really a *siyoko*, an evil spirit. He could feel the evil grip his heart, as surely as if it had come to him in a bad dream, and, in fact, he felt as though he were in the clutches of the pale *siyoko* now" (209). Charging Elk tries to flee: "the evening had become strange, as though the treacherous *siyoko* had called him to this street and now would wish to do him great harm, perhaps to steal his *nagi*" (210). But he finds himself turning around and going back to the bars of Rue Sainte whose function as brothels the sight of Breteuil has helped him to discover. "Perhaps the *siyoko* lived there and made it attractive to entice men like himself to enter", he muses (210). From a psychoanalytic perspective Charging Elk's sudden conviction that Breteuil is in fact a *siyoko* is not difficult to interpret: because of his fear of sexuality and his equally intense sexual desire (for women)—Charging Elk is twenty-seven years old and still a virgin—he escapes the resulting emotional quandary by a paranoid construction that puts the blame on homosexuality (fantasized as aggression) by taking up René's remark that "he is an evil one" and translating it into a Lakota mythological lexicon. This reading is corroborated by another small scene in which Charging Elk enters the red-light district for the second time and encounters a gypsy woman with a little child, whose grotesque appearance strikes him as another bad sign: "he couldn't help but feel that . . . she possessed some of the *siyoko*'s power" (216). Once again, Charging Elk's fear is related to a remark by René, who "told him that the gypsies contained l'*esprit malfaisant*." Charging Elk again feels the impulse to flee from the scene, but then he gives the gypsy a generous gift of money and feels that he has "passed a test" and is now free to "become a whole man finally" (217).

If there were only these two scenes, this reading would be convincing. But the narration also probes Breteuil's mind and presents his exoticist sexual fantasies, his pride in his social and cultural accomplishments, and his self-centeredness, aestheticized brutality, and utter coldness (254). Marie's shocked but ultimately helpless response to Breteuil's sinister plan is also represented in intimate detail. As a result, a psycho-

analytic reading such as the one elaborated earlier (arguing for a confluence of antagonistic psychological tendencies in a situation of intense
moral insecurity) loses credence because it exclusively concentrates on
Charging Elk's perceptions and feelings without taking his cultural
background or Breteuil's psychological makeup and action into account. Clearly, Marie's characterization of Breteuil as "pale villain" fits
the man (269). Inexplicable as it is, Charging Elk's sudden conviction
that he is dealing with a *siyoko* is shown as being based on an intuitive
perception of Breteuil's amoral recklessness. And the narrator concurs
with Charging Elk on that. Before the rape scene the text indicates the
imminent danger that Charging Elk himself is unaware of in terms that
give up the narrator's usual neutral stance and support Charging Elk's
mythological understanding of the world: "Charging Elk did not see Ol-
ivier and the pale *siyoko* arm in arm" (224). It is a significant moment in
which the epistemological foundation of the realist novel is appropriated and absorbed by Native American myth, investing Charging Elk's
perception with moral authority.

After Breteuil's death, the narration retreats to its former neutral
ground and concentrates on the interpretation of the killing by Charging Elk himself and by the French public, showing the incompatibility of
Western and Native American psychology and ethics. While waiting for
his trial, Charging Elk reflects on the killing of the *siyoko* in terms of the
war between the Lakotas and the *wasichus* over the land and conceives of
his deed as a heroic act of resistance (297 f). Charging Elk's ethics justify the killing, and his reflections rehearse tribal history, giving credit to
Bevis's observation that the presentation of violence in white and Indian
novels reflect "each culture's view of nature and civilization" (607). It
is the memory of Marie that interrupts a train of thought that comes
close to identifying *siyokos* with whites: "Charging Elk was confused in
a funny way. He knew he had done a right thing in killing the evil spirit,
but he also mourned the death of the woman who was to become his
wife and give him children and happiness. Were the two things related?
More important, was he to blame? If not for him, the *siyoko* would not
have come there and Marie would still be alive" (299). Because of Charg-

ing Elk's love for Marie, his understanding of the killing in terms of heroism and revenge is subtly undercut. He does not know yet that Marie is alive and that she has betrayed him. But at the trial it is Marie's feeling for Charging Elk that makes her admit to her participation in Breteuil's crime. She pays the price of public humiliation but saves Charging Elk's life. What brought Charging Elk and Marie together was not romantic love—even though Charging Elk wanted Marie to marry him—and their relationship did not provide mutual recognition. Built, rather, on mutual ignorance of cultural otherness and mutual misrecognition as individuals, their physical intimacy, however, did produce tenderness and compassion and respect for the other in a limited yet profound way. Welch's portrayal of Charging Elk's and Marie's relationship thus rewrites the trope of love as a reconciliation of the individual with society and challenges the sentimentalized reconfiguration of this trope as an image of overcoming cultural difference. The bonding of the two social outsiders demonstrates, rather, the severe limits of intercultural communication. Nevertheless, Welch does not denounce Charging Elk's desire for communion, nor does he deny Charging Elk and Marie the possibility of self-transcendence.

For Charging Elk the trial repeats earlier experiences of dehumanization: he is the savage on public display, an object of curiosity, of loathing, but also of philanthropic sympathy. Policemen charge him with vagabondage, doctors declare his racial incapacity to live in a civilized society, government officials define Charging Elk's status as an illegal immigrant, while, at the instigation of a journalist who wants to produce social action by some deft strokes of the pen, some students who "had led small demonstrations against the exploitation of the Algerians" passionately take up Charging Elk's case as the persecution of "the vanishing American" (335). When he is finally allowed to speak before the jury, Charging Elk begins to give his disposition in French but then goes on to explain himself by speaking Lakota because he lacks "the French words to explain about evil" (338). While for him this speech is a moment of self-realization and self-expression as a subject—standing up, he looks around at all the people in the room, looking into their eyes, hoping for recognition as a human being after years of invisibility—the whole courtroom "bursts into laughter" at the "savage gibberish" (339). The trial scene thus exposes the irreconcilable difference in Western and Native American ethics and underlines the victimization of racialized others by the ethnocentric presumptions of the judicial process.

3

The decision to join Buffalo Bill's troupe takes Charging Elk into the heart of whiteness: to France, the European country where, after all, primitivist notions of the noble savage were developed as part of an Enlightenment cultural critique directed against the self-serving glorious images of civilization and where modernist artists were to construct, but also reflect upon, a new version of primitivist otherness at the time of Charging Elk's predicament. With subtle irony Charging Elk is invoked as a naïf in the tradition of Montaigne's Indians or Montesquieu's Persians, who described Europe from the point of view of the "uncivilized".[4] For Charging Elk France is an alien territory, inhabited by people who speak a strange language, who observe foreign customs, eat disgusting things, and follow unintelligible rules. But Charging Elk is no ethnographer or cultural critic cast in Indian garb. Rather, his life in the city and the crises he goes through resonate with the cultural and material issues of colonialism. The route taken by so many colonial and postcolonial subjects—migration to the Western metropolis—is Charging Elk's as well. But while immigrants *sans papiers* are forced to leave, Charging Elk must stay where he never meant to. When he joins the colonial workforce in the factories and later on the docks of Marseille, he is regarded as another exotic other and treated as such, which includes being treated as sexual prey.

While this narrative construction is unique in Native American literature, it resonates with African-American experiences, as is indicated by Breteuil's sexual fantasies of "*nègres*" and "*indiens*," or by the demonstrators who link Charging Elk's fate with that of Algerians. In order to highlight the cultural politics of Welch's novel in the context of American minority histories, it is useful to compare it with an African-American novel also set in Marseille, namely Claude McKay's *Banjo* (1929). In a series of scenes McKay depicts an international subculture, a community of "wanderers" drawn from the peripheries of the "civilized" world (11). McKay's two African-American protagonists, Banjo and Ray, explore Marseille for different reasons. Banjo "would make his way anywhere"; he has "no plan, no set purpose," other than his love for adventure and his fascination for a life without rules and routines (12). Occasionally working on the docks, hanging out with friends, looking for women, playing jazz, Banjo and his friends are "handsome, happy brutes" (48), at least to Ray, an African-American intellectual expatriate who accompanies Banjo on his stints. A wanderer himself, who had lived in America "like a vagabond poet," Ray is acutely aware of French racism and compares France rather unfavorably to America, "that stupendous young creation of cement and steel" (65). Nevertheless, the docks of Marseille strike him as a place of "cruel beauty":

> Ray loved the piquant variety of the things on the docks as much as he loved their colorful human interest. And the highest to him was the Negroes of the port. In no other port had he ever seen congregated such a picturesque variety of Negroes. Negroes speaking the civilized tongues, Negroes speaking all the African dialects, black Negroes, brown Negroes, yellow Negroes. It was as if every country of the world where Negroes lived had sent Negroes drifting in to Marseilles. A great vagabond host of jungle-like Negroes trying to scrape a temporary existence from the macadamized surface of this great Provencal port. (68)

Ray loves Marseille more than any other European city because it reminds him of America, which he celebrates for "the terrible buffalo-tramping [sic] crush of life, the raucous vaudeville mob-shouting of a newly-arrived nation of white throats, the clamor and clash of races" (68). He lives in a self-chosen exile in Europe because he wants to be a writer and seeks the "necessary solitude" as a mode of self-exploration and a query into black self-definition (66), a condition that makes him an avid observer of—and later an avid participant in—Banjo's freewheeling existence. Observing the European way of life, he has come to despise it: "Oh, it was a great civilization indeed, too entertaining for a savage ever to have the feeling of boredom" (136). As "a child of deracinated ancestry" (137), he advocates a "getting down to our racial roots" to create a new African-American culture (200), a concept that seeks to rearticulate and revalidate notions of Western primitivism. For Ray's "poetical enthusiasm" for the "environment of common black drifters" is predicated on their non-assimilation into a civilization epitomized to him by the snobbish pride of the French (202). Banjo and his friends' careless manners and their ability to live in the present strike Ray as a profoundly new and promising way of creating a black modernity: he "gained from them finer nuances of the necromancy of language and the wisdom that any word may be right and magical in its proper setting" (321).

McKay clearly creates Ray as a conduit for his own concept of an emerging black cosmopolitan culture. He is not advocating an attempt at recuperating a precolonial past; rather, his idealization of the community of black drifters in Marseille functions as a repudiation of both his own former Marxist internationalism and of concepts of a racial uplift put forward by African–American middle-class intellectuals (324, 117). For Ray/McKay homelessness is an essential modern condition; in the novel Marcus Garvey's Back-to-Africa movement is repeatedly discussed with irony (76 f., 102). Banjo's travels, his libertarian sexual mores, his acts of solidarity with other outsiders, his storytelling, and his music are invoked to demonstrate the existence of a dynamic popular black counterculture that integrates various fragments from African tradition and experiences of exile into a new vibrant whole. That Ray defends and celebrates this culture as an accomplishment of black endurance rather than exposing its foundation in economic deprivation is presented as a consequence of his bitter feeling of having to "regulate his emotions by a double standard" if he wants to be recognized by white "civilized" society. "Rather than lose his soul, let intellect go to hell and live instinct!" therefore becomes Ray's maxim (164 f.).

This primitivist notion of a black modern culture is a modernist my-thologized narrative, but, insofar as it rests on an idea of (e)migration, it was shared by other African-American artists. As Paul Gilroy argued in his study on the black Atlantic diaspora, the experience of displacement is crucial for a tradition in African-American culture that moves beyond essentialist tenets of Afrocentricity: "Whether their experience of exile is enforced or chosen, temporary or permanent, these intellectuals and ac-tivists, writers, speakers, poets, and artists repeatedly circulate a desire to escape the restrictive bonds of ethnicity, national identification, and sometimes even 'race' itself" (19). Another, no less important aspect of such a black poetics of dislocation concerns the traumatic memory of slavery, which by these authors and artists is "actively reimagined in the present and transmitted in eloquent pulses from the past" (74). Yet for Gilroy, just as for McCay, slavery marks the irreversible creation of a black diaspora that renders the call for a precolonial African authentic-ity extremely problematic.

McKay's aestheticization of a transnational black subculture rests on a transgenerational experience of displacement. In contrast, Welch's his-torical novel tells a story of an isolated Indian's slow and painful adjust-ment to European life and mores. There is no equivalent to the black At-lantic of multiple transatlantic journeys and therefore no group of exiled or migrant Native Americans that Charging Elk could join.[5] The material conditions of his life in Marseille, however, are the same as those of other immigrants, and he feels sympathetic to their way of life, which reminds him of life at home. After his stay in the Soulas family, he chooses to live in Le Panier—"a hell-hole of North Africans and Turks, of thieves and cutthroats" (329), as the prosecutor describes the neighborhood. But the differences in language and cultural background preclude community, even though for the French both the African and Levantine immigrants and the Native American are racialized as colored people in a similar fash-ion. Charging Elk remains an observer to the life in Le Panier:

Charging Elk had reached his apartment building in Le Panier. It was on Rue des Cordelles, a narrow street which buzzed with many

tongues, mostly North African and Levantine. Children played in
the street until late at night, sometimes keeping him awake. But
more often than not, he found the laughter, the squeals, the cries,
the barking dogs somehow comforting, as though the constant
flurry of noise proved that he was not really alone. . . . In some
ways, this neighborhood reminded him of the village out at the
Stronghold. . . . These people were closer to his own than any of
the others he had come across since he left Pine Ridge. (190)

Charging Elk's isolation is aggravated by the fact that the trauma of colonial conquest and dispossession is a very recent experience for him. His
life in France and his former life at home exist side by side, to be ceaselessly compared with and juxtaposed to each other, creating the "contra-
puntal vision" of exile (Said 186). While Ray rejects Garvey's Back-to-Africa Movement as profoundly nostalgic, for Charging Elk the project of
going home, with its implications of cultural renewal, is constitutive of
his identity. While accepting the necessity of adjusting to the European
environment, Charging Elk is keeping the past alive in his everyday life.[6]

But Welch adds yet another perspective to this depiction by widen-
ing the narrative horizon to include events at the Lakota reservation.
As a consequence, Charging Elk's spatial distance from home and his
being out of sync with the developments there are highlighted and
held against the character's own deepest longings. But, if Charging
Elk's effort of maintaining a Lakota identity against all odds is questioned by the "new life of strangers" he is forced to adapt to (130),
this holds true for the Lakota on the reservation as well. Exile and estrangement are their predicaments and with them the feelings of loss
and uprootedness. It is a cultural condition that almost by necessity
produces reconstitutive cultural projects. Visions of the ghost dance
and of the massacre at Wounded Knee with which Charging Elk is
haunted throughout the book refer to such a project and to its horrible
ending, which repeats and even surpasses the earlier trauma of defeat
and dispossession.

At a structural level the visions represent Charging Elk's inscription

in a Lakota history of suffering that affects all members of the tribe
wherever they may live. At the level of story the visions present Charging
Elk with questions about his own cultural identity because he does not
know anything about the actual events and their circumstances but is
aware of a traumatic dimension that bears upon his own life. The vision
of the ghost dance held at the Stronghold—the place where Charging
Elk himself had in vain tried to escape white domination—is disturbing because he does not recognize the dance: "it was not rhythmic and
graceful like the old-time dances." Thinking about the dream, he comes
to the conclusion "that the crazy dancers were not Oglalas, not even
Lakotas"—a thought that subsequently makes him question his own
former decision to live at the Stronghold and cut himself off from the
tribe (128). He therefore reads the vision as a warning not to escape into
a dreamworld of tradition—"as though the *wasichus* had never existed, as
though our misery was just a dream" (433).

While it is historically accurate that the ghost dancers met at the
Stronghold, Charging Elk's vision of the massacre relocates it to this
place, effectively condensing individual and collective history:

In his dream he was standing on one of the sheer cliffs of the
Stronghold. Something was wrong and he was weeping. He wanted
to jump off the cliff, but every time he tried, a big gust of wind
blew him back. He tried four times, five times, ten times, but each
time the wind pushed him back, until he was exhausted from his
labors. But the next time he approached the cliff, too weak even to
attempt to jump, he looked down and he saw his people lying in a
heap at the bottom. They lay in all positions and directions—men,
women, and children, even old ones. They lay like buffaloes that
had been driven over the cliffs by hunters, and Charging Elk understood why he had been weeping. As he stood and looked down at
his people, he heard the wind roar in his ears like a thousand running buffaloes, but in the roar, he heard a voice, a familiar voice,
a Lakota voice, and it said, "You are my only son." And when he
turned back to his village at the Stronghold, there was nothing

there—no people, no horses or lodges, not even the rings of rock
that held the lodge covers down—not even one smoldering fire pit.
Everything was gone. (235)

Isolated as he is, Charging Elk erroneously interprets the vision as signifying the end of the Lakota tribe.[7] In a complicated meditation started
by the uncanny vision of the unfamiliar dance and the demand of the
familiar voice, he arrives at an understanding of his life as a life in-between: "His heart was not here; nor was it there, at the Stronghold. It
was somewhere he could not name just now" (235 f.).

After ten years in prison, Charging Elk is pardoned as a political prisoner because the French recognize the sovereignty of the Lakota nation.
A Catholic relief organization brings him to a small farm, where he falls
in love with the farmer's daughter Nathalie. He marries her and moves
with her to Marseille, which for him has become a place where he at
least knows how to make a living on his own, even though the city is
beset with troubling memories. Charging Elk finds work on the docks
and with it a community he can participate in: "[His fellow-workers]
accepted Charging Elk as one of them, a member of the union, in a way
that he hadn't been used to—not in the market when he had worked for
René; not in the soap factory; not even in prison. And he felt, for the first
time since he had left the Stronghold, that he was part of a group of men
who looked out for each other. And he liked it" (416). In conjunction
with Charging Elk's sympathetic responses to the immigrant quarter of
Marseille, this evaluation of the union is based on a notion of solidarity
that rests on a similarity of social position and a common goal of social
justice. Still, Charging Elk's cultural difference and his loneliness are
not erased. And Nathalie, who depends on Charging Elk, has to face the
metropolis as a frightening place, where she feels utterly isolated and
constantly dreams of her former life at the farm. Thus, both Charging
Elk and Nathalie are longing for a home that is lost to them, and they
need each other to make the "strange, sweaty city" into a place they both
will eventually declare home (414, 435). For, as it turn out, Nathalie's
pregnancy becomes the final step in a long process of Charging Elk's

acceptance of exile as his condition of life, when Buffalo Bill's Wild West Show returns to Marseille.

Charging Elk's meeting with the Lakota performers—sixteen years after he was left behind by the troupe—forms the climax of the novel. He watches the show with the crowd and realizes that he had always been a stranger in France. But his interpretation of the visions had been wrong: the Lakotas survive, his mother is still alive, and a return to Pine Ridge, which he has dreamed about for so many years, is within his reach. His choice to remain in France nevertheless and to continue living the life of a stranger is based on his responsibility for Nathalie and the baby. It is not predicated on the loss of tribal affiliation, however, as the conversation with Joseph, a young Lakota performer in Buffalo Bill's new show indicates. Asked about life on the reservation, Joseph says: "'They taught me many things—how to cut off my hair, how to wear clothes like them, how to use my knife and fork properly, how to say, "yes sir, yes, ma'am." Oh yes, they taught me many things so that I could be smart—just like them.' He snorted loudly, a sound of disgust that made Charging Elk aware of his own *wasichu* clothes" (432). Joseph's life and choice to turn himself into the image of the Native mirrors Charging Elk's in many respects. But Joseph did not escape reservation school and was forced to learn the white man's ways.

While Charging Elk lived in isolation in Europe without a possibility of talking with anyone in Lakota, without a possibility of participating in Lakota ceremonies, the Lakota were forbidden to speak their language and practice their religion. Joseph's decision to wear the mask of the Indian is thus an even more pronounced—if helpless—gesture of resistance than Charging Elk's once was. Too young to have personal memories of a tribal life in freedom, Joseph's performance rests on an identification with an image of the past that has been thoroughly appropriated by Euro-American culture. In turn, from Joseph's point of view (as Charging Elk imagines it), Charging Elk appears as a completely deracinated and assimilated Indian who has opted for an urban existence in Europe far away from family and tribe and has even married a white woman. But Charging Elk and Joseph find out that they still have something in common: as Lakotas—as they both continue to identify themselves—they share a history of traumatic dispossession and a sense of belonging to a sacred place, the Black Hills, which, precisely because it is a mythological place, cannot be taken away from them and is bound up with a desired but obstructed future for the dispersed tribe. And they share a vision of a possible future: "pitiful and powerless" as they are (435), the Lakotas have survived, and the imminent birth of Charging Elk's baby is a figure of continuity and hope.

4

Where is home? On the one hand, "home" is a mythic place of desire in the diasporic imagination. In this sense it is a place of no return, even if it is possible to visit the geographical territory that is seen as place of "origin." On the other hand, home is also the lived experience of a locality. Its sounds and smells, its heat and dust, balmy summer evenings, or the excitement of the first snowfall . . . all this, as mediated by the historically specific everyday of social relations. (Brah 192)

By having his protagonist move beyond the boundaries of America and live in exile, Welch provides the narrative framework for an interpretation of Native American identity as diasporic.[8] As Avtar Brah defines it, the concept of diaspora "refers to multi-locationality within and across territorial, cultural and psychic boundaries" and negotiates "'imagined' and 'encountered' communities" (197). This notion is wide enough to fit a vision such as Welch's that argues for a Native American identity based on the history and spiritual practice of the tribe but simultaneously recognizes the force of material conditions of economic and psychic survival that Native Americans have to struggle with and adapt to. Welch thus produces a modern subjective "location in the plural" (Kaplan 7).

As readers observe Charging Elk's thoughts and actions, they witness the emergence of a new Native American subject position. While this

position resonates with other histories of colonial conquest, dislocation, and dispersal, the narrative is committed to the specific terms and
turns of Lakota history. By aligning Charging Elk's and Joseph's decisions to work as Indian performers in Buffalo Bill's Wild West Show,
the geographical and psychical territories of exile and of the reservation
are shown to be interrelated by a common and transgenerational predicament of displacement and subordination.

Ultimately, The Heartsong of Charging Elk offers a narratively condensed
overview of twentieth-century Native American history: Charging
Elk's various stays in prison equals Indian life on reservations, his being awarded French citizenship equals the Native American reception
of American citizenship, his work on the docks and his marriage to a
Frenchwoman equals the move toward urban Indian culture and to intermarriage, his decision to stay abroad rather than return home signifies
a rejection of traditionalism. It is true: diaspora is no metaphor for individual exile (Brah 193)—but Charging Elk's individual exile in Europe
is a metaphor for an essentially diasporic condition that encompasses
both the Native Americans who live on the reservation and those who
live in an urban environment. As a consequence, the notion of home is
split and bound up with spatial or cultural distance, but Welch's representation of Native American identity as a distinct spiritual and ethical
practice of self built on a shared discourse of history and memory envi-
sions a community that succeeds in maintaining difference in a situation of cultural collusion.

Notes

This essay grew out of a presentation in honor of Hartwig Isernhagen at the
"American Ethnicities" conference, University of Geneva, November 2003. I
wish to thank Elvira Pulitano for helpful commentaries and suggestions.

    1. On this much-debated issue of cultural translation, see Cheyfitz; Niran-
jana; Krupat; and Siemerling (59–63). See also my essay "Mündlichkeit."

    2. Following Welch's spelling, I will use the French Marseille instead of the
English Marseilles throughout the essay.

    3. In his autobiography Lame Deer remembers having been threatened

with the *siyoko* by his grandmother: "When I didn't want to go to sleep, my grandma would try to scare me with the *ciciye* —a kind of bogeyman. '*Takoja, istima ye*—Go to sleep, sonny,' she would say, 'or the *ciciye* will come after you.' Nobody knew what the *ciciye* was like, but he must have been something terrible. When the *ciciye* wouldn't work anymore, I was threatened with the *siyoko*—another kind of monster. Nobody knew what the *siyoko* was like, either, but he was ten times more terrible than the *cicye*" (17). This anecdote indicates both the amount of shock and anxiety Charging Elk feels and his pride as a monster slayer.

4. The boat that takes the Wild West Troupe to Europe is named the *Persian Monarch* (64).

5. Welch makes up for this lack by constructing a complex intertextual network that relates Charging Elk's story to that of historical Lakota performers in Buffalo Bill's Wild West Show, such as Black Elk and Luther Standing Bear. I have elaborated these intertextual links in a different essay (Haselstein, "'This New Life'").

6. In the Lakota language the concepts of space and time are inseparable. As William K. Powers argues, "All temporal statements in Lakota are simultaneously spatial ones, and the reverse is true" (174).

7. The vision seems based on Lakota beliefs about the afterlife: "Somewhere at the end of the Milky Way [the *wanagi*, or ghosts of the dead] are met by an old woman who assesses their deeds on earth. Those who were good are passed along the way to a place which is reflective of their life with ni; those who were bad are pushed over a cliff, and their evil spirits are left to roam the earth, where they endanger the living" (Powers 53).

8. On the notion of diaspora, see Safran; and Clifford; see also Rushdie.

Works Cited

Bevis, William. "Native American Novels: Homing In." In *Recovering the Word: Essays on Native American Literature*. Ed. Brian Swann and Arnold Krupat. Berkeley: University of California Press, 1987. 580–620.

Brah, Avtar. *Cartographies of Diaspora: Contesting Identities*. New York: Routledge, 1996.

Cheyfitz, Eric. *The Poetics of Imperialism: Translation and Colonization from The Tempest to Tarzan*. New York: Oxford University Press, 1991.

Clifford, James. "Diasporas." *Cultural Anthropology* 9.3 (1994): 302–38.

Fisher, Philip. *Still the New World: American Literature in a Culture of Creative Destruction*. Cambridge: Harvard University Press, 1999.

Gilroy, Paul. *The Black Atlantic: Modernity and Double Consciousness*. Cambridge: Harvard University Press, 1993.

Haselstein, Ulla. "Mündlichkeit, Moderne, Markt als Faktoren literarischer Interkulturalität. Leslie Marmon Silko's Ceremony." In *Interkulturalität. Zwischen Inszenierung und Archiv*. Ed. Stefan Rieger et al. Heidelberg: Narr, 1999. 65–82.

———. "'This New Life of Strangers': James Welch's *The Heartsong of Charging Elk*." In *Authenticity, Sovereignty, and Indigeneity: Pursuing Social Justice in Native American Literatures*. Ed. Deborah L. Madsen. Forthcoming.

Kaplan, Caren. *Questions of Travel: Postmodern Discourses on Displacement*. Durham: Duke University Press, 1996.

Krupat, Arnold. "Postcolonialism, Ideology, and Native American Literature." *The Turn to the Native: Studies in Criticism and Culture*. Lincoln: University of Nebraska Press, 1996. 30–55.

Lame Deer, John (Fire), and Richard Erdoes. *Lame Deer, Seeker of Visions*. New York: Washington Square Press, 1976.

Niranjana, Tejaswini. *Siting Translation: History, Post-Structuralism, and the Colonial Context*. Berkeley: University of California Press, 1992.

Owens, Louis. "Earthboy's Return: James Welch's Acts of Recovery." *Other Destinies. Understanding the American Indian Novel*. Norman: University of Oklahoma Press, 1992.

Powers, William K. *Oglala Religion*. Lincoln: University of Nebraska Press, 1975.

Ruoff, A. Lavonne. "Images of Europe in Leslie Marmon Silko's *Gardens in the Dunes* and James Welch's *The Heartsong of Charging Elk*." In *Sites of Ethnicity: Europe and the Americas*. Ed. William Boelhower, Rocío G. Davis, and Carmen Birkle. Heidelberg: Universitätsverlag Winter, 2004. 179–98.

Rushdie, Salman. "Imaginary Homelands." *Imaginary Homelands. Essays and Criticism: 1981-1991*. London: Granta, 1992. 9–21.

Safran, William. "Diasporas in Modern Societies: Myths of Homeland and Return." *Diaspora* 1.1 (1993): 83–99.

Said, Edward W. "Reflections on Exile." *Reflections on Exile and Other Essays.* Cambridge: Harvard University Press, 2002. 173–86.

Siemerling, Winfried. *The New North American Studies: Culture, Writing and the Politics of Re/Cognition.* London: Routledge, 2005.

Vizenor, Gerald. *Manifest Manners: Postindian Warriors of Survivance.* Hanover NH: Wesleyan University Press, 1994.

13 Clowns, Indians, and Poodles

Spectacular Others in Louis Owens's *I Hear the Train*

> Crossing conceptual horizons can be, and
> in fact must be, hard work.
>
> LOUIS OWENS, *Mixedblood Messages*

When I met Louis Owens in his Parisian hotel lobby some seven or eight years ago, he was on a tour organized by his French publishers, Albin Michel, to promote the French translation of one of his novels. I had been a translator, off and on, for the same publishing house for some time, and, though the translation of *The Sharpest Sight*, to my great disappointment, had not been "given" to me, the editor of the "Terre indienne" collection had informed me of the fact that Owens would be "free" on that afternoon and arranged a meeting for my benefit. At the time I was amazed to be favored in such a manner, and I still cannot figure out what the reason was for helping a scholar like me, one of the academics the house did not like to see nosing into their translation policy too much, meet one of the most promising Native American authors of the day.

The man waiting for me in the rather dim, disheartening first-floor lobby turned out to be unexpectedly open and generous with his time, words, and ideas. The gist of our long conversation is immaterial, but the encounter moved and impressed me deeply—so much so that, when I heard about Owens's suicide in 2002, that did not quite come as a surprise to me. At the time, however, he had not confided in me any specifics about his personal life and certainly not that he was just then undergoing the kind of ordeal he was later to describe in "In a Sense Abroad." Anyway, even though I did not trust the publisher's interest in human beings, there was no way one could have suspected that the current experience could be so damaging for Owens. Had I known, I would have tried to help—but I was too young, certainly, too shy in the presence of a writer I admired, to trust my impressions that something was amiss. I failed to see the seriousness of what was going on, and I have felt guilty of some sort of coarse insensitivity ever since; the feeling will not go away.

Reading "In a Sense Abroad" rekindled those emotions, and, unlike other critics in the field, what I am aware of in those pages is no masterly touch of humor. On the contrary, I am struck again and again by the pathetic, now become tragic, tone of trapped sincerity and betrayed naturalness. Here, then, is to Louis Owens, in respectful, too late, affectionate memory.

I Hear the Train (2001) is divided into three main parts: "Reflections" consists of ten autobiographical texts, two of which relate travels, respectively, in France and in Italy; "Inventions" contains seven fictional stories, with one of them, "The Dancing Poodle of Arles," bearing interesting resemblances to the ninth section of the first part, the one about France; finally, "Refractions" is a series of three critical essays on Native American literature.

Because both "The Dancing Poodle of Arles" and "In a Sense Abroad" explore the same themes, albeit in very different styles, I propose to focus on those two pieces, while keeping an eye on what Owens expresses as his literary concerns elsewhere. Now, to make my intention clear from the outset, in a sort of friendly mimicking and echo of Louis Owens's own statement—"As an American of deeply mixed heritage and somewhat unique upbringing, I speak on behalf of and from the perspective of no one else" (IHTT 207)—I will readily concur and state that, being myself a Frenchwoman (or am I?) of deeply mixed heritage and somewhat unique upbringing, I will speak on behalf of and from the perspective of no one else.

I would also like to stress that I believe my reaction to "In a Sense Abroad" cannot be too offhandedly explained away by my being more or less a French citizen, equipped with a predictably peeved chauvinism;

I rather intend to demonstrate that in its deepest meaning, Louis Owens's account is less an offense toward the French than it is problematic per se for what it tells us about Owens himself, and as such should be a thorn in the flesh of the currently numerous advocates of heterogeneity, hybridity, dialogism, all enemies of the so-called Western binary structures.

In this section Owens's feeling of at times unbearable discomfort is—at least partly—easily accounted for because of the truly disturbing experience he went through. No doubt the context in which his tours took place is extravagantly crazy, and there is no exaggeration on his part as concerns the most unbelievable tricks that were played on him on a number of occasions.

Among the "true" elements he tells about in his story are the following facts: his French publisher was Albin Michel in Paris, his editor was "Francis," and the public relations person's first name was Christine. His portrayal of "Francis" is delightfully true to life: he was (and not in that instance alone, in fact) "fresh off the powwow circuit"; he "tried to anticipate and avoid all problems or confusions by answering all questions about Indian things before any of the indigenous Americans with him could speak" (109); and he has an "always-happy-but-suspecting-trouble-ahead voice" (115). So is the fact that he "had tricked [Owens] into devilishly bizarre touring arrangements and circus shows" (114). In addition, it is very likely that the pistol Louis Owens had won as a *roman noir* literary award was indeed sent to him in a package illegally and falsely labeled "LIVRES" (116). He also hits the mark when he writes: "life would be much better for me in France if I looked more appropriately like a Plains warrior, preferably Lakota"—for there lay his publishers' preferences—and "the French do not take 'No Smoking' signs with any degree of seriousness whatsoever" (115). Also, "the well-known Native activist," "a real Plains Indian leaning halfway out a cab window at 2 a.m. screaming extraordinarily creative expletives at surprised tourists on the Left Bank" (108), probably is one of Albin Michel's best-selling authors, whose name is not to be revealed here if Louis Owens chose not to do so himself.

Indeed, what sells well is stereotyped views on life and, among others, on Native Americans: pictures of Indians in full regalia, stories that ceaselessly plough the same furrow—the Indian is close to nature, the Indian is our victim, the Indian is doomed, the Indian's past is glorious; now he has become a (noble) remnant of an irrecoverable pristine age, who nevertheless retains unfathomable wisdom. Publishers' prosperity the world round is based on similar stereotypes in all fields: the corrupt politician, the good-hearted prostitute, the mysterious ways of other cultures, and so on. What stereotyping there is with commercial publishers encompasses more than racialism, than sexism, than class divisions: it really thrives on simplification, on the erasing of subtleties, on the shrinking of the range of possible meanings and complexities. So, even if the events told by Owens in this section seem hard to believe, they are not unexpected. Anyway, they are also documented: in my opinion they can rightfully account for his very bitter reaction to his "discoveries in France."

Keeping that in mind, let us now address the comic turn Owens purports to give to the section called "In a Sense Abroad: Clowns and Indians, Poodles and Drums—Discoveries in France" (IHTT 105-16). Right from the title, this piece evinces a sort of promise that the reader will be told "a good one." The two parallels, "Clowns and Indians" on the one hand, "Poodles and Drums," on the other, build unexpected, hence laughable, associations of Indians to clowns and of Indian creativity (drums and music) to poodles—that is, animals transformed into ridiculous semblances of real dogs. As a consequence, the artificiality of a poodle, and a "blue poodle" at that (113), is put on a par with Native American music, while Native Americans themselves are implicitly likened to clowns. The two parallels reinforce one another, and, because the formulation is so plain, well balanced, and immediately understandable, the association "Indian" = "laughable and artificial" sounds self-evident. As for the last part of the subtitle, "Discoveries in France," it serves the function of an explanatory note: it is in France, indeed, that such insulting equations can be experienced, and the author "discovers" that possibility there.

Of course, there is an amusing reversal here in that Europeans (among whom are French people) are wrongly said to have "discovered" the "New World," while it is now the turn for a member of those "discovered" people to realize that his and his people's identity can be so misunderstood and despised as to be likened to clowns and associated with poodles. One could also argue that there seems to be another layer of humor here with the use of the word *discoveries*, as a reminder of Gerald Vizenor's favorite term to qualify the output of anthropology and social science research (*Narrative Chance* esp. 10).

True, Owens's tone undoubtedly aims at irony. As Jacquelyn Kilpatrick remarks in the introduction to her collection of essays, after quoting a delirious episode when Owens is on television with "Shirley MacLaine, men in drag, and life-sized puppets" (IHTT 110): "In this amazing bit of story, the barefoot boy from the Mississippi and California riverbanks *nests rather cozily* inside the *internationally famous author*, the one informing the other and each keeping the other honest. The illusion of naïveté is nicely undercut by *the irony of his cultural tease*, his use of the Indian-as-artifact in his response to Christine's 'Open your eyes, Louee.' Coyote is indeed speaking in France" (12; emphases mine). Indeed, Owens does use what Kilpatrick terms "his cultural tease," and there is honesty in those pages. But it is a wounded, even if humorous, honesty; and there is also dismay at the "amazing" events around him. Irony, in fact, requires distance and simply cannot coexist with involvement of any kind. You can handle the hurt if you manage to remain unaffected, whereas the most striking feature here is the distress that exudes from the text as a whole. Actually, there is no sense of coziness at all in those pages but one of hectic nonsense. Owens himself, in contradiction to Kilpatrick's wishful thinking that he is an "internationally famous author," states repeatedly that he is not known at all: "For me it was stardom qualified by the fact that the night before the show I had to wash my Levi's and best shirt out in the hotel shower and semidry both with intense applications of a hair dryer. Real celebrities didn't do such things, I was certain. . . . I am confident that Shirley MacLaine, who looked fresh and lovely . . . did not wash her clothes in her hotel shower before the show"

(110–11). Two pages earlier Kilpatrick had stated that "Owens uses humor and literary irony masterfully" in his novels—then she chooses a piece of nonfiction to assert her point. Although I would readily agree that Owens's use of irony is indeed masterful in his novels, I am quite concerned that this is not the case at all when he tackles very sour memories of the way he was treated in France. The deriding of the French way of mispronouncing the English language, together with repeated expressions of bewilderment, betrays a highly uncomfortable sense of being (mis)taken for a purely commercial object. For example, Owens writes a phonetic rendering of the French pronunciation of such words as *Paris* ("Paree," 106), *Louis* ("Louee," 110, 111; "Louie," 113; "Louees," 115), and *big* ("Smile beeg," 110, 113) as well as the phrases "there is a problem" and "It is a gun, a pistol" ("zere ees a problehm," "Eet ees a gun, a peestol," 116)—surely a worn-out form of local color mockery.

He also makes fun of the French way to pronounce the first name Francis ("Frahncees," 115). Here the laugh unfortunately is on the intolerant foreigner: Natives do pronounce native nouns in a Native way. In addition, by mixing Spanish ("Que será será," 112) with lame English and improbable French, Owens undoubtedly gives the impression of a disturbingly nonsensical language environment. Although Owens concludes that he "absolutely" does not speak French (115), he nevertheless sprinkles French adjectives, adverbs, and phrases throughout his story, in a way that is hardly ever appropriate—for example, "were *beaucoup* handsome" and writing the noun *indienne* without a capital letter and the related adjective without an *s* in the plural (106). Also, the phrase "trop gauche" to qualify the alleged French people's insistence that everybody should drink wine, "even when one valiantly attempts to demur," is utterly fanciful and meaningless here (108). As is blatantly so the assertion that Owens's voice having been translated by a young Vietnamese-French woman would elicit the exclamation "Qu'est-ce que c'est, Coyote?" from the French, for two obvious reasons: first, that French phrase would not convey any meaning given the context; second, there have been French-speaking Vietnamese in Vietnam for generations, and those Vietnamese who have come to live in France since the end of the "Guerre d'Indochine" very seldom, except in the older generations, sound anything but French, so that nobody in a television audience would be likely to hear the girl's spoken French as "not authentically French"—I insist that his interpreter would not have any accent and would not be spotted as a Vietnamese by a French audience. A good way to make this point clear would be to imply that an American of Swedish, Irish, or Asian origin in the United States would sound Swedish, Irish, or Asian after two or more generations in the country—or else does he mean a female interpreter can give no fair rendering of his male voice?

There is another instance of cultural misunderstanding in Owens's text when he rightfully remarks that "a surprising number of the French intelligentsia have impressive knowledge about the Leonard Peltier case and are properly outraged over America's brutally racist politics exemplified by the case" and then adds that "they are not at all amenable to discussing the darker aspects of French minority politics" (115). I do not wish to contend the absurd idea that French people would readily discuss those matters with a foreigner, nor am I denying that the French can often be obnoxiously arrogant. But I do think it necessary to point out that there are different cultural ideas and feelings about assimilation in France and in the United States. Now, what is probably hinted at in Owens's remark is the large proportion of immigrants from North Africa, some of whom have only recently started claiming a special status, in the wake of the dynamic evolution of Islamism the world over, a delicate situation, no doubt, but not uniquely French.

Not knowing about France's history is no sin, but debunking the French out of an inability to see, or even suspect, that they must perforce (by law of life and history) be different, while at the same time claiming for oneself a right to be "different," proves slightly incoherent and unfair in the eyes of the observer. Anyway, it reveals a lack of understanding, hence the impression that Owens finds himself at a loss in France.

Another clue to Owens's uneasiness with "illogical" behaviors is how he ridicules the objects of his observation by using an oxymoron in "the marvelously polluted bay of Marseilles" (111; emphasis mine), with the etymology of the term ("pointedly foolish") underlining the stupidity of the two French actresses who want to go skinny-dipping—all the more so as the whole context is so ludicrous, with "Francis" telling Owens that the venture could be dangerous and Owens "concurr[ing]." That is not the only instance pointing to some inveterate obtuseness and illogical behavior in French people, for at other times Owens writes of "French gullibility" (which provokes him into "making up wild 'Indian' stories to see what they'd buy"), of "the unceasing demand for clichéd romance" (106), of "the onslaught of essentialist, romantic, unshakably confident French pronouncements upon *les indiennes*" (107). A rhetorical device that also betrays how upset Owens is appears when he indulges in generalizations of the French, hence stereotyping them, using indefinites such as "some incredulous Frenchman" (105); this is all the more striking as it is in stark contrast to the opening of the text in medias res, eleven lines earlier, with a definite article applying to Native Americans: "The four boys from the Northern Ute and Blackfoot reservations." For the sake of fun he also generalizes in an outrageous way when he spuriously asserts: "I have learned that as an Indian in France one should have a real 'Indian' name and be angry as much as possible about things done to one's people, that the average citizen in France knows a great deal more about American Indians and U.S. history than I do, and that one out of two Frenchmen and women have been given Indian names, been adopted into one or more tribes, been to Crow Fair, and been on vision quests, often in the Bois de Boulogne" (115). That people should expect an "Indian" to have an "Indian" name is not distinctively French; I would say this is most probably true in many other countries around the world, including the United States. As for the economy of anger, it seems to me that, should anybody consider that Indians have no right to express any anger, then we would have good cause to feel concerned. As for the rest of the statement, it is likely that New Age practices such as those described here exist in France, but no more than in the United States, for example, and they are far from involving any significant number of people; anyway, I doubt any circle of Indian aficionados around the world would give the onlooker a different impression. Owens nevertheless relentlessly attacks the French by making fun of what he deems "represents" or "looks" French at large: "As we all know, the French do take art very seriously, however. The French read Proust and they have produced Robbe-Grillet" (115). Of course, the French do not read Proust, for his style and concerns are too difficult and exacting for an "average citizen," and probably not one out of a hundred French people know that Robbe-Grillet is not a tennis player. What Owens does in the lines quoted here is precisely what we think is "not fun," actually, when that kind of stereotype is built up at the expense of other people. "As we all know" is a typical "appetizer," so to speak, for unaccountable statements because it does not mean anything. "As we all know," the sun revolves around the Earth, for that matter. Owens's misconception and ignorance of French reality fail to raise a laugh the moment we consider the French as deserving more than a flippant description as a mad crowd, at which a Native American poet and rap artist can shout his anger while they, those "loving French audiences" (109), obtusely refuse to react sanely. Any essentialist pronouncement is plain abuse, not depending on the target of the process but because the process itself is unacceptable. Using it for one category of human beings shows disrespect to any other community of human beings.

This lowering of one's standards in one as sophisticated as Louis Owens does not, of course, result from sheer insensitivity but, rather, stems from a taxing dismay about what is going on around him, which in turn annihilates his capacity to react as (self-)trained to, from want of the knowledge that would be necessary in those circumstances. Had Owens been more self-confident, he would not have taken "Francis's," Christine's, French "Indianistes'" crass behaviors for what they in fact reveal: their own personal/class deficiencies in the service of a big publishing house—a business ethos he cannot but have come across earlier elsewhere; such operators are not remotely "the average French citizen." Owens gives the reader "a reversed gaze" in an unexpected manner, distorted images of a binary structure, closed upon itself, rejecting "the other."

What becomes visible, then, is that, while some passages in the "In a Sense Abroad" section may be termed ironic, yet the controlled distance

at times is painfully short and reveals that, in the absence of any mediat-
ing clues, too close a contact becomes unacceptable because it is simply
unbearable. In those instances Owens's subtle and responsive nature
shows through, while his—normally highly—sophisticated style is at
pains to cope with the brand of such naked utilitarianism that his publishers, foremost among others, unashamedly display. His use of facile
exoticism and of a recurrent set of parallels, antitheses, and generalizations demonstrates that the account of this dismaying experience as
"an Indian," and a spectacular one at that, unfortunately conveys both
his puzzlement at strange and incomprehensible behaviors and his own
retreat—confined as he is in an attitude of bewilderment—into in turn
seeing the French as "spectacular." "Others" are after all difficult to
make sense of, and the "visiting" other, once seared, is apt to have his
capaciousness and mellow sensitivity impaired.

In this plight Owens calls forth the figure of Coyote to picture the
situation he finds himself in. One of Vizenor's condensed definitions
of the trickster, sometimes featured as Coyote, will help to understand
Owens's stance here: "The tribal trickster is a liberator and healer in a
narrative, a comic sign, communal signification and a discourse with
imagination. . . . The trickster is a language game in a comic narrative"
(*Narrative Chance* 187). Unfortunately, even though he feels he does not
belong, Owens cannot escape personal pain, as would Coyote; he is
stuck in the slot he was forced into. In this harrowing situation he does
not succeed as a "liberator and a healer"; he is not the "contradancer"
who can act, play, and move on, to use still another of Vizenor's words
(*Interior Landscapes* 262). Indeed, he does play tricks on Christine, but
never is he benevolent. Unlike in his novels, or even in other sections
of the same book, or again in *Other Destinies*, he does not manage to fully
cope with this disregard for his humanity. He is at pains to get through
the surface of what he sees, remains at the level of what meets the eye,
and, suffering from being used in a series of more or less formal shows,
feels trapped by the others' vision of him: he is spectacular to them. In
his turn he sees them but cannot make sense of what he sees: they all of
them remain spectacular to him, stereotypes of incomprehensible and

ridiculous, "gullible" French face-to-face with a stereotype of a sour, dour "Indian" (106). They are as much an absence of French as he is an absence of Indian.

Elvira Pulitano's contention—though it refers specifically to Native American critical theory—that a Native-centered position is untenable, if only because there is no such thing as "pure" Native traditions, thought, or literature, seems particularly relevant here: in the present instance Louis Owens has fallen prey to stereotypes and a simplified view of the other. What Pulitano has found in the course of her study of Native American critical theories rings a more general truth about how we should deal with different cultures if we are to avoid the pitfalls of reifying, stereotyping, reducing, and simplifying the people we are looking at: "Any kind of Nativist approach . . . ultimately ends up perpetuating the categories of an us/them universe, merely reversing the terms of the opposition and granting the Indian a privileged position" (*Toward a Native American Critical Theory* 189). Along the same lines, in his book on Owens Chris LaLonde remarks, "A danger lurking in the act of telling, of the construction of an other discourse, is that the dominant culture and its discourse will be so essentialized that we are left with narratives that do to them precisely what they do to Natives." But he adds that Owens's texts skirt that pitfall "by incorporating historical and cultural particularities" (18). Sadly, this is not the case in the section about France in *I Hear the Train*, for Owens's narrative here is severed from a historical context he has not cared to inquire about. He finds himself alone throughout the experience, a spectator of the beautiful Indian dancers as well as of the mad incivility of his French "hosts." While in *Mixedblood Messages* Owens praises James Clifton's notion of "frontier" as a definition of where he himself wants to stand, in that "culturally defined place where peoples with different culturally expressed identities meet and deal with each other" (*Mixedblood Messages* 52; quoting Krupat quoting Clifton, in *Ethnocriticism* 5), here he has failed to find that "culturally defined place."

French philosopher Pierre-André Taguieff, who has worked extensively for the past thirty years or so on the notion of racism, its forms and varieties, states: "'Essentialist thought' appears as a mode of perception and of categorization that is rudimentary and at the same time freezes human groups in time: it condenses and hardens the given characteristics, which it eternalizes by fixing them into stereotypes, or, 'race characteristics'" (*La Force du préjugé* 31; my translation). Analyzing Durkheim's reading of Vacher de Lapouge and Ammon, Taguieff concludes that racists "'naturalize' what is cultural and/or social (both being considered as biologically given) and also consider as 'inescapable,' 'bound to happen' the course of human history, contingency being disguised/converted into necessity, and necessity into fate" (34). A "derealization" is worked on the subject, giving birth to the belief that any individual represents a whole group, a group that in turn supposedly gives the individual his or her essential "identity" (36). This is why "a group of human beings embodies the essentialized victim, who, in turn, by way of self-legitimizing inversion is considered the aggressor" that is then logically denounced, condemned, and fought against (34).

I would propose that the notion of derealization, the cutting off from reality, is a quite satisfactory translation of Vizenor's contention that "the indians are the romantic absences of the natives" (*Fugitive Poses* 14). Similarly, Owens's French editor, "indianistes"—or more exactly tiny groups of ignorant, romantic Indian lovers—the French intelligentsia, the "average citizen," caught in a "carnival of madness" (109), are the ridiculous absences of the French natives. As Shorty Luke, the narrator—or the storyteller, rather—in *Dark River* puts it, to oppose the anthropologist's view of what the Apache should do: "This ain't no disco, this ain't no theme park" (209). True, but then freeze-framing the Natives of France is no more acceptable than freeze-framing the Natives of America.

On the other hand, Owens remains understanding and even admiring as concerns the Native dancers who take part in the same talk show as he does. To quote Priscilla Oats in her essay "The First Generation of Native American Novelists," "Whether showing the effect of alienation or assimilation, the Native American writer stresses the basic humanity of his Indian characters and always emphasizes this. Regardless of the miseries of life, tribalism and family love shine through" (*Critical*

Perspectives 85). Owens himself does not depart from this stance. Although he is prone to self-derisive statements, he approves of the young Indian dancers, singers, and drummers he describes in his text. Positive terms abound concerning them: "three extraordinarily beautiful young girls," "handsome warrior," "powerfully built grass dancer," "imposing and dignified," "a pillar of maturity and responsibility" (105), all those young Natives perfectly at ease, and "far too sophisticated to have contemplated chaperones in the first place" (107), never uncomfortable in an utterly unknown and potentially dangerous environment. All the Blackfeet youth had flown to Paris alone; one girl, aged fourteen, missed her plane in Great Falls but later caught a flight by herself, changed planes a couple of times, and managed to get from Charles de Gaulle Airport into Paris without a word of French. "She arrived grinning and happy as a new songbird about this strange foreign world, chattering at once with the other girls about the weird human beings and cute boys served in France" (107). Now, this commodification of French boys does not sound offensive unless you consider that some people deserve to be commodified and some do not.

In "In a Sense Abroad," then, the pleasure of telling a "good" story unbalances the responsibilities the artist has endorsed and pulls him down from his commitment to fighting ignorance and prejudice. As Jesse Peters plainly puts it in his essay "'You Got to Fish Ever Goddamn Day': The Importance of Hunting and Fishing through I *Hear the Train*," "After all, frontier space has never been about certainty, and if one truly wants to understand who he or she is, then that person must be willing to explore, to hunt, not just between the lines, but beyond them" (Kilpatrick 241). Peters further suggests that doubt is at the core of Louis Owens's work, especially in I *Hear the Train*—hence the book's subtitle, "Reflections, Inventions, Refractions" (226)—and that Owens's approach to writing, and life in general, is at core that of a hunter, for hunting allows one to become other. If that casting be true, Owens's hunting skills, in the case of his French tour, are somewhat challenged. The story of this experience abroad reveals more about his vibrant concern for mutual respect and human values than it displays the hunter's cool inquiry. Clearly, hunting an other, to become him/her/it, if only "for a privileged time," becomes impossible if this other behaves in accordance with unknown, weird, and possibly crude rules. As a consequence, both the observer and the observed are doomed to remain at the surface, merely spectacular and pathetically shallow, so that there is no way for salvation or fleeing from oneself in the end.

It seems to me that Owens's suffering is both existential and specific to his sense of being "invisible." A good example of this sort of obsession about "visibility," if only because the lexical field is strikingly similar to that in the story of his French tour, is to be found in another text of the same book, the essay entitled "The Syllogistic Mixedblood: How Roland Barthes Saved Me from the *indians*" (IHTT, 90–104), set just before "In a Sense Abroad." Musing on the "otherness" of his great-grandfather in a photograph, he states: "he looks distinctly like some kind of 'other,' and I have diverse reasons for valuing that discovered otherness in my ancestor" (90). Later in the text he remarks: "These photographs taken in Indian Territory are records of invisibility, and it is within the invisible that I locate mixedblood identity. There is no space for mixedbloods within the national fantasy; therefore they remain uninvented" (102).

And he goes on, brooding on the fact that nobody could in fact "look Indian," because it is "something that never existed" (103), ending with the following assertion: "I see in these mixedblood ancestors the kind of suspicious yet resolute indeterminacy that I feel in my own life and see in my own face, a kind of Native negative capability. The Indian has never been real in the mirror" (104). Clearly, being visible/invisible looms large in his reflections upon his own identity, with an insistence on what is to be seen, that is, determined about one, about the "spectacle" of one's identity. So it seems Owens is aggrieved by people's repeated failure to see him, which logically feels as abandonment and betrayal. The same is true in his intellectual life; for example, in his essay entitled "As If an Indian Were Really an Indian" (IHTT, 207–26), Owens underlines the peculiar situation of Native American literature—it is very seldom taught within university English departments—and adds, "In fact, surprisingly, it would not take much time spent browsing through contemporary critical/theoretical texts—including especially those we call postcolonial—to discover an even more complete erasure of Native American voices" (209).

What he fears is erasure, invisibility, oblivion, betrayal, all awfully exacting and painful manifestations of his being to a great extent "expendable."

There nevertheless appears to be one way out of pain, discontent, and disorientation, and that is the solace of art. In his preface Owens states, for example, that storytelling helps us in the midst of the confusion in the world that surrounds us: "As Vladimir Nabokov knew and showed us so brilliantly in *Pale Fire*, we make stories in order to find ourselves at home in a chaos made familiar and comforting through the stories we make, searching frantically for patterns in the flux of randomly recorded events, a world in which endings stalk us and we can only keep inventing ways to both explain and forestall closure" (xiii).

In a similar way Chris LaLonde ponders Vizenor's statement in his autobiography that he did not follow the political stance of the American Indian Movement (AIM) but had turned to literary activism instead: "I listened to the voices, the racial politics, the ironies, the lies, and tried to turn the sound of drums in my heart into a dream song, into literature" (*Grave Concerns, Tricksters Turns* 189; quoting *Interior Landscapes* 235). In these lines LaLonde had just come to the obvious—namely that, like Vizenor, Owens had decided to be a fighter in and through literature, never on the political terrain, asserting that he "meshes the traditional and the Euroamerican in order to count coup on ignorance" (186).

It seems appropriate, then, to have a look at the sort of parallel that the fictional, hence more "artistic," story "The Dancing Poodle of Arles" sets up alongside the autobiographical "In a Sense Abroad." In the same way "Finding Gene" (IHTT, 3–15), as an autobiographical piece, informs *The Sharpest Sight*, even if the novel cannot be reduced to that aspect, and in the course of *I Hear the Train* there are some "Inventions" that reflect and reverberate with the events of Owens's life as he tells about them in the first part, called "Reflections."

A third-person narrative, "The Dancing Poodle of Arles" features a Native American man coming from Spain and going through the south of France, to Geneva in Switzerland, with his girlfriend or wife. Between midnight and 6 a.m. they stop in the station then walk around Arles, waiting for the train to the "cool blue of Geneva" (180).

What comes to mind immediately when reading this piece is again the feeling of a shaky, hectic, and somewhat dangerous environment that may have once been magical but is now mainly absurd (176; "madly," 180), eliciting a feeling of disorientation in the narrator ("How did I get here?") as well as of violence ("rage against the French" [177]), full of nonsense, in a din of incomprehensible languages ("a language they could not understand" [178]). Although the text is only five pages long, there are a great many repeated and nostalgic references to home ("back home on the reservation," "thinking of home"; "back home," "the kids at home," "another world" [176–77]), as if to recover balance in this general madness. Toward the end, however, the narrator senses that there is a familiar story here, but he cannot make out which one. In spite of his efforts to understand his surroundings, what he feels in Arles is discomfort and displeasure. Then, in the course of their aimless walk, the two travelers come to a house and are attracted to the light coming out the window. They peep between the shutters, into a room where the narrator sees a man with red hair and sharp cheekbones sitting on a bed, his eyes "like dark whirlpools":

On a tumbled bed a scarlet coverlet was turned back from the sheets and pillows of light greenish lemon, and on the edge of the bed sat a man with an emaciated, luminous head outlined with tangled red hair, the lines of the hair heavy, as if laid on an impulse of thick strokes. The man's high, pale forehead angled down to razor-edged cheekbones, hollow cheeks, and a sharp chin under a sparse confusion of orange beard, and wrapped around the head and under the chin so that it covered one ear with a thick pad was a white rag. (180)

The lexical field here is that of painting ("luminous", "outlined," "an impulse of thick strokes"), with colors that are disturbingly either unnatural or unusual in everyday life but can quite arguably have been chosen by a painter's eye: "scarlet coverlet," for one, but most of all the "orange beard" and the "pillows of light greenish lemon."

Of course, the description is that of Van Gogh's room in Arles, either from *Van Gogh's Room at Arles* (1889), which is in the Musée d'Orsay in Paris, or *Vincent's Room, Arles* (1888), at the Vincent Van Gogh Foundation Museum in Amsterdam. The man described here is one of the painter's self-portraits, either the 1889 one or the 1888 *Self-Portrait in front of the Easel*, but, even more obviously, his famous *Self-Portrait with Bandaged Ear* (1889), in which there are also pictures on the room walls.

Also, the visually disturbing description of the landscape, with its green flames of cypresses against the blue lines of a mountain, its tormented wheat, clearly refers to Van Gogh's famous paintings, *Cypresses* (1889), *Wheat Field* (1889), or again *Wheat Field under Threatening Skies* (1890). Even the fact that the protagonists look at the landscapes through the train windows reminds one of the frame around a painting: "Through the broad windows of their compartment, he could watch a world of shocking turbulence, a stormy sea of wheat fields, grain like patterned sand tossed with rolling bushes, and the green flames of cypresses quivering upward against blue, knobbed mountains curling in waves upon themselves. Overhead, a swirling pale-blue sky and thick lines of angular black crows above stubble cornfields and a curving swath of red-green road" (180).

No doubt Owens's story of passing through Arles and the description of landscapes around the town reveal a deep attraction to Van Gogh's paintings. This must account for the fact that the town feels familiar to both characters: "'Arles,' she said, musing on the sound of the word. 'There's *something familiar about that town.*' *He knew what she meant,* and he remembered the old stories. *The strongest colors should be used bravely,* he thought, for *time will only soften them too much*" (181; emphases mine). Owens manifestly admires Van Gogh's "brave" strokes of "the strongest colors" and fears what softening time might effect on this strength.

He also is delicately discreet on what this "familiar" picture of the man in the room may arouse in him, even if the text states there is a "painful contrast" between the man himself and his peaceful environment: "The tiny room, with its broad lines of furniture, portraits, and wrinkled clothes hung on pegs, expressed a deep, inviolable rest in painful contrast with the man on the bed" (180).

The story, then, fruitfully illuminates the meaning of the "nightmare tour" in "In a Sense Abroad" (109). One remarkable link between the two pieces is actually the poodle, "a small blue poodle" in the autobiographical one and "a large blue-gray poodle" in the "invented" story, the word being also present in both titles (113, 178). The protagonist who smiles at his wife in "The Dancing Poodle in Arles" has seen and recognized Vincent Van Gogh, the painter associated with the town of Arles, the one who painted out of the chaos of what he saw and who shot himself dead about one year later, in July 1890, "for the good of all."

I Hear the Train was published in 2001, and Owens shot himself in 2002.

This is why I can see no "masterful irony" in "In a Sense Abroad," simply the pain of inadequacy when forced to confront the wild upsurge of unaccountable, unheard of, mad behaviors one feels unable to cope with—that incoherent power over the self that seems to overcome even the bravest of strong words on the page and colors on the canvas.

Works Cited

Fleck, Richard F., ed. *Critical Perspectives on Native American Fiction.* 1993. Pueblo CO: Passeggiata Press, 1997.

Kilpatrick, Jacquelyn, ed. *Louis Owens: Literary Reflections on His Life and Work.* Norman: University of Oklahoma Press, 2004.

Krupat, Arnold. *Ethnocriticism: Ethnography, History, Literature.* Berkeley: University of California Press, 1992.

LaLonde, Chris. *Grave Concerns, Trickster Turns: The Novels of Louis Owens.* Norman: University of Oklahoma Press, 2002.

Owens, Louis. *Other Destinies: Understanding the American Indian Novel.* Norman: University of Oklahoma Press, 1992.

————. *The Sharpest Sight*. 1991. Norman: University of Oklahoma Press, 1992.

————. *Mixedblood Messages: Literature, Film, Family, Place*. Norman: University of Oklahoma Press, 1998.

————. *Dark River: A Novel*. Norman: University of Oklahoma Press, 1999.

————. *I Hear the Train: Reflections, Inventions, Refractions*. Norman: University of Oklahoma Press, 2001.

Pulitano, Elvira. *Toward a Native American Critical Theory*. Lincoln: University of Nebraska Press, 2003.

Taguieff, Pierre-André. *La Force du préjugé. Essai sur le racisme et ses doubles*. Paris: La Découverte, 1987. Trans. Hassan Melehy. *The Force of Prejudice: On Racism and Its Doubles*. Minneapolis: University of Minnesota Press, 2001.

Vizenor, Gerald. *Interior Landscapes: Autobiographical Myths and Metaphors*. Minneapolis: University of Minnesota Press, 1990.

————. *Fugitive Poses: Native American Indian Scenes of Absence and Presence*. Lincoln: University of Nebraska Press, 1998.

————, ed. *Narrative Chance: Postmodern Discourse on Native American Indian Literatures*. Albuquerque: University of New Mexico Press, 1989.

14 Oklahoma International

Jim Barnes, Poetry, and the Sites of Imagination

Bones beneath my feet, I make
a song for all of them.
JIM BARNES, "A Song for All of Them"

In another country, I push
aside the leaves, and my own loss begins
to fade.
JIM BARNES, "In Another Country"

Wherever I go, it seems I never get too far away
from home but what I am reminded of it.
JIM BARNES, On Native Ground: Memoirs and
Impressions

Issish ibakana, a Choctaw phrase Jim Barnes himself glosses as "mixed-blood from Oklahoma" in his fine-grained prose and verse autobiography On Native Ground: Memoirs and Impressions (169), offers a point of departure. For if he has dwelt fondly upon his American family plait of Native, Welsh, and English origins, at the same time, and likely not a little in consequence, it has been accompanied by the insistence on not being bound to any single categorization. To his often self-acknowledged consternation this includes Native American writer. Rather, with Native America but one realm of lineage—however wholly and without doubt important—Barnes has given his now considerable range of poetry, fiction, life writing, and discursive work to an unfolding variorum of sites both in and beyond America.

These different geographies of his life, moreover, provide a double seam, physically lived-in sight and sound yet always the figural landscape of feeling or memory. They begin for Barnes with the Great Southwest, as he calls it, the eastern Oklahoma Somerville of his birth in 1933 and hard-scrub upbringing in LeFlore County's Fourche Maline and Holson Creek. It was there, during a Depression-era and World War II boyhood with parents pressed to find ranch and herding work and obliged, albeit within a limited perimeter, to move the family from one house to another (he speaks of them as "gray" in *On Native Ground*), that he acquired his poet's abiding sense of the importance of site as at once exterior but intricately, and always, inward landscape. A brief poem such as "Surveying near Ellsworth, Kansas" in the collection *La Plata Cantata* (1989) succinctly, and dramatically, gives emphasis to the point:

All that's left is hard,
the bone-dry creek,
the knife shade of a single tree,
the prairie burned brown by a screaming summer sun,
and a lone marker,
stone, belonging god-knows-where:
scalped 1853.[1]

Oklahoma's *tierra* of smallholding, farm, pasture, bluff, ridge, pond, tree, river, orchard, wind, bird and animal life, season and skyline, not to mention the small-town life of high street and school, sheriff's office and jail, church and store, and each residual Choctaw burial mound and arrowhead, has long featured for him as a first archive. Of all the sites in Barnes's poetry none quite matches in weight of association, a timeline of mind as much as place, and whether literal topography or the layers of Native and settler history or his own arriving consciousness. Even so, he has resisted any temptation to romanticize Oklahoma, however beguiling its Choctaw, Anglo, and Celtic fashioning along with the human *métissage* to which it has given rise. In this respect, if no other, he invites comparison with a range of contemporary Native authorship taken up with mixed dynasty and the migrations and sitings that has entailed, as notably as anywhere, the writings of Gerald Vizenor, Diane Glancy, Louis Owens, and Betty Bell.

Restless, chafed, stir-hungry, in 1951 he would step westward from Summerfield, Oklahoma, to Eugene, Oregon, where he had family, and to employment in logging through the years 1954–59 in the Cascades and Willamette Valley. The Pacific Northwest's mountain forestry, nature and commerce, again has stayed with him, a vital next source of place in his writing. It was in Oregon that the same call to writing, long nascent, became yet more emphatic: the emerging first stories and verse, the early imitations of Faulkner and Hemingway. A liberal arts degree from Oklahoma State in 1964 and then a master's degree and doctorate from the University of Arkansas in 1965 and 1970, with a brief teaching stint at Northeastern Oklahoma State University, have led to more than three decades (1970–2003) as professor of English and Comparative Literature at Truman State University, Kirksville, Missouri, and editorship of the literary and translation journal, the *Chariton Review*. In 2004 he took up a Distinguished Faculty position at Brigham Young University, Utah, carrying the journal with him. For its part Missouri, and the ambient local Midwest of townships and people, rivers and land, becomes necessary further landscape in his verse.

Beyond America he has made little secret of relishing his stints as overseas author-resident. The trajectory includes successive stays in Lake Como's Bellagio on Rockefeller Foundation Fellowships (1990, 2003), a Senior Fulbright year at the University of Lausanne (1993–94), guest residencies and funding in Munich (1995) and then Stuttgart (2000), and two Camargo Fellowships at Cassis within the painterly landscape of Arles and *le midi* in general (1996, 2001). The French capital, in its turn, has exerted a uniquely powerful influence, the inspiration for his recent volume simply called *Paris* (1997) and a continuation of his taste for closely worked personal observation within the silhouette of encompassing larger cultural reference. Oklahoma, Oregon, Missouri, Italy, Switzerland, Germany, and France: the sense of site, America or Europe, has been of the essence.

But another desideratum has equally always held for Barnes, the call for and to craft, a deliberated force of compositional style and whether for his own writing or that of others. Citing his longtime editorial experience at the *Chariton Review*, he berates in *On Native Ground* all contemporary tendency to "pretentious self-absorption" (191), the absence of due regard for "complication," "irony," "vantage point," and "tone" (235). This need to be concerned with "the art of making," he has gone on insisting, serves as the prophylactic against being "doomed to have only subject to work with" (236). A contribution to the *Dictionary of Literary Biography*'s *Contemporary Authors Autobiography Series* (1997) amplifies on "form and structure" as literary prerequisite, the need for the "true sentence" within "this world of Po-biz."[2]

Beginning from two slim and soon out-of-print verse collections, *This Crazy Land* (1980) and *The Fish on Poteau Mountain* (1980), these concerns of craft, the close, deliberated working with image and voice and with the pathways of memory and forms of unsentimental cultural nostalgia, have clearly been acted upon in his own writing. Each subsequent collection adds confirmation, whether *The American Book of The Dead* (1982), *A Season of Loss: Poems* (1985), and *La Plata Cantata: Poems* (1989)—the three reissued in a single volume as *On a Wing of the Sun* (2001)—or *The Sawdust War* (1992), along with the 1997 publication of *Paris*. There needs to be added story writing like his personal favorite, "The Reapers," and the considerable span of anthology and international journal publication from *American Poetry Review* to *Paris Review*, *Kenyon Review* to *Poetry Wales*, *Ploughshares* to *Italian Americana*. Barnes, throughout, has fused a commitment to verse as both "life" and well-wrought urn, the drama of the one or another site but always within an idiom assiduously honed to match.

In a general sense Barnes's poetry might be thought to belong somewhere inside a long elegiac tradition threading forward from the Horatian ode, be it the late-Augustan English poetry of Gray and Collins with, in their wake, Wordsworth (whose "Nothing can bring back the hour / of Splendour in the grass" he cites in his memorial World War II poem "Decades"), the darker pastorals of Thomas Hardy and Robert Frost, or the wry-cautionary poems of the veteran Munich writer Dagmar Nick in volumes such as *Summon and Sign* (1980) and *Numbered Days* (1998), for which Barnes has acted as admiring and deservedly prize-winning translator. The monograph that arose from his doctoral thesis, published as *The Fiction of Malcolm Lowry and Thomas Mann: Structural Tradition* (1990), strikes a shared note. The emphasis falls on how both authors explore the destructive element in human affairs, life interpreted, not to say magnified, through a glass darkly. Nor, for a moment, is this to overlook other shaping influences from a Native sense of word, be it spoken or written, or an array of other European, British (to include Welsh), and American literary sources.

None of this, at any point, is to lessen Barnes's own strong personal distinctiveness of vision or style right across, to date, his eight published volumes of poetry. But a number of shared perspectives can be discerned: the contemplative temper, the recognition of the ironies and sway of time, the care for exactness of image. All necessarily act, and interact, as markers in his poetry's engagement with its different sites.

On Native Ground, at once life writing and credo and typically meticulous in its voicing, supplies Barnes's own sense of career. The sitings in play each are given their due recognition, whether Native America, the Oklahoma and Missouri of his upbringing and professional career, the Pacific Northwest, or the successive locales of Europe. If, for immediate purposes, one begins with indigenous legacy, it is less to identify Barnes as some exclusively Native author than to emphasize how that aspect of his heritage has richly, and movingly, drawn his imagination. A considerable litany of poems can be said to serve.

In "Contemporary Native American Poetry" (*The American Book of the Dead*) Barnes offers a species of likely ironically titled, yet respectful and admiring, witness. For the poem's speaker Native history may look fugitive, a one-remove from his own time and place. But that history lies wholly, and quite inescapably, engrained in his consciousness:

For one thing, you believe it:
the skin chewed soft enough to wear,

the bones hewn hard as a totem
from hemlock. It's a kind of scare-

crow that will follow you home nights.
You've seen it ragged against a field,
but you seldom think, at the time,
to get there it had to walk through hell.

The imagery gives off the perfect memorial resonance. The buffalo
leather acts as a mnemonic for both food and clothing. Bones, hem-
lock-hard like a "totem," call up tribal ceremony. The well-judged hy-
phenation, and then the line break, of *scare-crow* summons the crow as
both warning emblem and trickster icon. As to "Native poetry" itself,
that, indeed, and in its every inclusive implication of culture, has been
to keep Native word, Native meaning, vibrant against history's nightmare. How, by implication, not to think of "relocations" such as the
1835 Cherokee Trail of Tears or 1862 Navajo Long March? These, and
other enforced marches, literally were "to walk through hell" and to
seek survival against odds of disease, each and every act further of dispossession. The history implied has its one-sided encoding in Manifest
Destiny or the winning of the West. However so, Barnes, at the same
time, far from implies simply loss, or even evisceration. This is Native
continuance against all of history's field line. Little wonder the opening
line gives the certifying assurance of "For one thing you believe it," testimony to Native poetry as intimately felt and dwelt-in history.

With "A Song for All of Them" (*A Season of Loss*) Barnes again blends
a dual sense of place and time, the poem's first-person voice pitched as
though to speak to remembered tribal voices. An immediately met with
nature, likewise, doubles with nature as the continuum of bones, bodies, ghosts, dust, sky, song, and name:

Hills where my father hid the bones
lie dark about me. I look for
trails hacked hard in trees and lined

in stones all years war with. I am
here this one night to find the farthest
corner of the sky, to place my body
one with the earth, sky, to talk with ghosts
long silent, long dark . . .
Bones beneath my feet, I make
a song for all of them. My name,
earth name, is sacred as the sun.
My name goes with me out of this world.

The sense of land, "hills," as the tribal repository of both body and spirit, has long been a feature of Barnes's poetry. The "trails" of the poem thus point to entry into both past habitation (flint knife, bears, hunters) and unfolding time (ghosts, bones). These, in turn, fold into the speaker's sense of his "earth name," its signification of arrival, existence, and future exit from the world. A one name, as may be, it is linked by the poem into the many, a "sacred" tribal sense of being bound up in the encompassing larger inscription and unerasability of all Native nomenclature.

"Ghost Fog" (*A Season of Loss*), a species of reverie set in Palo Duro Canyon, summons the dying of Poor Buffalo, a hunted nineteenth-century Comanche fighter. The "false dawn" of a present-day Tule Creek camp (near to Texas's Prairie Dog Town at the fork of the Red River) locates the poem inside the one time scheme. But another presses close from behind, one of "ancient campfires," the pitch of "an eagle-bone whistle," the "flap of sacred owl-skin," and the bones both of Poor Buffalo and his Tonkawa enemy K'ya-been. Within the immediate "dark dawn" reverie, confirms the poem, a "hundred years flowed back," present and earlier time, together with site, joined. The "heavy smell of a prairie dog town" thereby abuts a "shadow world," the uneasy cohabitation down through history of white settler and tribal Texas. But as memory steps back from the campsite into a ceremonial "place to die" for Poor Buffalo, so, once more, present-time noisily intrudes:

Then out of the pitch black west
A low and rumbling thunder set me straight.
Here was now: a trucker, damn his tunneled eyes,
Barreling-ass down the Amarillo-Lubbock run.

"Here was now" indeed runs the accompanying, and not a little accus-
ing, cryptic gloss. A historic tribal death, a sense of land, the playback
of memory, have all become inhumed within, or beneath, modernity's
speed, the "low and rumbling thunder" of the truck upon the oil-fumed
Amarillo-Lubbock highway. The camp serves as both location and chronology, two specifics of place and time and, at least by implication, all
the disjunctive human inter-layers between.

With "In Memory of a Day Nobody Remembers: September 26, 1874"
(A Season of Loss) Barnes looks to actual history, the attack under Colonel
Ranald Slidell Mackenzie (1840–89) of the Fourth United States Cavalry
upon peaceably encamped Kiowas and Comanches in Palo Duro Canyon and the next-day slaughter of more than a thousand of their horses
at Tule Creek. MacKenzie had fought as a Union officer, led black troops
in the Civil War, and in the wake of the so-called Red River War and the
defeat of southern Plains tribes such as the Comanches, Kiowas, and
Apaches, eventually taken over regional command of the Black Hills
down to Texas in the wake of George Armstrong Custer's death at the
Battle of Little Big Horn in 1876. It is not Mackenzie, however, who is
the subject of this dirge but, rather, Poor Buffalo, Kiowa leader, and
those like him prejudicially designated "Indian raiders." His death, as
that of his comrades, remains ethereally in the air, spirit residue in the
face of all the Texas-Oklahoma landgrab.

Barnes opens "In Memory of a Day" on a note of "ubi sunt?" but one
colloquially pitched—"Who is left to recall the sacred earth/where
Poor Buffalo bit the dust?" He works back to the historic skirmish and
then the killings, through the local spectacle of "Town Indians drunk
on Chock and Thunderbird." These addled tribal descendants have become lost to the hollow log creation story of the Kiowa (famously imagined in N. Scott Momaday's memoir The Names), to the life ritual of the

sun dance, and above all, to "the massacre / of men, and horses dead." The word *massacre* is fittingly deployed for what has occurred, the brute white military assault on both warriors and steeds. Invoking yet other figures of tribal resistance—Isatai, Maman-ti, and K'ye-been—the poem enjoins them to ghost-dance their way into the mellowing, almost Keatsian, autumnal leaves. If only for a moment, the tribal dead might thus live again, their presence caught in nature's own evanescent beauty: "Dance, ghosts, among the yellow leaves / Before they turn to dust."

Almost all of Barnes's Native-referenced, or perhaps more accurately, Native-shadowed, poems in *A Season of Loss* make use of this associative imagery of bones, runes, stones, flint, and, most notably, glyph. The poetry thereby offers as much a temporal as physical topography, an implied tribal scale both of chronometer and site. "Bone Yard" turns exactly, and engagingly, in this way. Two contrastive images of a "hundred" buffalo, their bodies seemingly "live," though as if slowed by sludge, and then truly remnant and skeletal, as if having become a graveyard, give the poem's opening:

A hundred buffalo
knee-deep in sludge.

Bones bleached to pebbles
and white sand.

The effect might almost be that of haiku, the totemic buffalo slowed, destroyed, bone-exposed and whitened, and finally reduced to "pebbles / and white sand." Yet within the "long-spent bones," "this dried waterhole," and "the land's cracked hide"—a nice elision of buffalo hide and earth—and the dead trees, sounds can be imagined to echo from earlier herd, and so tribal, life. At a prior time man and beast have met within a shared order of nature, a shared chain of being. The poem speaks of the tramping "ghosts of hoofs," "hot wind," the remembered live stillness of the beasts in the "dead of winter." The dynamism of these animals persists even as they are seen through their present desiccation. The prairie's memorial "bone yard" notwithstanding, the poem winningly insists upon the re-embodied and hovering buffalo spirit of life.

"Paiute Ponies," using a shared contrast, looks to these tribal horses as ancestral energy, beauty or physique, and yet to be set against the arriving contemporary diesel truck. Their silhouette stands sharp against "a ringed moon." The ancient "tracks" may have become yet another modern highway, but one that leads into Nevada's tribally named Winnemucca. No explicit Native allusion is used other than in the title, but the implication is unmistakable, the perennial within the given moment, an old power of site within the new. The middle stanza suggests precisely this overlap, almost as though a haunting:

Mane and tail hanging vertical as ice,
They sleep dead centuries,
or if ponies dream they dream.

Not unlike W. B. Yeats's swans at Coole or Wallace Stevens's thirteen blackbirds, Barnes's Paiute ponies carry time in their very composure. Even the truck fails to impede their continuance:

The diesel warns again, begins its roar, passes.
They raise their heads like automatons, blink,
then drop once more into centuries or dreams.

These closing lines, roaring diesel truck set against ponies, give the perfect synopsis. Modernity's engine speed is almost mocked by the Paiute-ancestral timeline, each pony its own law of motion, full of enduring dream and even insouciance. The effect is considerable and not a little magical.

An implicit Native seam similarly runs through two Barnes poems of the Arkansas-Oklahoma border, both with settings tied into the Ouchita Mountain range. In "Trying to Hide Out on Rich Mountain" the poem opens with a mixed report on the mountain's history: a well-known Dutch inn flattened to bedrock, "lightning" lizards, ruin, "rotting moss and fresh crap," "a Caterpillar's track." These provide the backdrop for the speaker's own parlous emotional or psychological condition, be it the lies that have made up his life or the hope to fool "the woman that you love this late" with a "phoney suicide" or his retreat to the mountain as escape or camouflage. The panorama, however, does not stop there. It looks to the "weekend tourists out of Tulsa," their calling cards spent beer cans and the barroom "hard rock about mountains they will / never have to climb." But from beyond this wry complicity of commercially intruded-upon mountain or of the speaker-self as against the weekenders, the eye turns to the vista of open day and wide sky:

> The day stays open.
> Wide. Wide as all the skies your forebears watched
> eagles in. You wonder if you'd know their kind.
> But it's too hot to pray Indians out of stone.

The allusion to a domain in which "your forebears" saw soaring eagles signifies an altogether greater, and better, field of vision, one of implied grace and sweep of spirit, in all the perfect counter-balance. The closing notion, even so, of a Southwest heat torpor to inhibit "pray[ing] Indians out of stone" acts as both a sense of self-loss (the irony, surely, caught up in the name "Rich Mountain") and self-reprimand.

"Stopping on Kiamichi Mountain," from *The American Book of the Dead*, offers a companion piece in which the one kind of outdoor hunting shadows the other. The speaking voice is all latter-day business: his Mustang driven past the sign for Sulphur Spring, the canyon below with its "snakes and tarantulas as fierce / as fire in jack pines," the desultory trail, the spring reduced to a trickle and full of bad sulfur smell, the incoming thunder and the tornado it portends, and the beckoning further sign for Antlers (the Oklahoma township in Pushmaha County). The scene is one of impending threat, a possible tornado or twister. Can the prospect of a beer, or even a binge-like "drunk," ease the sense of foreboding and "put a handle on the wind"? The transition is once more into other time, an Oklahoma of shared dangerous "wind" but whose indigenous name bears the necessary warning. The point, the contrast, is brought to the closing sequence:

> You head the Mustang straight into
> the dark and pray the only times you ever
> do that you know the wind by Indian name.

To one degree or another the "Native" poems throughout *A Season of Loss* work in this manner, indigeneity or at least its remembrance as a kind of collaborative and working substratum. A few, undoubtedly, are more explicit. "Song of I-see-o," told as though in the voice of a celebrated Kiowa warrior scout, invokes Rainy Mountain as pathway into the Fourth World. "Four Things Choctaw"—*Nashoba* (wolfsong), *Isuba* (horse), *Baii* (oak), and *Abukbo* (feather)—act, as Barnes offers them, as the passed-down Choctaw inventory of self within nature, the touchstones of tribal culture's equilibrium. "Reading Santa Fe" looks to "the drummer drums," "the angles of this land," which, almost mysteriously, compel the speaker to contemplate a site beyond the invitations to give poetry readings, visit the city's museum, gaze upon the cathedral historic statue of Bishop Lamy, or assuredly, take part in the New Mexico of tourist razzamatazz. "Choctaw Cemetery" speaks beautifully to the one and many tribal deaths, each as always with its own timeline, but also to be memorialized through the ancestral emblem of the "four winds" as a right mode of situating self within the universe:

> Stones,
> hand-hewn symbols
> touching four winds.

Barnes knows, too, that a complex animist universe has always held in that same Native universe, from trickster coyote to turtle creator. "Crow," a prose-poem, contains no explicit Native markers, but it would be hard not to have in mind the bird's familiarity in tribal lore as variously wiseacre, clown, or scout. At quite the same time, and undeniably, a Wallace Stevens blackbird again can plausibly, and quite fairly, also be invoked or any of the avian imagery in creature poems by, say, Gerard Manley Hopkins or Ted Hughes. But the unspoken Native provenance is hard to avoid. Each step in the interchange of voice and eye, the "conversation," more than hints of such. The crow's caw, however closely imitated by the speaker, fails to fool the bird. Three times repeated, it causes the bird merely to ascend to the higher tree branches, from which it looks down with "sidewise looks." It then lowers itself to immediate "eye level," twanging the lower limbs of the tree. In an exchange of mutual sightings the poem's self observes with no little irony, "I can see the world behind me in his black pupils." The crow's eyes act as perfect reflector, man and bird, self and world.

La Plata Cantata yields the further run, not least in its use of "glyphs" as recurrent Barnes metaphor. A poem such as "Trying to Read the Glyphs," told as the climbing of a vertical cliff face, turns upon "hand chiseled glyphs" each respectively "abstract," "open," or "riddled." Climbing upwards toward the glyphs, the speaker meets spirals of wind rising from hidden caves, "cold stone," a want of footholds, the tumbling reflection of a waterfall "a thousand years dead," his own sweat, and the echoing inward sensation that "my mind is full of bones." The lines become a gathering ode as much to time as place. The river beneath is likened to "a glacier hunting for / the sea." The shadow of a pivoting hawk implies timeless avian habit. The setting sun completes this day as it has all others before. The poem's voice, synoptically, speaks of the consciousness of "bones I never knew I was heir to." This is nature as alive in the present, immediate and kinetic, yet also a site to be understood through a wholly more ancient lexicon.

"Paraglyphs" reads to shared effect, a seven-part verse sequence given over to signs registered as though again past inside present, the older "language" borne down from Native to modern America. A Missouri cave so yields:

Two fish,
definitely carp,
picassoed in stone.

The seaming of Picasso as modern art's ranking name into an ancient
cave wall does symptomatic service, Nature's continuity of visual mark-
ing. Each ensuing section adds its confirming specificity. An "arc of
moon," "this scythe," with a "shining" hawk overhead in its light, is
seen etched on sandstone as though eternal configuration ("What's lost
concerns me / more than what may be"). A similarly engraved "red ochre
snake" suggests both "enemy" and "vein of life." A sea turtle is said to
bear "a road map on its back. Holson Creek, after rain, yields three arrowheads, a spearhead, the ax-like adze, and the clay pot and human
shinbone fragments amid the riverbank's oak fruit—a collage, as it
were, of old and new habitation. Big Sur, seen from an overhead plane
flight, becomes a tropic California of love and radicalism. Cuzco, Peru's
fabled city to which the Incas are supposed to have descended from Lake
Titicaca, is remembered from traditional Native cosmography as the
place where sun and earth "stood still." Taken together, Barnes's vivid,
imagist vignettes build into a serial of markings, the linked diversity of
human signature preserved upon an unfolding scroll of sites.

The Sawdust War yields four sequences. As a run of title poems, "The
Sawdust War" turns upon childhood and war memory. "After the Great
Plains" looks to landscapes and their histories spanning Oklahoma,
Missouri, and Montana. "Elegies for John Berryman and Others" develop literary tributes not only to the Berryman born in McAlesker, Oklahoma, and for whose Mistress Bradstreet (1956), 77 Dream Songs (1964),
and His Toy, His Dream, His Rest (1968) Barnes has long shown admiration, but also to Malcolm Lowry and Ernest Hemingway. "In Another
Country," Hemingway's story the apt footfall, takes on different scenes
and habitations in Italy. Of these "After the Great Plains" gives the strongest focus to the America he calls "this long land" of Native and settler,
most typically in a poem such as "Wolf Watch: Winding Stair Mountain
1923." The panorama invoked embraces meadow, pine, cattle, sheep,

fish, quail, crows, and centrally, the wolf, with a human quotient in a scene of preacher and flock, a waiting wife, and a dead herder. The note is one of both American time and space, a shared siting of Native and settler, prairie and homestead.

In "Crow White" and "Crow Firesticks" Barnes writes two canny avian vignettes. Both enact myth-fables suitably told in speaker-trickster voice, the one to do with the origins of the bird's crow-black color and the other with nature's chance ironies of fire and water told as the bird trapped inside a whale. "Postcard to James Welch in Missoula" can be thought to work a shared vein, one of the many "postcards" Barnes has made over into poems. Cast in the form of a verse epistle, it suggests, teasingly, how an "Indian" sense of rain and sound, sky and river, eludes the modern "inner ear." The old weather rain dance has gone, the bass refuse to bite, and the rivers and corn have become dry and dust laden. The poem closes ruefully, and as though in shared affectionate envy with Welch, of quite other understandings of a day's forecast:

> Remember when you were here, how the sky
> Was right with clouds and the winds scalped
> us down to the skull. You told us in a glance
> the moving days are best, when sounds strike
> the inner ear from places only the hawk
> can name and some wild damned Indian,
> eyes full of rainbows and fast jacks. *Achukma!*

The closing *Achukma!* the Choctaw term for "It is good" or "I am fine," strikes just the right note. Two mixed writer-heirs to Native history, fellow American moderns yet with their own pathways into American indigeneity, look to heritage, legacy. How, for either, to belong completely to the present-day world while actually, and residually, always conscious of nature's sights and sounds seen or heard by "only the hawk" or "some damned wild Indian" whose eyes give off a vision of "rainbows and fast jacks"? The personal and shared ancestry of site could not be more evident, self and place, self and time.

With "Fourche Maline Bottoms" Barnes nicely, and economically, fuses his natal Oklahoma with Native heritage. Fourche Maline, French for "dirty fork or path" (though here "river" or "bottoms") acts as the site for memory-within-memory. In childhood the speaker is told by "raucous neighborhood boys" that "*you won't find nothing down in them bottoms / worth a shit.*" In fact he finds a massive plenty, albeit a private plenty, at once a lift to the spirits and the sustaining link into his own memorial past:

> The joy
> Of finding arrowheads beneath the crumbl-
> ing leaves was something I could never come
> to trade for any neighbor's game.

The affection for the arrowheads, and through them once again the accompanying sense of entering Native American time as well as place, the poem summarizes exactly in its closing quatrain:

> For seven years I sifted coal-black dirt,
> found arrowheads so keen I knew I'd seen
> into my own ancestral past where hurt
> and harm stood taller than neighbor boys had been.

"Coal-black dirt," "arrowheads," "ancestral past." Together they supply just the right collocation, a Native past-into-present as necessary and correlative larger context for the speaker's boyhood-into-adulthood. The images are precise, and appropriately temporal and physical, those of a burrowing into the American earth for both artifact and self-meaning.

The further repertoire of sites in Barnes's poetry, whether America, Europe, or Japan and other Asia, deserves full and matching recognition. Select poems must do duty for the larger round, each given to a site full and sharp in particularity yet within the continuing overall register. In a well-taken recent appraisal of *On a Wing of the Sun*, for *Sewanee Review*,

Sam Pickering speaks of "letting [Barnes's] poems ferment through darkening nights. The names of places reverberated across lines: Tom Fry Hollow, Big Piney River, Goats Bluff, Horsefly, Marshalltown, Pyramid Lake and Winding Stair Mountain."[3] Selecting these picture-like, mosaical names points in the right direction, an America-sited contemplative poetry especially inviting of the reader's "fermentation."

This sense of site, a much traveled Southwest and West heavy in mulled-over feeling, recurs. "The Cabin on Nanny Ridge" calls up halcyon Oklahoma boyhood ("Time / backed for us"), even as "Europe burned." By contrast "Military Burial, Summerfield Cemetery: A Late Eulogy" recalls the European war actually carried into Oklahoma—"An honor guard brought the gray box down from / Tinker Field." The note is one of sad respect, a remembrance of death in the skies ("For all who had the will / for wings I have only words I wish were more"). In "At 39: The View from Sycamore Tower" (*La Plata Cantata*) a sense once again of boyhood life past ("scrub oak / or sparse pine where I stepped barefoot / on my first rattlesnake") joins with the adult present ("I came / too many miles and from a woman / I could have been drinking bourbon with"). Within the perimeters of Buffalo Mountain and the Tower both supply memory sites for self-inquiry. Little wonder the air of the mountain is said to be "chock-full / of ghosts and insects" and home "always ten thousand miles away."

"La Plata, Missouri: Clear November Night" (*A Season of Loss*) sees the Midwest township under "an avalanche of stars," "snowing light," a heartlands at once literal yet preternaturally illuminated. "Driving through Missouri," a mid-autumn night vista, prompts thoughts of love and its call. The site at hand, at once close at hand and yet far away, is cast as wistful, real enough yet distant with hope and desire:

I gather all my light love

into an artifice of now, see a snow
drifting at the bottom of my eye, although

I am contending with the real, the road.
I'd like to clap my hands and sing the woods

rich in rainy, salmon leaves and new light,
set a course for stars deep in softer night,

a night I could make a song on. Out of
this pale time there's still a thing or two to love.

"On the Beach at Manzanita, Oregon" (*The American Book of the Dead*) casts its gaze to the further west with a vision of "cryptic stone faces seaward" and "the ageless Chinook." Yet these "chords of memory," in turn, bring back to mind the almost defunct Yuchis of Oklahoma.

As inviting a triumph as almost any of Barnes's America-sited poems is to be encountered in "Notes for a Love Letter from Mid-America," his four-part rumination with a preface from Chief Seattle ("There is no death. Only a change of worlds"), and which blends remembrance of a past lover with a past Midwest. The missing object of affection is situated against "dead November," "glacial drift." A winter of heart and land contrasts with "white-water sounds" and "salmon mad with love." The runes of love, close-lived and lost, overlap with nature's own changing seasonal and topographical runes. Locale is both the physical exterior of mountain, cornfield, moss, and rapids, and at the same time, reverberatingly, the inward terrain of feeling ("I miss my breath / in your hair," "A sense of place / allowed us room to love"). The mutuality of both sites, here as so often in Barnes's poetry, supplies a wholly distinctive signature.

Europe has greatly supplied Barnes with working poetic terrain, nowhere more so than in the seventy or so poems that make up the collection *Paris*. Barnes's itinerary is busy, alive with appetite for the city—whether "Le Métro" with its "air brakes wheezing on the rails" and "rupturous light," "On Rue de Fleurus" as homage to Gertrude Stein and Alice B. Toklas ("a flowering, a shining"), "At the Tomb of Baudelaire" ("Nothing about this place seems dull: / the stone flowers have a luster that grows full / as day goes down," or "Rodin's Garden" with its museum of "praying hands and walking men / and lovers locked in time" and grounds where "a white and silent peace abounds."

Italy likewise exerts its pull, rarely to more imaginative good purpose than in a poem such as "Above Bellagio, Looking North to Varenna" (*The Sawdust War*). Gulls are said to circle the lake where rocks, and even graves, have fallen into the waters. Nearby Tremezzo reminds us of where Mussolini, Il Duce, was shot. Hydrofoil and ferry cross, the latter with foghorn at full blast. Switzerland just about hovers into view ("the waves reflecting Alps / in their white caps"). Pliny and Dante are invoked. And the poem ends with its own eulogy, a site of true place, true feeling:

> No cantos are large enough
> to hold the spirit of this place. The water is deep
> and the Alps lean hard into Lombardy's shifting winds.

It could not be more appropriate to link this Europe with Barnes's America. "Anasazi Rocks" (*Paris*) strikes the right note, a vignette of purchasing "a crude necklace" from an old jewels and lace shop in the city's Rue St. André des Arts:

> We had no thought of buying things
> So far from home. On touch I felt the red
> Canyon de Chelly sand and the drumming
> Of dry thunder and dread.
>
> I felt my blood pulse slow and paid too much,
> as any tourist would. The stones were dull
> and real, their faces heavy to our touch.
> On quai d'Orsay we pulled
>
> them free of the German silver bases
> and threw them wide into the rising Seine
> to ride the earthy current into sea
> and home on wind and rain.

The poem gathers many of Barnes's characteristic interests. The idiom is immediate though tinged with a certain reflective *tristesse*. Necklace, colors, the act of casting the stones into the Seine as connecting world river, and the linking of France's quai d'Orsay with Native America's Canyon de Chelly, make for a deep, inward continuity of travel, heritage, time. As latest work-in-progress is announced—the story collection "A Good Place in the World"—and new verse to be called *Visiting Picasso*, it supplies the yet one more site in a poetry of lasting distinction.

Notes

1. Jim Barnes, "Surveying near Ellsworth, Kansas," *La Plata Cantata: Poems / On a Wing of the Sun*, 180.

2. "Jim Barnes," *Contemporary Authors Autobiography Series* (Farmington Hills MI: Thomson Gale, 1997), 28:17–32.

3. Sam Pickering, "Time Ever Slow and Long," *Sewanee Review* 112.3 (Summer 2004): 468.

Works Cited

Barnes, Jim, ed. *Five Missouri Poets*. Kirksville MO: Chariton Review Press, 1979.

———. *The Fish on Poteau Mountain*. Stillwater OK: Cedar Creek Press, 1980.

———, trans. *Summons and Sign: Poems by Dagmar Nick*. Kirksville MO: Chariton Review Press, 1980.

———. *This Crazy Land*. Flagstaff AZ: Inland Boat Series, 1980.

———. *The American Book of the Dead: Poems*. Urbana: University of Illinois Press, 1982.

———. *A Season of Loss*. West Lafayette IN: Purdue University Press, 1985.

———. *La Plata Cantata: Poems*. West Lafayette IN: Purdue University Press, 1989.

———. *The Fiction of Malcolm Lowry and Thomas Mann: Structural Tradition*. Kirksville MO: Thomas Jefferson University Press, 1990.

———. *The Sawdust War: Poems*. Urbana: University of Illinois Press, 1992.

———. *On Native Ground: Memoirs and Impressions*. Norman: University of Oklahoma Press, 1997.

———. *Paris: Poems*. Urbana: University of Illinois Press, 1997.

————, trans. *Gezählte Tage / Numbered Days: Poems by Dagmar Nick*. Kirksville MO: New Odyssey Press, 1998.

————. *On a Wing of the Sun: Three Volumes of Poetry*. Urbana: University of Illinois Press, 2001.

————. *Visiting Picasso: Poems*. Urbana: University of Illinois Press, 2007.

Chariton Review. Ed. Jim Barnes. 1976–present.

"Jim Barnes." *Contemporary Authors Autobiography Series*. Farmington Hills MI: Thomson Gale, 1997. 28:17–32.

Contributors

HELMBRECHT BREINIG is Professor and Chair Emeritus in American Studies at the University of Erlangen-Nürnberg and former Director of the Bavarian American Academy, Munich. He has taught at the universities of Freiburg, Mannheim, Stuttgart, Bamberg, and Erlangen as well as UC–San Diego and UC–Berkeley and held visiting scholarships at Berkeley, Harvard, and the University of British Columbia–Vancouver. His more than a dozen books include monographs on the American satirical novel, Mark Twain, and Washington Irving. He has published widely in the fields of American fiction from the eighteenth through the twentieth centuries, modern American poetry and poetics, Inter-American Studies, cultural theory, and Native American Studies. His most recent book is a collection of essays and literary texts by European and North American scholars and writers, *Imaginary (Re-)Locations: Tradition, Modernity and the Market in Contemporary Native American Literature and Culture* (2003), and a bilingual, annotated anthology of poetry thematizing New York City, *Poetischer New York–Führer* (2005).

BRIGITTE GEORGI-FINDLAY is Professor of North American Studies at the Technical University of Dresden. Major areas of research are the cultural history of the American West (Native Americans, women, the urban West), travel writing, American photography, and, most recently, transatlantic relations. She is the author of *The Frontiers of Women's Writing: Women's Narratives and the Rhetoric of Westward Expansion* (1996).

KATHRYN NAPIER GRAY is Lecturer and Head of American Studies at Plymouth University. She is the author of several articles on Early American and Native American literature and is currently working on a monograph entitled "Communicative Acts: John Eliot, Praying Indians and Seventeenth-Century Colonial Performances," which considers speech acts, performances, and colonial encounters in Puritan New England.

ULLA HASELSTEIN is Professor of American Literature at the John F. Kennedy Institute, Freie University Berlin. She has published widely on modernist and postmodernist literature, the captivity narrative, Native American Studies, Gender Studies, and literary theory. Her books include *Entziffernde Hermeneutik* (1991); *Die Gabe der Zivilisation* (2000); *Iconographies of Power: The Politics and Poetics of Visual Representation*, coedited with Berndt Ostendorf and Peter Schneck (2003), *Cultural Transactions: Fifty Years of American Studies in Germany*, coedited with Berndt Ostendorf (2005), and *Aesthetic Transgressions: Modernism, Liberalism and the Functions of Literature*, coedited with Thomas Claviez and Sieglinde Lemke (2006).

HARTWIG ISERNHAGEN is Emeritus Professor of American Literature at the University of Basel. His publications in American Studies include *Ästhetische Innovation und Kulturkritik: Das Frühwerk von John Dos Passos, 1916–1938* (1983) and *Momaday, Vizenor, Armstrong: Conversations on American Indian Writing* (1999) as well as numerous articles on the theory and history of twentieth-century fiction (modernism/postmodernism), American Indian literature, and the humanities in transition.

YONKA KRASTEVA is Director of the American Studies Program at the University of Veliko Tarnovo, "St. Cyrill and St. Methodius," Bulgaria, currently teaching at Friends University, Kansas. She has taught at Basel University, Switzerland; at Bilkent University, Turkey; and at the Catholic University of Lublin, Poland. She was also the recipient of two Fulbright research grants—in 1982 at the University of Michigan and in 1989 at Stanford University—and of an American Council of Learned

Societies (ACLS) grant at Arizona State University. Her publications include *The West and the American Dream: Studies in Twentieth Century American Literature* (1997) as well as numerous articles on contemporary American literature and culture and on issues of cultural encounters, especially between the West and the East.

A. ROBERT LEE, British born, taught American Studies and literature at the University of Kent, UK, before becoming Professor of American Literature at Nihon University, Tokyo. His nearly thirty books and essay collections include *Designs of Blackness: Mappings in the Literature and Culture of Afro-America* (1998), *Ethnics Behaving Badly: U.S. Multicultural Narratives* (2001), and *Multicultural American Literature: Comparative Black, Native, Latino/a and Asian American Fictions* (2003), which won an American Book Award. Among his essay collections are *Other Britain, Other British: Contemporary Multicultural Fiction* (1995), *Beat Generation Writers* (1996), the four-volume *Herman Melville: Critical Assessments* (2000), and *China Fictions/English Language: Essays in Literary Diaspora* (2006). His books *Gothic to Multicultural: Idioms of Imagining in American Literary Fiction* and *Japan Textures: Sight and Word*, with Mark Gresham, appear in 2007. His Native American interests are reflected in *Postindian Conversations*, with Gerald Vizenor (1999); *Loosening the Seams: Interpretations of Gerald Vizenor* (2000); and the four-volume *Native American Writing: Critical Assessments* (2006).

DEBORAH L. MADSEN is Professor of American Literature and Culture at the University of Geneva. She is currently President of the Swiss Association for North American Studies. She has published short pieces on such Native American writers as Gerald Vizenor, Michael Dorris, Louise Erdrich, Leslie Marmon Silko, and Joy Harjo. Her book *American Exceptionalism* (1998) discusses Native responses to the U.S. national narrative; other books include *Allegory in America: From Puritanism to Postmodernism* (1996) and *Understanding Contemporary Chicana Literature* (2000). She edited *Visions of America since 1492* (1994), *Beyond the Commonwealth: Expanding the Postcolonial Canon* (1999), and *Beyond the Borders: American Literature and Post-Colonial Theory* (2003). Her current research focuses upon comparative multiculturalisms, trauma theory, and American exceptionalism.

SIMONE PELLERIN is Professor of American Literature at the University Paul-Valéry in Montpellier. She has published a number of articles on various nineteenth- and twentieth-century American authors and on the history of Native American literature, including analyses of texts by authors ranging from Samson Occom to David Treuer, and a monograph, *Première leçon sur N. Scott Momaday* (1997). She is also the French translator of Robert M. Utley and Wilcomb E. Washburn's *Indian Wars*; of short stories in *Spiderwoman's Granddaughters*, edited by Paula Gunn Allen (by Anna Lee Walters, Zitkala-Sa, Louise Erdrich, Leslie Silko, Elizabeth Cook-Lynn, Humishima, and Mary TallMountain); and of *American Indian Myths and Legends*, edited by Richard Erdoes and Alfonso Ortiz. She is currently working on the specificity of the relationship between Native American literature and American literature at large.

GAETANO PRAMPOLINI teaches literature of the United States at the University of Firenze. His writings cover a wide range of topics from the colonial period to the present. In the field of Native American literature he has written extensively on N. Scott Momaday (whose *The Way to Rainy Mountain* as well as a selection of shorter pieces he has also translated into Italian) and has been the coeditor of "Indianamericana," a series of texts by contemporary Native American writers in translation.

ELVIRA PULITANO is currently an Assistant Professor in the Ethnic Studies Department at California Polytechnic State University. A Fulbright scholar from Italy, she received her doctorate from the University of New Mexico, specializing in Native American literatures and postcolonial studies. She is the author of *Toward a Native American Critical Theory* (2003) and of various essays on Native American and postcolonial literatures. Her interests in cross-cultural global approaches to contemporary Anglophone studies include Caribbean literatures, literatures of the black Atlantic, transnationalism, diaspora, and human rights discourse. She is currently working on a monograph exploring literary representations of diaspora in Anglophone Caribbean writing. From 2002 to 2006 she taught postcolonial literatures and theory at the universities of Geneva and Lausanne in Switzerland.

BERNADETTE RIGAL-CELLARD is Professor of North American Studies at the University Michel de Montaigne–Bordeaux 3. She studied there and at the University of California–Santa Barbara. As a specialist of contemporary North American religions and Native literatures, she teaches graduate seminars focusing on the modes of adaptation and representation of traditional myths, intermythology, and postcolonialism. She serves on the editorial board of the *European Review of Native American Studies* (ERNAS). Her publications in English include *Scott Momaday, House Made of Dawn* (1997); a collection of essays on the novel *House Made of Dawn* (1997); as well a number of essays on Paula Gunn Allen, Louise Erdrich, Tom King, Louis Owens, Gerald Vizenor, James Welch, Native American autobiographies, and various aspects of American and Canadian Native cultures (including religions, treaties, and films). In French she has published *Le Mythe et la plume* (2004), a study of North American Native literatures.

MARK SHACKLETON is currently Acting Professor in the Department of English, University of Helsinki, and is Codirector of the University of Helsinki project "Cross-Cultural Contacts: Diaspora Writing in English." He has published on postcolonial writing, especially Native North American writing, including articles on Tomson Highway, Thomas King, Monique Mojica, Gerald Vizenor, Louise Erdrich, and Simon J. Ortiz.

PAUL BEEKMAN TAYLOR was born in London and educated in the United States and Norway before becoming Professor of Medieval English Language and Literature at the University of Geneva. He published translations from the Old Norse with W. H. Auden and wrote extensively on Old Norse, Old English, and Middle English topics. Following a sabbatical year in New Mexico, he turned his attention to Chicano and Native American Literature and published articles on major novelists such as Rudolfo Anaya, N. Scott Momaday, Leslie Marmon Silko, Linda Hogan, and Louis Owens. He is retired and lives in Geneva.

REBECCA TILLETT is Lecturer in American Studies at the University of East Anglia, where she is the cofounder of the Native Studies Research Network, UK. Her work focuses on twentieth- and twenty-first-century multiethnic American literature and film, particularly contemporary Native American writers and filmmakers; and race, postcolonial, and ecocritical theory. She is the author of several articles on Native American literature, and her book *Contemporary Native American Literature* appears in 2007 as part of the British Association for American Studies (BAAS) series.

Index

CPSIA information can be obtained at www.ICGtesting.com
Printed in the USA
BVOW05s0428270315

393553BV00015B/57/P

9 780803 260344